Early Reviews For the ALL NEW
5th EDITION

*"For anyone seeking employment with the government, **The Book of U.S. Government Jobs** provides a clear roadmap through the federal maze. Getting to your destination — a job — will be a whole lot easier with the help of this book."*
— **William Stothers, editor, MAINSTREAM Magazine**

"Damp does a very credible job of presenting the tremendous opportunity in federal employment and pointing the way to capitalizing on it. Some of the best jobs in America are easier to land thanks to Damp's clear direction. A valuable part of every federal job hunter's library."
— **Peter E. Ognibene, Publisher, FEDERAL JOBS DIGEST**

*"The place to start if you want to work for the federal government is Dennis Damp's **Book of U.S. Government Jobs**. Damp makes sense of the federal government's oft confusing employment system and smoothly guides you through the federal hiring labyrinth."*
— **Daniel lauber, author, Government Job Finder**

*"**The Book of U.S. Government Jobs** is a valuable resource for anyone interested in entering or advancing in the federal work force. It is a comprehensive and well organized guide. Highly recommended."*
— **Paul Endress, President, DataTech Software**

"Dennis Damp has sorted through the vast amount of information, resources, and procedures required to obtain a government job and has laid out a map that will guide you step-by-step through this hiring maze."
— **Roxanne S. Rogers, Human Resource Consultant and Host of "The Career Connection", WHO Radio, Iowa.**

"This book will be a great time saver for any government job hunter."
— **Will Cantrell, Editor & Publisher, International Employment Hotline**

Reviews for earlier editions of
The Book of U.S. Government Jobs

*"Damp's **The Book of U.S. Government Jobs**, an updated, comprehensive how-to guide, provides an in-depth understanding of the federal government employment system. Written in a clear, readable style, this reference answers myriad questions from civil service exams and federal pay schedules to employment opportunities. This title is recommended as a worthy, affordable addition to career collections."*
LIBRARY JOURNAL (1/92)

*"**The Book of U.S. Government Jobs** is an easy to read book with plenty of graphics and well-written text. It clearly introduces students to the Uncle Sam's world."* **The Career Opportunities News**

*"Anyone interested in obtaining government employment will find **The Book of U.S. Government Jobs** by Dennis V. Damp a **Treasure Trove of Information,"** Diane Donovan, Mid West Book Review*

"Extremely helpful and informative..." **Small Press Magazine**

Books by Dennis V. Damp

The Book Of U.S. Government Jobs (January 1994 release)
Health Care Job Explosion! Careers In The 90's (April 1993 release)
Dollars & Sense (March 1989 release)

What they are saying about the
Health Care Job Explosion!

*"With the growth of the health care industry, **Health Care Job Explosion** will be a boon to those seeking jobs... well rounded and special. Recommended for general collections; **this book will be in demand.**"*
LIBRARY JOURNAL (3/15/93)

*"...This **thorough book** will help the seeker find job sources and ways of locating positions in the health care area... well done. **A fine addition to career collections.**"*
KLIATT (5/93)

*"The information is extremely well-organized, accurate, and up-to-date. The **Health Care Job Explosion** will be enormously useful to individuals seeking employment opportunities or information about particular jobs in the health care field. It should be available in every academic and public library as a resource."*
Robert C. Aber, M.D., Associate Dean of Medical Education
Penn State University, College of Medicine

*"**Health Care Job Explosion: Careers In The 90's** is without question the most comprehensive source of information on the health care profession that I've seen. Not only does the book explore the multitude of jobs within the health care industry, it also covers the major topics related to the job-search process. I can't imagine any graduate wishing to pursue a career in health care who wouldn't benefit from this valuable resource."*
Eileen Nester, Editor, Career Woman Magazine

"...An ambitious round-up of advice and resources to help health field job seekers make a good connection. Unless you're a research professional, you'd probably not uncover a number of the resources mentioned. A real time saver!"
Joyce Lain Kennedy, Nationally Syndicated Careers Columnist

*"If it weren't so comprehensive, I'd call Dennis Damp's **Health Care Job Explosion**, Careers In The 90's a gem. At over 384 pages of detailed job resources, descriptions of health care fields and their career potential and tips on preparing and landing jobs, I'd have to call it a gold mine. This book is a detailed road map through the promised land of career opportunities. It helps you figure out where to go and shows you what it will take to get there."*
Steven Czetli, Executive Business Editor,
The Pittsburgh Press

THE BOOK OF
U.S. GOVERNMENT JOBS

Where They Are, What's Available, and How to Get One

Fifth Edition

Dennis V. Damp

D-AMP PUBLICATIONS
Moon Township, PA

THE BOOK OF
U.S. GOVERNMENT JOBS
Where They Are, What's Available, and How to Get One

By Dennis Damp

Fifth Edition

Disclaimer of All Warranties and Liabilities

The author and publisher make no warranties, either expressed or implied, with respect to the information contained herein. The information about periodicals and job services reported in this book is based on facts conveyed by their publishers and operators either in writing or by telephone interview. The author and publisher shall not be liable for any incidental or consequential damages in connection with, or arising out of, the use of material in this book.

Publisher's - Cataloging In Publication
(Prepared by Quality Books Inc.)

Damp, Dennis V.
    The Book Of U.S. Government Jobs: Where They Are, What's
Available, and How to Get One / by Dennis V. Damp. - 5th ed.
    p. cm.
    Includes bibliographical references and index.
    Preassigned LCCN: 93-070449.
    ISBN 0-943641-09-8

    1. Civil service positions--United States. I. Title.

JK716.D36 1994   353.001'03
                                    QBI93-21879

For information on distribution or quantity discount rates, Tel. 412/262-5578 or write to: Sales Department, D-AMP PUBLICATIONS, 401 Amherst Avenue, Moon Township, PA 15108. Distributed to the trade by Publishers Distribution Service, 6893 Sullivan Road, Grawn, MI 49637, Tel. 800-345-0096. Library distributors include Quality Books, Unique Books, BRODART, FOLLETT, and Baker & Taylor.

CONTENTS

FOREWORD

Conducting a job search in the 1990's is a complicated task that requires an in-depth knowledge of the hiring process for very different industries and hiring circumstances. For those seeking employment in the public sector, and in particular with the federal government, the attempt can quickly become a nightmare of trying to discover what specific jobs are available in the federal government, where the jobs are located, who actually conducts the hiring for these positions, and how to obtain the proper testing and application forms to begin the process. And all of that is just the beginning.

Dennis Damp has sorted through the vast amount of information, resources, and procedures required to obtain a federal government job and has laid out a map that will guide you step-by-step through this hiring maze to your goal of government employment. Most importantly, Dennis Damp has continuously revised his original work so that this 5th edition contains the most current requirements and necessary procedures that you must complete to reach your employment goals.

The Book of U.S. Government Jobs; Where They Are, What's Available, and How to Get One incorporates the same job search methods that I advocate on my radio program, for my clients, and for all job seekers. These are methods proven to be successful for a job search in the highly competitive workplace of the 1990's. The guidance offered in this book will save you enormous amounts of time, effort, and frustration in your job search for obtaining a federal government job.

Roxanne S. Rogers

Human Resource and Training Consultant
Host of *"The Career Connection"* WHO Radio, Des Moines, Iowa

PREFACE

This book's primary purpose is to steer job seekers through the maze of the federal hiring process and to present realistic job search strategies and viable options to landing a job with Uncle Sam. There are numerous and welcomed efforts underway to streamline the federal hiring process. I know only too well the complexities and problems that plague federal personnel policies and the hiring process in general.

Vice President Al Gore's *National Performance Review Committee* issued their first report titled "*From Red Tape To Results; Creating A Government That Works Better & Costs Less*" on September 7, 1993. This report is an integral part of President Clinton's plan to "*Reinvent Government*". The majority of what this report supports is long overdue and if implemented will benefit job seekers and reduce the overall cost of government. I couldn't help relate its findings to my 25 years of federal work experience, the last nine years as a mid-level manager. If half of the proposals are implemented, all will end up winners. Job seekers will find the federal employment process tremendously simplified. Federal managers and individual agencies will finally have a greater voice in the selection process, exceptional employees will benefit from new performance incentives, and we will have a leaner, more efficient government.

From Red Tape To Results states, "*This report represents the beginning of what will be — what must be — an ongoing commitment to change. It includes actions that will be taken now, by directive of the President; actions that will be taken by the cabinet secretaries and agency heads; and recommendations for congressional actions.*" Many of the personnel issues, including the hiring process, must be changed by congressional legislation. If the recommendations pass congressional scrutiny it will take years to fully implement the significant proposals of this plan simply because of the maze of rules, case law, and regulations that now exist. The NPR reports, "*Year after year, layer after layer, the rules have piled up. The U.S. Merit Systems Protection Board reports there are now 850 pages of federal personnel laws — augmented by 1,300 pages of OPM regulations on how to implement those laws and another 10,000 pages of guidance from the Federal Personnel Manual.*"

Summaries of the *National Performance Review's* (NPR's) proposed changes and their impact are outlined throughout this text. These changes are tentative and only time will tell if and when they will be implemented. My hope is that the American people will not let these proposals die. The issues are far too significant to ignore and we must not continue to pay for ineffective and wasteful practices. I commend Vice President Gore and the NPR for presenting to the American public viable alternatives to improve government efficiency.

The NPR announced plans to eliminate 252,000 federal employees over the next five years. Initially this sounds tremendously high and the announcement may prevent job seekers from investigating the federal job market. This number is large by any standard; however, you must look at the overall federal employment picture. Fifty thousand positions will not be filled each year for five years. Most of the positions will be eliminated through attrition. Uncle Sam employs an average of 437,000 new workers each year to replace employees that transfer to other jobs, retire, or stop working for other reasons. **Considerable job opportunities will remain for those willing to seek them out.** The federal government workforce will remain close to 2,800,000 strong after downsizing.

Actually, more entry level positions may become available due to the administration's strategy to dramatically reduce mid-level managers and supervisory positions. The thrust is to reduce total salary by eliminating a large number of GS-13 through GS-15 positions and reducing the supervisory to employee ratio to 10 employees for every supervisor. Currently, many agencies have supervisory ratios of 6 to 1 or less.

Retirement incentives, proposed by President Clinton, could prove to be a **bonanza** for those seeking federal employment. If it is offered to all federal agencies as proposed, any federal employee with 25 years service at any age or age 50 with 20 years service can retire early and receive a cash incentive to do so. Employees taking early retirement are assessed a 2% penalty against their retirement annuity for each year they are under age 55. Thousands may opt to leave early. If this happens, look for a tremendous hiring push like that of 1990 when the federal government hired over 700,000 workers in one year.

The NPR also proposes decentralizing personnel policies and they will ask Congress to pass legislation decentralizing authority over recruitment, hiring, and promotions. Their intent is to give all departments and agencies authority to conduct their own recruiting and examining for all positions, and abolish all central registers and standard application forms.

The Office of Personnel Management has experimented with this practice on a limited basis over the years. *The Book Of U.S. Government Jobs* explains the *Direct Hire* and *Case Examining* authorities in detail and the new procedures proposed by the NPR will closely parallel these programs. They also propose establishing a government-wide employment information system that will allow the public to go to one place for information about all job opportunities in the federal government. The new 5th edition provides abundant resources for you to locate government jobs, including OPMs latest telephone job hot lines and computer bulletin boards. Even if the NPR recommendations are adopted it will be difficult for the government to list all federal jobs in one central system due to different special hiring programs in the Department of Defense and overseas programs.

There are also proposals to simplify the federal job classification system including reducing career paths to four-to-six broad bands within each path.

If you're looking for good pay and excellent benefits, pursue the federal job market and don't be put off by rumors or pending changes. The proposed changes will do much to simplify the complex federal hiring process to your benefit. Many of the recommendations give employees a greater voice in the workplace and will shift the focus of government from a top down bureaucracy to entrepreneurial government. Use this book's resources to begin your personal job search. The Job Hunter's Checklist in Appendix A will help you organize your search and keep you on target.

Dennis V. Damp

ACKNOWLEDGEMENT

Since we published the previous editions of *The Book Of U.S. Government Jobs*, D-AMP Publications has noted a considerable improvement in the dissemination and availability of employment information from numerous federal agencies and departments including the Office of Personnel Management (OPM). Leonard Klein, OPM's Associate Director for Career Entry, responded to a recent GAO audit that indicated problems at Federal Job Information Centers. Mr. Klein responded by listing numerous improvements that were either just initiated, in the planning stages or close to implementation. I commend Mr. Klein and his staff for these improvements and throughout our research I was amazed at the professional response that we received when networking with OPM and other agencies. During previous research efforts we frequently had to have our Congressmen and Senator call various offices to obtain needed information.

A special thanks must go to William Stothers, editor *Mainstream Magazine* - Peter Ognibene, editor *Federal Jobs Digest* - Roxanne Rogers, Human Resource Consultant and Host of "*The Career Connection*" WHO Radio in Des Monies Iowa - Will Cantrell, Editor *International Employment Hotline* - Veltiseszar Bautista, author of *The Book of U.S. Postal Exams* - and Paul Endress, president of DataTech Software, developers of the federal application software package *Quick & Easy 171s*, all of whom were kind enough to review the 5th edition's manuscript and to assist us with presenting to our readers the most up-to-date federal career guide available. A special thanks must also go to Daniel Lauber, author of the Job Finder Series, for setting the publishing standards for job resource lists including his latest effort *The Ultimate Job Finder*. Daniel Lauber's insightful comments, recommendations, and editorial input were tremendously helpful and appreciated. His input significantly contributed to the professionalism of this production.

The publishing industry lost a good friend recently, Muriel Turner, Joyce Lain Kennedy's assistant. Ms. Turner unexpectedly passed away from a serious illness. I will miss Muriel's kind words, encouragement, and sympathetic ear. She always had time to refer lost souls, like myself, to the proper resource. She was a valuable asset to Ms. Kennedy's staff and I know that Joyce, myself and hundreds of publishers nationwide will sorely miss Muriel.

It was refreshing to read Vice President Gore's National Performance Review (NPR) report titled, "*From Red Tape To Results: Creating A Government That Works Better & Costs Less.*" This wealth of information and change agent should revolutionize federal government and particularly the hiring process for those seeking federal employment. I commend the architects of this valiant effort and trust that principals of the plan will stay the course to insure implementation. This farsighted and indepth report must be the catalyst for "*Reinventing Government*". In my 25 years of federal employment I witnessed numerous half hearted efforts to streamline government and improve overall efficiency. Most fell through the bureaucratic trap door to oblivion. I truly believe that the present administration has the opportunity of a lifetime to commit this country to significant change with the mandate of most Americans. Let us not let this opportunity slip past or become muddled in the politics of the day. I fear that this monumental effort might take a back seat to health care reform and/or the NAFTA agreement. If it does, we all will surely lose the opportunity of a lifetime to streamline an overburdened and archaic bureaucracy.

There are legions of dedicated, knowledgeable, and hard working federal workers who may perceive the NPR's report as derogatory and critical of their service. This couldn't be further from the truth. The government today operates effectively only because of these dedicated gate keepers who are forced to work with outdated policies and burdensome regulations. There are hundreds of thousands of quality federal workers who are micromanaged and placed in compromising situations due to an industrial-era bureaucracy operating in the informational age. The government's top-down management style has impeded inventiveness and discouraged entrepreneurial efforts. Agencies make it almost impossible for an employee to submit suggestions that would streamline operations or improve a process. The paperwork trail for suggestions is unbelievably complex and individuals often wait two to three years to receive a response.

I have not listed all of the authorities and sources consulted in the preparation of this book. To do so would require more space than is available. The list would include a large number of federal departments and agencies, libraries, institutions, periodicals, and many individuals. I sincerely thank all of the people that played a part in the development of *The Book of U.S. Government Jobs*.

Illustration Credits: All illustrations in this book, including the cover design, are original art work by James Wright, 3307 Garbett St., McKeesport, PA 15132 - Phone (412) 673-0848.

Cover by James Wright

CHAPTER ONE

INTRODUCTION TO GOVERNMENT EMPLOYMENT

SHOULD YOU CONSIDER WORKING FOR THE FEDERAL GOVERNMENT? Consider the numbers. Uncle Sam employs over **3,041,000** workers and hires an average of **437,000** new employees each year to replace workers that transfer to other federal or private jobs, retire, or stop working for other reasons.[1] The U.S Government is the largest employer in the United States, hiring 2.5 percent of the nation's civilian work force.

Even when you consider the proposed cuts of the Clinton/Gore National Performance Review (NPR), described below and in the preface, tremendous job opportunities remain for those who know how to tap this lucrative job market. All government hiring is based on performance and qualifications regardless of your sex, race, color, creed, religion, disability, or national origin. Where else can you apply for a high paying entry level job that offers employment at thousands of locations internationally, excellent career advancement opportunities, plus careers in hundreds of occupations?

Federal workers enjoy excellent benefits with the average annual white-collar salary exceeding $34,664, professionals $43,477, and administrative reaching $39,366.

The NPR's recommendations may ultimately create a hiring bonanza for those seeking federal employment. Early retirement incentive packages and significant reductions in mid-level management and supervisory positions may create a mass exodus of senior employees with 20 or more years of service.

The Clinton administration has proposed eliminating 252,000 federal civilian jobs, roughly eight percent of the total federal civilian workforce, over a five year period. Vice President Gore said, "*Most of the personnel reductions will be concentrated in the structures of over-control and micromanagement that now bind the federal government: supervisors, headquarters staffs,*

---

[1] Government Pamphlet PWI 9301, Federal Civilian Workforce Statistics, Employment and Trends, March 1993.

personnel specialists, accountants, and auditors." The NPR's goal is to eliminate unnecessary layers of management and nonessential staff.[1] Many of the displaced workers will retire or they will be offered jobs with other agencies.

The NPR's findings are proposals - **NOT LAW**. The report states, *"If Congress enacts the management reforms outlined in this report, we will dramatically cut costs."* The President does have executive powers over some areas. No one knows what recommendations will make it through congress. Continue to explore the lucrative federal job market. Enter the job search with your eyes open and with these program highlights you'll be aware of proposals that may affect your job search down the road.

Five agencies employ 75 percent of the work force or 2,280,750 employees. Of the 116,000 federal employees stationed abroad, 72,582 are U.S. Citizens. The remaining 43,565 are foreign nationals.[2]

TABLE 1-1
THE FIVE LARGEST FEDERAL AGENCIES

TOTAL WORKERS	3,041,714	100.00 %
Legislative Branch	38,381	1.27 %
Judicial Branch	28,018	0.93 %
Executive Branch	2,975,315	97.8 %
USPS & PRC *	781,438	25.0 %
DEFENSE	958,976	32.0 %
VA	263,427	08.0 %
TREASURY	172,606	05.0 %
HHS	131,625	04.0 %
ALL OTHERS	719,842	24.0 %

* USPS & PRC is the United States Postal Service and Postal Rate Commission

SOURCE: Federal Civilian Workforce Statistics, Employment/Trends - March 93, PWI 9305

---

[1]Excerpts from the Report of the National Performance Review, "From Red Tape To Results", September 7, 1993.

[2]THE FACT BOOK, Office of Personnel Management, PSOG/OW1-2, June 1992

The changes in Table 1-1 from the previous 4th edition are revealing. The two largest agencies shrunk while employment increased for the remaining three. The largest change was in the (DOD) Department of Defense; from 1,076,462 employees in October of 1989 to 958,976 for a loss of 117,486 workers. The USPS decreased by 43,364 workers. This trend is projected to continue in the Defense Department. When military bases close civilian DOD total employment decreases. The VA, *Veterans Affairs*, and HHS, *Health & Human Services*, grew by 25,952 workers. This trend supports the Bureau of Labor Statistics projections that total employment growth in health care will lead all other fields through the year 2005. Between 25,000 and 30,000 new jobs will be added to national health care payrolls each month through the year 2005. This includes both private and public sectors.

NATURE OF FEDERAL EMPLOYMENT

The U.S. federal government affects the lives and livelihood of every American. Uncle Sam represents American interests abroad, defends Americans against foreign aggressors, provides public services, enforces laws that protect American's safety, health, rights, and administers various public assistance programs. All of our lives are affected with such diverse activities as weather forecasting, air traffic control, rail transportation and highway regulations, meat and poultry inspection, workplace safety regulations, savings deposit guarantees, and home mortgage programs. Workers employed by the federal government play a vital role in all these and many other facets of American life.[1]

The constitution of the United States divides federal government into three branches: legislative, judicial, and executive branches. The executive branch is the largest of the three, employing 97.8 percent of all federal workers. The executive branch is composed of the Office of the President, the 14 executive departments, and over 90 independent agencies. Appendix C provides detailed information on federal agencies including employment offices and phone numbers.

WORKING CONDITIONS

Almost every working condition found in the private sector can also be found in the federal government. Most white-collar employees work in office buildings, hospitals, or laboratories, while blue-collar employees generally work in factories, warehouses, shipyards, airbases, or construction sites. Others spend much of their time outdoors, such as those employed in national parks and forests. Work environments can range from very controlled and relatively relaxed while other environments are quite hazardous and stressful - such as those of law enforcement officers, astronauts, or air traffic controllers.

Many federal workers' duties require travel away from their duty station to attend meetings, complete training, or perform inspections while others - such as auditors, instructors, field engineering crews, and safety investigators - may require extensive travel for weeks or months at a time. Some employees are on continuous travel and receive lump sum payments to cover

---

[1]Career Guide to Industries, U.S. Department of Labor, September 1992

travel costs. *Alternative work schedules* are available to many workers through negotiated union contracts that permit *flexitime or compressed work schedules*. Some agencies are experimenting with *flexiplace* which allow workers to perform some job duties at home and many larger federal workplaces now offer child care facilities for working parents.

Over sixty percent of all agencies recently surveyed have some form of *(QWL) Quality of Work Life or Employee Involvement* program implemented throughout their workforce. These programs encourage employee participation at all levels to improve overall efficiency, productivity, and working conditions.

OCCUPATIONS

Federal workers are employed in almost every conceivable occupation. Approximately 2 out of every 3 federal workers are employed in *professional specialty, administrative support, or executive, administrative, and managerial occupations*. Secretaries are the largest administrative job series, employing over 100,000 workers.

College degrees are held by 35 percent of the total federal workforce. Certain jobs require a general 4-year bachelor's degree and some positions require a specific concentration. A graduate or professional degree is necessary to enter some professional jobs. Since the Department of Defense employs over half of all non-postal federal workers, it employs some workers in almost every occupation.

Almost all professional specialty jobs require a 4-year college degree or at least 3 years of non-clerical work experience. Some, such as engineers, physicians, and life and physical scientists, require a bachelor's or higher degree in a specific field of study. Engineers work in every department of the executive branch. Most are employed by the Department of Defense, a significant number work in the National Aeronautic and Space Administration (NASA) and the Department of Transportation.

Systems analysts and computer scientists are the largest professional specialty groups, employing about 50,000 workers throughout government. This specialty is needed to write computer programs, analyze data processing related problems, and to keep computer systems operating.

Almost 75 percent of all federal *health care workers* are employed by the Department of Veteran Affairs (VA) at one of their 172 VA hospitals, 233 outpatient clinics, and 120 nursing homes. The VA fills approximately 15,000 job vacancies each year due to retirements and to replace those who choose to leave. *Health Care Job Explosion! Careers In The 90's* is available from the publisher and it provides complete information on health care jobs in the public and private sectors. There are positions for audiologists, various technologists and technicians, medical records specialists, librarians, counselors, physicians, nurses, and dietitians. Other professionals include life scientists including geologists, meteorologists, and physicists. The Department of Agriculture employs the majority of life scientists, but physical scientists are distributed evenly throughout the executive departments.

Executive, administrative, and managerial workers are primarily responsible for overseeing federal government operations. Because most people advance to these jobs from professional occupations, most have a bachelor's degree or at least 3 years of non-clerical work experience. Others provide management support. Accountants and auditors develop financial records and check operations for fraud and inefficiency. Inspectors and compliance officers enforce regulations and tax examiners determine and collect taxes. In addition to the DOD, many of these workers are employed by the Department of the Treasury, and almost all of the tax examiners, inspectors, and compliance officers employed in the country work for the government. Other management support workers include purchasing agents, administrative officers, and management analysts.

Administrative support workers usually need only a high school diploma. They aid management staff and include secretaries, typists, word processors, and various clerks. All agencies hire administrative support workers.

Technicians and related support occupations aid professionals in research, analysis, or law enforcement, and often their tasks and skills are quite specialized. As a result, many technicians are required to have some vocational training or extensive work experience. Many have two year associate degrees. Engineering technicians are most common. Others include health technicians, such as dental hygienists and radiologists, legal assistants, or air traffic controllers.

Most federal jobs in other occupations require no more than a high school degree, although some departments and agencies may prefer workers with some vocational training or previous experience. Over half of the precision production, craft, and repair occupations are mechanics, such as vehicle and mobile equipment mechanics, who fix and maintain all types of motor vehicles, aircraft, and heavy equipment, and electrical and electronic equipment operators, who repair electric items and telephone and cable television lines. Others include the construction trades, painters, plumbers, electricians, and other skilled trades.

Service workers are relatively scarce in the federal government. About half of all federal workers in these occupations are firefighters and police officers. The federal government employs relatively few workers in fabricator, operator, and laborer occupations; agriculture, forestry, fishing, and related occupations; and marketing and sales occupations.

OUTLOOK

The Clinton administration plans to cut total federal employment by 250,000 over the next five years, roughly 8 percent of the federal civilian workforce. Considering that Uncle Sam hires an average of 400,000 people each year to replace workers that transfer to other federal or private jobs, retire, or stop working for other reasons, considerable job opportunities will remain. Most of the cuts will be achieved through attrition.

Opportunities for entry level positions may increase as management and supervisory positions are either eliminated or reduced. The Bureau of Labor Statistics projects that distribution of employment is expected to change with reductions anticipated in the Department of Defense. Also, if Congress approves the administration's *Reinventing Government* plan, reductions among the remaining executive agencies may occur over the next five years.

DOD employment is expected to gradually decline due to the end of the cold war as well as increasing concern over budget deficits. Employing half of all federal workers, the DOD should gradually reduce its workforce through attrition over the next decade. Blue collar workers, 3 out of 4 work for the DOD, may be particularly hard hit.

Federal employment is generally not affected by cyclical fluctuations in the economy, as are employment in may construction, manufacturing, and other private sector industries. However, political changes can influence staffing levels. Each presidential administration may have different public policy priorities that result in greater levels of federal employment in some programs and declines in others. Layoffs, called *reduction in force*, have occurred in the past; however, they are uncommon and generally affect relatively few workers.

Over the past decade the federal government hired an average of 437,000 workers yearly to fill vacancies. Competition is keen for federal positions, especially in time of economic uncertainty.

GETTING STARTED

In the past it was difficult for job seekers to obtain up-to-date job information, applications, and guidance from *(FJICs) Federal Job Information Centers*. The United States General Accounting Office reported the severity of this problem in July of 1992.[1] The Office of Personnel Management (OPM) is aggressively working to resolve these problems. OPMs Director of Federal Workforce Future Issues reported that OPM is building a job information network that utilizes the latest in telecommunications technology. The system is in transition from separate local information centers to a nationwide network.

The Book Of U.S. Government Jobs walks you through the latest government sponsored and private company job information networks including available electronic bulletin boards, self-service job information computers, the 24 hours a day, 7 day a week telephone information systems, toll-free services, (TDD) telephone device for the deaf systems, computer-based reference systems, and explores and exposes all facets of the federal job search.

Readers will find up-to-date information on how the federal employment system works from an insiders prospective and how to locate job announcements through various methods and resources. Services are also listed that review applications to determine the federal jobs that you are qualified for. You'll learn about special hiring programs for the physically disadvantaged, veterans, students, and scholars, thousands of job opportunities, Civil Service Exam requirements, overseas jobs, Postal Service jobs, how to complete your employment application, and much more. Appendix A provides a comprehensive checklist that will take you through the entire federal employment process. Use Appendix A throughout your job search.

The four appendices include; an easy to use federal job check list, Federal Job Information Centers listing, complete lists of federal occupations, and comprehensive agency summaries and contact lists including employment office addresses and phone numbers.

This book will guide you step-by-step through the federal employment process, from filling out your first SF-171 employment application to locating job resources and hiring agencies. Follow the guidelines set forth in this book to dramatically improve your chances of landing a federal job.

PAY & BENEFITS

Job security and excellent pay are among the top reasons most seek federal employment. There are eight predominate pay systems. Approximately half of the workforce is under the *General Schedule (GS) pay scale*, twenty percent are paid under the *Postal Service rates*, and

---

[1]July 1992 GAO/GDD-92-116 - Poor Service Found at FJICs - GAO Report to Congressional Subcommittees

about ten percent are paid under the *Prevailing Rate Schedule (WG) Wage Grade classification.* The remaining pay systems are for the *Executive Schedule, Foreign Service, Nonappropriated Fund Instrumentalities scales,* and *Veterans Health Administration.*

General Schedule (GS) pay varies from the GS-1 level at $11,903 per annum to $86,589 per annum at the top GS-15 grade. The Senior Executive Service salary tops out at $115,700 per annum. The president adjusts federal salaries to levels that are competitive with the private sector. The average annual salary for full time non-postal employees increased to $34,664 over the past year.[1] Starting pay depends on your level of experience, education and the complexity of the position applied for. A complete GS pay schedule is printed in Chapter Two.

Each GS grade has ten pay steps. Currently, a GS-9 starts at $27,789 for step one and reaches $36,123 per year at step ten. At the GS-9 grade each pay step adds $926.00 to the annual salary. Pay steps are earned based on time in service and the employee's work performance. General Schedule employees are referred to as white collar workers under the federal classification system. Approximately 17 percent of total federal non-postal employment is classified under the Wage Grade (WG) blue collar pay schedules. See Appendix D for a complete list of occupations.

VACATION & SICK LEAVE

All employees receive: 10 paid holidays, 13 days of vacation for the first three years, twenty days of vacation with three to fifteen years service and after fifteen years twenty-six days. Additionally, 13 sick days are accrued each year regardless of length of service. Sick leave can be accumulated and applied towards retirement.[2]

Military time counts towards benefits. If you have 3 years of military service you begin with 4 weeks paid vacation and 3 years towards retirement.

HEALTH BENEFITS & LIFE INSURANCE

Medical health plans and the *Federal Employees' Group Life Insurance*, FEGLI program, are available to all employees. The medical plan is an employee-employer contribution system and includes HMO and Blue Cross and Blue Shield programs. There are hundreds of plans to choose from. The FEGLI program offers low cost term life insurance for the employee and basic coverage for your family. FEGLI offers up to 5 times the employee's salary in death benefits.

One of the primary benefits of federal employment is the satisfaction you experience from working in a challenging and rewarding position. Positions are available with the level of responsibility and authority that you desire.

---

[1] Occupations of Federal White-Collar and Blue-Collar Workers - US Dept. of Commerce PB93-140804

[2] Various sections of the Federal Personnel Manual.

RETIREMENT

The federal retirement system was significantly changed for individuals hired after January 1, 1984. Social Security is withheld and a new employee contribution system is fashioned after a 401k defined contribution plan. You can elect to contribute up to 10 percent of your salary into a *THRIFT savings 401k plan*. The government will match your contribution up to 5 percent. This is effectively a 5 percent pay increase. Your contributions are tax deferred and reduce your taxable income by the amount contributed. The retirement benefit is determined by the amount that has accumulated during the employee's career. This includes the interest earned and capital gains realized from the retirement fund.

The employee can elect to invest his contributions in one of three mutual funds. There are many withdrawal options including lump sum and various fixed term annuities. The contribution plan payout is in addition to the social security benefits that you will be eligible for at retirement.

> The Employee Benefit Research Institute indicates that people retiring in 2010 will derive 37.7% of their retirement income from Social Security, 36.6% from employer sponsored pensions, and 25.7% from savings and investments.

TRAINING & CAREER DEVELOPMENT

Federal agencies offer extensive career advancement programs. Employees normally receive orientation and skills training and can take advantage of career advancement opportunities. Many federal departments and individual agencies, such as the Office of Personnel Management, Federal Aviation Administration, United States Department of Agriculture, Federal Bureau of Investigation, National Oceanic and Atmospheric Administration, Department of Defense, and all branches of the armed forces have large full time training facilities for mandatory employee training in technical and management fields. These training facilities offer many college level courses that are accredited by the American Council on Education. College credits can be earned while attending work related training.

TYPES OF TRAINING

- **■ ORIENTATION TRAINING (NEW EMPLOYEES)**
- **■ TECHNICAL SKILLS TRAINING**
- **■ PROFESSIONAL TRAINING**
- **■ SUPERVISORY TRAINING**
- **■ EXECUTIVE AND MANAGEMENT TRAINING**
- **■ CAREER DEVELOPMENT TRAINING**

Career development programs are offered by most agencies for target positions and personal long term career goals. Each agency offers its own unique programs. However, they are all authorized by the same federal regulations and many similarities exist between agencies. The following is a sampling of currently offered career development programs.

CAREER DEVELOPMENT PROGRAMS

● **SECRETARIAL DEVELOPMENT PROGRAM** - The Department of Education provides opportunities for well qualified secretaries to follow a career track and to grow professionally by developing a high degree of proficiency. This program is a certificate program open to all Department secretarial/clerical personnel. Individual training programs and developmental assignments must be completed to obtain certification.

● **UPWARD MOBILITY PROGRAM.** This program allows employees (below GS-9 or equivalent), who are in dead-end jobs, to obtain positions with greater career advancement potential. Extensive training is provided to eligible employees to gain the necessary qualifications for higher paying positions.

● **INDIVIDUAL DEVELOPMENT PLANS.** This program offers employees the opportunity to sit down with their supervisor and design a career development program. A target position is identified and training is provided to help the employee reach his/her goal. Training programs are tailored to meet specific goals and can include formal college courses at government expense. (**The amount of tuition reimbursement depends on availability of funds. Agencies typically fund 50 to 100 percent of the tuition if the student maintains a C average or better.**) Correspondence programs are available and lateral work assignments are encouraged to provide exposure to diverse aspects of the target position.

● **MANAGEMENT INTERN DEVELOPMENT PROGRAM.** This program provides details to a Division Manager's office to complete career development training. Each participant is assessed on the knowledge and skills obtained during the detail. Details are for periods of from one month to one year and the employee is placed on full travel expenses for the duration of the assignment.

● **SEMINAR FOR PROSPECTIVE WOMEN MANAGERS.** (Offered by the Department of Transportation) This seminar provides opportunities for women who demonstrated high abilities and motivation to enter a management position.

LOCATING A JOB

Fourteen cabinet departments and over 100 independent agencies comprise the federal government system. These departments and agencies have offices in all corners of the world. The size of each agency varies considerably. Several agencies have as few as one employee: Commission On Minor Business Development, and the Commission on Interstate Child Support. The five largest agencies are listed in Table 1-1. The larger the agency the more diverse the opportunities. These large agencies hire a broad spectrum of occupations, professional and blue collar.

If you desire to travel, government jobs offer abundant opportunities to relocate within the continental United States and throughout the world. Chapter 7 provides information on thousands of overseas employment opportunities. Twelve federal agencies and departments offer employment abroad for over 72,733 civilian U.S. citizens. The Department Of Defense Dependent Schools system employees hundreds of teachers for military dependent schools overseas.

California has the largest number of federal workers, 312,207, and Vermont the least with 5,708 workers. All of the 315 (MSA) Metropolitan Statistical Areas in the U.S. and Puerto Rico had federal civilian employees in December of 1992 as listed in the Central Personnel Data File. Small towns and rural areas outside of MSAs had 361,362 federal workers.[1] The actual number of federal civilian employees is greater than the above figures. The Defense Intelligence Agency, Central Intelligence Agency, and the National Security Agency do not release this data. Chapter Three provides job resources including magazines and newspapers that list thousands of national job openings and job placement services. Special hiring programs are explained for *Outstanding Scholars*, the *Career America Program*, and thousands of student employment opportunities. Appendix B provides detailed listings of Federal Job Information Centers and Appendix C provides a comprehensive agency contact list that includes national and regional personnel office contacts.

---

[1]Federal Civilian Employment By State & Metropolitan Areas by OPM statistician Christine Steele.

TABLE 1-2
FEDERAL EMPLOYMENT BY STATE 12/31/92

STATE	TOTAL	STATE	TOTAL
Alabama	58,055	Nevada	11,581
Alaska	15,897	New Hampshire	8,358
Arizona	40,437	New Jersey	73,738
Arkansas	20,723	New Mexico	27,700
California	312,207	New York	149,200
Colorado	57,029	North Carolina	50,798
Connecticut	24,498	North Dakota	8,313
Delaware	5,476	Ohio	93,538
Florida	114,218	Oklahoma	45,667
Georgia	93,480	Oregon	30,920
Hawaii	25,287	Pennsylvania	132,307
Idaho	11,293	Rhode Island	10,262
Illinois	106,163	South Carolina	32,775
Indiana	42,878	South Dakota	10,102
Iowa	19,801	Tennessee	53,872
Kansas	26,381	Texas	178,973
Kentucky	38,022	Utah	35,442
Louisiana	35,051	Vermont	5,708
Maine	16,234	Virginia	167,735
Maryland	135,717	Washington	68,592
Massachusetts	62,291	Washington DC	389,427
Michigan	58,536	West Virginia	17,391
Minnesota	33,790	Wisconsin	29,934
Mississippi	25,871	Wyoming	6,582
Missouri	65,989	OVERSEAS	119,088
Montana	12,392	*Unspecified	41,601

* Mostly Judicial Branch (62%) and the FBI (37%).

EDUCATION REQUIREMENTS

In the federal government 65 percent of all workers do not have a college degree. The level of required education is dependent upon the job that's applied for. Each job announcement lists needed skills and abilities including education and work experience. However, the more education and work experience that you have the more competitive you will be when ranked against other applicants. A sample qualification statement is presented in chapter 2 for the Training Instructor Series (GS-1712). The majority of positions within the government have a published qualifications standard similar to the provided example.

You can review a specific qualification standard, called X-118s, at your local Federal Depository Library. Many large college and private libraries are designated depository status and they can help you locate specific government publications including the X-118 qualification standards for your particular skill.

CAREER SEARCH

If you are uncertain about which career to enter or if government jobs are right for you *The Book of U.S. Government Jobs* is a good place to start. Chapter Three outlines detailed informational interviewing techniques that will help you investigate primary and alternate career paths and the all new and expanded 5th edition provides over a thousand resources to help you make a connection. The Federal Jobs Checklist in Appendix A guides job seekers through the federal employment system beginning to end.

The *Federal Jobs Digest* offers a *Federal Job Matching Service* to help you determine what career is best suited to your education, training, and background. They evaluate your Federal Employment Application and send you a list of federal job titles and grade levels for which you qualify. The fee for this service is $25 for subscribers and $30 for non-subscribers. Call their Federal Job Matching Service toll free number (800-824-5000) for further details.

There are many excellent resources available to assist you with your job hunt. A few select books and software programs are offered for sale by the publisher in the back of this book for your convenience. Books and services that we mention but don't offer for sale will have ordering information printed with the notation such as *Joyce Lain Kennedy's Career Book*. This book is by far one of the most complete, informative and useful career guide on the market today. It helps people decide what they want to be - what must they do to get what they want -and how to move ahead once they enter a career. This valuable reference and work book motivates, presents valuable tools to help one make a career selection, then propels you through the rigors of college to landing your first job. Available at bookstores and libraries, or you can order a copy toll free at 800-323-4900 for $17.95 plus shipping.

CIVIL SERVICE EXAMS

Tests are required for specific groups including secretarial/clerical, air traffic control, and for certain entry level professional/administrative jobs. Chapter Four offers detailed information on testing requirements and provides sample test questions. *Outstanding Scholars,* college graduates with top grades, can be hired on the spot. Entry-level professional and administrative job applicants will earn eligibility by either:

- Earning a college grade point average of 3.5 or above on a 4.0 scale and impressing agency recruiters with experience and technical abilities during an interview.

- Passing a job-related skills test and a new Individual Achievement Record test. Both measure relevant personal qualities required for successful job performance.

CHAPTER TWO

UNDERSTANDING THE FEDERAL
EMPLOYMENT SYSTEM

Most government personnel specialists do not have the time to counsel prospective employees. Examples of some common questions are: Must all applicants take extensive written exams? What is a federal register, appointment, series and announcement? What training and experience is required? Who in government is currently hiring? What jobs are available state-side, overseas and with the U.S. Postal Service, and what can he/she expect to achieve? There are too many questions and too few answers.

COMPETITIVE SERVICE

About 12 percent of all federal jobs are in Washington D.C. Government employees work in offices, shipyards, laboratories, national parks, hospitals, military bases and many other settings across the country and overseas. Approximately 57 percent of civilian jobs are in the *competitive service*, which means that people applying for them must be evaluated by the Office of Personnel Management (OPM). Chapter Three explains the various services into which you can be hired.

COMPETITIVE EXAMINATIONS

Hiring for federal jobs is generally through a *competitive examination*. There are exceptions to this rule and non-competitive appointments are available for certain veterans, the physically challenged or handicapped, and other groups. New employees are hired for their ability to perform the work advertised in the job announcement. An applicant's ability is determined through an evaluation of educational background, work experience, and skills testing for certain job series.

DETERMINING YOUR ELIGIBILITY

Eligibility is determined through evaluating an applicant's education **AND/OR** work experience. For example, an entry level radio operator would start at a GS-2 pay grade, $13,382 per year, if he/she was a high school graduate **OR** had at least three months of *general experience*. That same radio operator could start at a GS-4, $16,393 per year, if he/she had six months of general experience and six months of *specialized experience*, **OR** 2 years of education above high school with courses related to the occupation.

GENERAL EXPERIENCE

This is any type of work which demonstrates the applicant's ability to perform the work of the position, or experience which provided a familiarity with the subject matter or process of the broad subject areas of the occupation. Specialized experience can be substituted for general experience.

SPECIALIZED EXPERIENCE

This is experience which is in the occupation of the position to be filled, in a related occupation, or in one of the specialized areas within that occupation, which has equipped the applicant with the particular *knowledge, skills, and abilities* (KSA's) to perform the duties of the position.

WRITTEN TESTS

An *examination announcement (job opening notice)* may or may not require a written test. In many cases the examination consists of a detailed evaluation of your work experiences and schooling that you list on your employment application. Of the 446 white collar job series, just over 90 require written tests under the new Administrative Careers With America program. Additionally, jobs in Air Traffic Control and other specialized fields require written tests. The 90 administrative careers that require tests are listed in chapter four.

The **NPR** will ask congress to pass legislation decentralizing authority over recruitment, hiring, and promotion. Under this decentralized system, agencies will also be allowed to make their own decisions about when to hire candidates directly - without examinations or ranking.

The federal government evaluates each candidate strictly for his/her ability to perform the duties of the position. **ABILITY IS OBTAINED THROUGH EDUCATION AND/OR EXPERIENCE.** Even engineering positions are rated this way. For example, there are several alternative non-degree paths that allow applicants to rate eligible for engineering positions. OPM qualifications for engineering positions require either a 4 year engineering degree OR four year college level education, and/or technical experience. Chapter three provides specific details on the *Engineering Conversion Program.*

> Each employee is classified within a highly complex system of some 459 job series, 15 grades and 10 steps within each grade. The **NPR** suggests a simplified system with as few as five career paths - professional, technical, specialist, administrative, and clerical.

JOB SERIES

Each job announcement describes the required experience, education, job location, pay and miscellaneous details needed to apply for a position within a *job series*. A complete occupational job series listing is provided in Appendix D. Job series are identified with a title and series number such as:

JOB SERIES EXAMPLES	
TITLE	**SERIES**
Accountant	GS-510
Secretary	GS-318
Engineer-Electrical	GS-801
Computer Specialist	GS-334
Equipment Mechanic	WG-5800
Paperhanging	WG-4103
Laboring	WG-3502

THE FEDERAL REGISTER

The *federal register* is a list of applicants who pass an examination with a score of 70 out of a maximum of 100 points. If you are a veteran you may qualify for an additional 5 or 10 points depending on your discharge status. Veterans preference is discussed in Chapter Six.

Examination announcements are issued by the Office of Personnel Management and by agencies that have *direct hire* or *case examining* authority for job openings in specific areas. Area offices of the Office of Personnel Management (OPM) issue **"FEDERAL JOB OPPORTUNITIES LISTS"** that provide information on current needs for anticipated job vacancies within their servicing area. Interested individuals would call, visit or write their Federal Job Information Center, FJIC, see appendix B, to request open job announcements or call the Office of Personnel Management's Telephone Message Directory, OPM's electronic job bulletin Board, contact individual agencies that have direct or case hiring authority, or call the telephone hot lines listed in chapter three or in the appendices. State employment offices also receive copies of these lists.

Examination announcements are advertised for periods from several weeks to months depending on the agency's critical needs. Exceptions to these rules apply to Vietnam Era, recently discharged, disabled veterans, and the handicapped. You must obtain examination announcements from the FJIC, Federal Job Information Center, or directly from agencies that have direct hiring or case examining authority. FJICs and direct hire authority agencies are responsible for hiring in their specific territory.

CASE EXAMINING

The Office of Personnel Management has implemented new case examining hiring procedures to assist agencies that have critical hiring needs. Applicants can apply directly to various agencies for positions that meet specific qualifications. Under these procedures, when an agency has a vacancy they issue a vacancy announcement, not OPM. This announcement lists the title, series and grade of the position; gives the opening/closing dates and duty location; provides information concerning the duties, responsibilities and qualification requirements of the position; and gives the name and phone number of a contact person in the recruiting agency. To obtain announcements applicants must contact the agency where the vacancy exists.

The agency reviews the applicant's basic eligibility. The final ratings are done by OPM and the candidates are ranked according to total score. OPM does maintain a centralized listing of open case examinations through Federal Job Information Centers and Testing Services. See chapter three for complete information on how to obtain current announcement information for case examinations.

DIRECT HIRE AUTHORITY

Direct hire authority is granted to agencies with specific hiring needs in one or several job series. The Office of Personnel Management delegates hiring to certain agencies for critical needs. Agencies with this authority advertise job openings, rate applicants, establish their own eligibility lists and registers, conduct interviews and hire. Job seekers must contact individual agencies to identify direct hire job openings or subscribe to one of several private companies' federal jobs listing services. OPM only delegates limited direct hire authority for certain job series within an agency. Agencies can have direct hire authority in one large metropolitan area due to a large population of a particular series and the same agency in other areas must hire through OPM area offices.

THE EMPLOYMENT APPLICATION

After identifying a desirable announcement you must submit the requested paperwork. *The SF-171 form, Federal Employment Application*, and all other requested announcement forms must be filled out in detail.

> Inadequately prepared application forms prevent many highly-qualified candidates from making the eligible list.

There are vast differences between industry's standard brief RESUME format and the detailed information you must supply on the SF-171 application. **The RESUME is generally one to two pages long. The SF-171 application will be four to five pages for a new employee with minimum education and experience to over sixty pages for career government managers**.

The federal government rates *bidders*, "applicants" on their work experience and education. The personnel specialist rating you generally knows little about the job you bid on. This specialist will rate you by referring to the Federal Qualification Standards, called X-118s; see a sample qualification standard on the following pages. These standards break most job series down to general and specialized qualifying work experience and required education. You must have a certain number of years of both general and specialized experience for various starting pay grades. Past work experience and training must be noted on your application. Describe the specific duties, responsibilities and accomplishments performed in each job held and include special assignments and details. Refer to chapter five for step by step guidance on how to complete your SF-171.

When submitting your application, SF-171, you don't have to send the original. Copies are acceptable. However, you must have an original signature on the copy you send in. Keep the unsigned original for copies needed for other announcements and for the interviewing process.

LITTLE KNOWN FACTS

If you visit a FJIC and view their current list of available positions it may not be all inclusive for that area. Some agencies have direct hire or case hiring authority for specific job skills and many agencies can hire college graduates non-competitively under the *Career America Program*. These agencies do not advertise openings through OPM. The Career America program is explained in Chapter Three.

To locate other potential job openings contact individual agency's personnel or human resources departments at locations that you wish to work. Also, contact OPM or your local Federal Building's Federal Executive Board, FEB, to obtain local agency listings.

Review the Blue pages in your white page directory. Blue pages list government agencies in your area. The yellow pages also offer comprehensive government listings.

To obtain specific information about a particular agency first refer to Appendix C and then look up the *United States Government Manual* at your library for additional details. This highly informative book is published and revised yearly and lists each department and agency. Contact names, addresses, and a brief agency description is provided along with some employment information.

Don't overlook your local state employment office. The Office of Personnel Management supplies current employment lists to all state employment offices and often direct hire agencies forward their lists to state agencies.

HOW JOBS ARE FILLED

Selecting officials can fill positions through internal promotions or reassignments, reemploying former employees, using special noncompetitive appointments such as the *Veterans Readjustment Act program*, or by appointing a new employee that is on a Federal Register.

NONCOMPETITIVE APPOINTMENTS

If you can qualify for a special NONCOMPETITIVE APPOINTMENT, you should contact agencies directly. The following chapters explain the various special appointments that are available.

> Agencies seek out job applicants who can be hired through non-competitive appointments.

Agencies often hold off on hiring until close to the end of the fiscal year, September 30th. They evaluate their attrition, projected retirements, and staffing allowances throughout the year. However, they hold off recruiting because of the uncertainty of the system.

> Federal managers fear that if they don't hire up to their authorized employment ceiling in the current fiscal year, congress will, with the stroke of a pen, reduce their employment ceiling next year.

Adding to the confusion, federal employees are eligible to retire at age 55 with 30 years service or at age 60 with 20 years service. Some job series offer early retirement with as little as 20 years service. Many eligible employees opt to remain long after their retirement anniversary date. After age 55 is reached agencies don't know when employees will elect to retire. One day agencies are fully staffed and the next day 50 people submit their paperwork.

All of this uncertainty causes agencies to go begging for new employees at or close to the end of a fiscal year. Unfortunately, if agencies advertise through the Office of Personnel Management it can take from three to six months before the job is advertised, applicants rated, and the selection made.

Noncompetitive appointments and former employees can be selected and picked up the same day. If you qualify for any noncompetitive program multiply your chances by going directly to each agency in your area. Send them a signed copy of your SF-171 and write a cover letter explaining who you are, what program you qualify for, and when you can start working. Be tactful and don't demand employment. Agencies don't have to hire anyone non-competitively if they choose not to.

REINSTATEMENT

Reinstatement is the noncompetitive reentry of a former federal employee into the competitive service. Formal federal employees are not required to compete with applicants for federal employment on an OPM list of eligibles. Reinstatement is a privilege accorded in recognition of former service and not a "right" to which the formal employee is entitled. Reinstatement is completely at the discretion of the appointing agency.

Former employees entitled to veterans preference who served, or who were serving, under appointment that would lead to career status and nonveteran employees with career tenure may be reinstated regardless of the number of years since their last appointment. Career status is obtained when an employee works for three full years with the federal government in a career position.

Former nonveteran career-conditional employees, those who worked less than three years with the federal government, may be reinstated only within three years following the date of their separation. Certain types of service outside the competitive service may be used to extend this three year limit.

Employees seeking reinstatement should apply directly to the personnel offices of the agency where they wish to work. Complete information on reinstatement can be found in Chapter 315 of the Federal Personnel Manual.

TABLE 2-1
ANNUAL SALARY RATES
General Schedule (GS) - January 1994

GRADE	1	2	3	4	5	6	7	8	9	10
GS-1	$11,903	$12,300	$12,695	$13,090	$13,487	$13,720	$14,109	$14,503	$14,521	$14,891
2	13,382	13,701	14,145	14,521	14,683	15,115	15,547	15,979	16,411	16,843
3	14,603	15,090	15,577	16,064	16,551	17,038	17,525	18,012	18,499	18,986
4	16,393	16,939	17,485	18,031	18,577	19,123	19,869	20,215	20,761	21,307
5	18,340	18,951	19,562	20,173	20,784	21,395	22,006	22,617	23,228	23,839
6	20,443	21,124	21,805	22,486	23,167	23,848	24,529	25,210	25,891	26,572
7	22,717	23,474	24,231	24,988	25,745	26,502	27,259	28,016	28,773	29,530
8	25,159	25,998	26,837	27,676	28,515	29,354	30,193	31,032	31,871	32,710
9	27,789	28,715	29,641	30,567	31,493	32,419	33,345	34,271	35,197	36,123
10	30,603	31,623	32,643	33,663	34,683	35,703	36,723	37,743	38,763	39,783
11	33,623	34,744	35,865	36,986	38,107	39,228	40,349	41,470	42,591	43,712
12	40,298	41,641	42,964	44,327	45,670	47,013	48,356	49,699	51,042	52,385
13	47,920	49,517	51,114	52,711	54,308	55,905	57,502	59,099	60,696	62,293
14	56,627	58,515	60,403	62,291	64,179	66,067	67,955	69,843	71,731	73,619
15	66,609	68,829	71,049	73,269	75,489	77,709	79,929	82,149	84,239	86,589

SCHEDULE 4 - SENIOR EXECUTIVE SERVICE

ES-1	$92,900
ES-2	97,400
ES-3	101,800
ES-4	107,300
ES-5	111,800
ES-6	115,700

SCHEDULE 5 - EXECUTIVE SCHEDULE

LEVEL I	$148,400
LEVEL II	133,600
LEVEL III	123,100
LEVEL IV	115,700
LEVEL V	108,200

PAY REFORM

Congress passed a locality pay reform bill for federal employees in 1991. High cost areas such as New York City and Los Angeles received an 8 percent premium over their basic rate. These areas were scheduled to receive additional increases through 1994. Locality adjustments were instituted to provide pay comparability between federal employees and the private sector. Typically, government agencies in high cost areas have had a difficult time recruiting. These differentials were designed to attract new employees and to encourage existing employees to stay with the government.

President Clinton has delayed full implementation of pay reform to help ease the federal deficit. Federal civilian workers, excluding Postal workers, will not receive a cost of living increase until June of 1995 and the payscale in table 2-1 will remain in effect until that time.

QUALIFICATION STANDARD SAMPLE

The following Qualification Standard example will give you an idea of what raters look for and how all job series standards are written:

QUALIFICATION STANDARD
TRAINING INSTRUCTION SERIES
GS-1712

Training Instructor, GS-5/13
Supervisory Training Instructor, GS-9/15
Training Administrator, GS-9/15
Training Specialist, GS-5/14

DUTIES

Incumbents of positions covered by this standard perform work involved in a program of instructional training in an occupation or other subject, when the work requires practical knowledge of the occupation or subject to be taught and a practical knowledge of the methods and techniques of instruction. They may be instructors or supervisors of instructors in specific subject areas, may develop or review special subject-matter course materials, training aids, and manuals for training programs, or may administer training programs. The duties of some positions will include demonstration in the use of equipment, techniques, principles and practices of the subject being taught.

EXPERIENCE AND TRAINING REQUIREMENTS

Except for the substitution of education provided below, applicants for these positions must have had general and specialized experience of the length specified in the table below and of the nature described in the statements that follow:

	General (years)	Specialized (years)	Total (years)
GS-5	3	0	3
GS-7	3	1	4
GS-9	3	2	5
GS-11-15	3	3	6

General experience - practical and progressive experience or training in an occupation or subject appropriate to the position to be filled. This experience must show evidence of sufficient knowledge and ability to demonstrate, explain, and instruct students in the use of equipment, techniques, principles, or practices of the occupation, or subject.

Evidence of this knowledge and ability may have been demonstrated by one of any combination of the following:

1. Experience as a teacher or instructor.

2. Satisfactory completion of a formal course or an on-the-job training program in basic principles and techniques of instruction which included supervised practice teaching.

3. Performance of duties involving the supervision or on-the-job instruction of fellow workers in the use of equipment, techniques, principles, or practices of an occupation or subject.

4. Successful completion of a formal vocational training program for the appropriate occupation, in which the applicant demonstrated an unusual and marked aptitude for learning and applying the principles, practices, and techniques of the occupation or subject-matter field.

Specialized experience -- Experience in teaching or instructing in an adult education program, secondary school, college, or industrial establishment in the particular functional or subject field(s) for which the applicant has applied, or in supervising such instruction work; in training program administration; or the development or review of course materials or training aids.

QUALITY OF EXPERIENCE

For positions at all grade levels, experience shown must have been at a sufficiently high level of difficulty and responsibility to demonstrate the ability to perform the duties and responsibilities of the position for which the candidate is applying. Therefore, at each grade through GS-11, six months of the required experience must have been at a level of difficulty and responsibility comparable to that of the next lower grade in the federal service, or at least one year of that experience must have been a level of difficulty and responsibility comparable to that of the second lower grade in the federal service. For each grade above GS-11, one year of the required experience must have been at a level of difficulty comparable to that of the next lower grade in the federal service. To determine the level of difficulty of the applicant's experience, refer to the appropriate position classification standard.

SUPERVISORY POSITIONS

For supervisory positions use the qualification standard for "Supervisory Positions in General Schedule Occupations" in part III of this handbook in conjunction with this standard.

SUBSTITUTION OF EDUCATION

For general experience:

Study successfully completed in schools above high school level, including appropriate vocational schools, may be substituted for general experience at the rate of 1 academic year of study for 9 months of experience, provided such study included at least 6 semester hours (or equivalent) in a subject directly related to the particular subject-matter or functional option for which the applicant is being considered.

For a maximum of 1 year of specialized experience:

One academic year of study completed in a school above high school level, not already used in substitution for general experience, may be substituted for one year of specialized experience, provided such study include at least 9 semester hour credits (or equivalent) in a combination of subject field and education courses, with a minimum of 3 semester hours in each.

BASIS OF RATING

Applicants will be rated on a scale of 100 on extent and quality of their experience, education, and training relevant to the duties of the position. The evaluation will be based on information contained in the application, supplemented by information received through qualifications inquiries in terms of factors such as the following, as appropriate:

(1) Extent of special subject-matter knowledge as reflected by the particular subject field.
(2) Ability to establish and maintain effective personal working relations.
(3) Ability in oral and written expression.
(4) Degree of difficulty of subject dealt with.
(5) Initiative, interest, and capacity in devising special methods to serve special needs, or for program improvement.
(6) Degree of responsibility and nature of work involved in planning a program of training, or phase of a program, or in development of operational plans, or in the development of instructional material and training aids.
(7) Ability to select, develop, and supervise a staff.

MEDICAL QUALIFICATIONS STATEMENT

Applicants must be physically and mentally able to efficiently perform the essential functions of the position without hazard to themselves or others. Depending on the essential duties of a specific position, usable vision, color vision, hearing, or speech may be required. However, in most cases, a specific physical condition or impairment will not automatically disqualify an applicant for appointment. The loss or impairment of a specific function may be compensated for by the satisfactory use of a prosthesis or mechanical aid. Reasonable accommodation may also be considered in determining an applicant's ability to perform the duties of a position. Reasonable accommodation may include, but is not limited to: the use of assistive devices, job modification or restructuring, provision of readers and interpreters, or adjusted work schedules.

Also, all positions involving federal motor vehicle operation carry the additional medical requirements specified in Federal Personnel Manual Chapter 930, Appendix A, Physical Standards for Motor Vehicle Operators and Incidental Operators.

TABLE 2-2
The "TYPICAL" Federal Civilian Employee
Non-Postal Employment

INDIVIDUAL CHARACTERISTICS	1980	1991
Average Age	41.9	42.5
Average Length of Service	14.0	13.3
Retirement Eligible		
CSRS	NA	8.0%
FERS	NA	3.0%
College Educated	28.0%	35.0%
Gender		
Men	61.0%	56.0%
Women	39.0%	44.0%
Race & National Origin		
Minority Total	23.0%	27.7%
Black	15.7%	16.8%
Hispanic	4.3%	5.4%
Asian/Pacific Islander	1.5%	1.9%
Native American	1.5%	1.9%
Disabled	7.0%	7.0%
Veterans Preference	42.0%	28.0%
Vietnam Era Veterans	9.0%	15.0%
Retired Military	NA	4.7%
Retired Officers	NA	.5%

Sources: Central Personnel Data File, Office of Workforce Information; Federal Civilian Workforce Statistics, Affirmative Employment Statistics, Publication PSOG/OWI-2, June 1992.

CHAPTER THREE

WHAT JOBS ARE AVAILABLE

The traditional approach to obtaining federal government employment is to call or write Federal Job Information Centers listed in Appendix B and request information on currently open job announcements. Federal Job Information Centers (FJICs) will discard your letter if job vacancies aren't immediately available in your specialty. Job seekers can duplicate their first letter at a local print shop and send copies to the FJIC on a recurrent basis until they receive a job announcement.

Additional avenues are now available to locate open job announcements including; OPM sponsored job hot lines, job fairs, electronic bulletin boards, computer generated data bases, resume matching services, directories, and periodicals that publish job listings. These resources are listed in this chapter under *Common Job Sources*. Specific hiring programs are discussed following the job resource listings such as; the Outstanding Scholars program, Administrative Careers with America, student hiring, and engineering conversions programs.

> **"Reinventing Government"** proposals include the establishment of a government-wide, employment information system that allows the public to go to one place for information about federal government jobs. The **NPR** suggests a centralized system to replace federal registers. If approved by Congress, it may take several years to centralize lists.

Individual agency personnel offices should also be contacted to obtain job announcements. Regional offices are the most productive and a complete listing is included in Appendix C. A consolidated listing of Washington, D.C. Federal Personnel Departments is provided following the Common Job Resources section in this chapter. If an agency has direct hire or case examining authority they advertise jobs independently from the Office of Personnel Management

(OPM). OPM doesn't maintain a consolidated list of direct hire job announcements. Occasionally OPM conducts job fairs throughout the country. Job fairs are announced on OPM's Telephone Message Directory that is listed in this chapter.

Chapter six explains the Veteran Readjustment Appointment (VRA) Program and Veterans Preference. Postal Service jobs are explained separately in Chapter Eight. The U.S. Postal Service, USPS, does not advertise job openings through OPM and the federal Handicapped Hiring Program, new to this edition, is discussed in chapter Nine.

IMPROVING YOUR CHANCES

The more contacts you make the greater your chances. **Don't get lost in the process.** Too many job seekers pin all their hopes on one effort. They find an open announcement, send in a bid, then forget about the process until they receive a reply. Federal jobs are highly competitive. The more announcements you bid on the better your chances.

If you're not using a computer program to generate your SF-171 employment application, before sending in your first completed SF-171 application have it duplicated at a local print shop. Then you can send copies to bid on other announcements. Copies are acceptable as long as you have an original signature on the copy you send in. Don't sign the original. Use the original as a master and sign each copy.

Use the list of FJICs and Regional Offices in Appendix B and C and the common job resources listed in this chapter to improve your chances. If you're willing to relocate request job announcements from FJIC servicing centers and individual agencies in other areas. Several of the job resources listed in this chapter publish comprehensive national federal job listings. Each FJIC maintains it's own geographical listing. Also, contact agency regional offices and find out what is currently available, what's coming up, and how to apply.

The informational interviewing methods presented in this chapter will help you develop contacts and networks within agencies. You aren't locked into the first job or, for that matter, location that you are originally selected for. Once hired, you'll have opportunities to bid for jobs in-house. Many agencies have offices at hundreds of locations and you can bid to any one of those locations for future promotions or to enter a related field under your job series. Check with employing agencies to see if they have offices located in or close to the area you want to eventually live. If offices are at a desired location find out if they hire your specialty. If so, more than likely you will have an opportunity to bid on future openings at that location.

COMMON JOB SOURCES

This section presents resources that can be used to locate federal job announcements. After reviewing the listed resources refer to Appendix D for a complete list of federal occupations. Appendix B lists all FJICs throughout the country. A number of the periodicals and directories listed in this chapter are available at libraries. *The National Business Employment Weekly*, published by Dow Jones & Company, is widely distributed to libraries. Others, such as *CareerWoman*, are free to women within two years of graduation. Many publishers will send complimentary review copies of their publications upon request. Others, like *USA Today*, are available at most news stands.

Resource headings include job openings, placement services, directories, and general information. Job openings include publications with job ads, job hotlines, and computer bulletin boards. The general information section lists related books, pamphlets, brochures, and computer software. All job sources are listed alphabetically with the <u>larger publications underlined</u>.

JOB OPENINGS

PERIODICALS & NEWSPAPERS WITH FEDERAL JOB ADS

Affirmative Action Register for Effective Equal Opportunity Recruitment - AAR, Inc., 8356 Olive Blvd., St. Louis, MO 63132; 800-537-0665, 314-991-1335, Monthly magazine, $15 annual subscription rates. Lists university, state, federal, and other publicly-funded positions for veterans, women, minorities, and handicapped job seekers.

Business and Industry Bulletin - Career Development and Placement Services, Campus Box 14, Emporia State University, Emporia, KS 66801; 316-343-5407, $56.50/year subscription rate, weekly 3 page newsletter includes federal government positions.

Equal Opportunity Publications - 150 Motor Parkway, Ste. 420, Hauppauge, NY 11788; 516-273-0066. This company publishes a number of excellent target audience publications including **Career Woman, Minority Engineer, Woman Engineer, Equal Opportunity, CAREERS & The DisABLED, and Independent Living** magazines. Display ads feature national employers including the federal government seeking applicants for many varied fields. Each issue offers a dozen to sixty or more display job ads. Call for subscription rates.

Federal Career Opportunities - Federal Research Service, 243 Church St., NW, Vienna, VA 22180; 703-281-0200, bi-weekly, $38/three month subscription. Provides approximately 4,000 federal job vacancies in each issue.

<u>**Federal Jobs Digest**</u> - Breakthrough Publications, P.O. Box 594, Dept D30, Millwood, NY 10546; 1-800-824-5000, published bi-weekly, $29 for 3 month subscription, $54/six-month subscription. Up to 30,000 federal job vacancies listed per issue. Compiles vacancies from OPM, regional announcements, overseas vacancies, and schedules for U.S. Postal exams. Provides comprehensive federal career articles with each issue and lists updated personnel office contacts.

Federal Research Report - Business Publishers, Inc., 951 Pershing Drive, Silver Spring, MD 20910; 301/587-6700, weekly, $16.50/yearly subscription. Provides information on federal grants and research and development contracts.

Federal Times - 6883 Commercial Dr., Springfield, VA 22159; 703-750-8920, weekly; $48/year subscription rate, $24 for six months. Publishes several hundred vacancies with brief descriptions under "Jobs" starting at the GS-7 level.

Journal of Minority Employment - 2210 Goldsmith Office Center, Ste. 228, Louisville, KY 40218; 502-451-8199, published monthly, twenty or more job classifieds listed under "Job Mart". Annual subscription $24.

Mainstream - Magazine of the Able Disabled - Exploding Myths, Inc., 2973 Beech St., San Diego, CA 92102; 619-234-3138, $24/year, $3.50 for single copies, monthly. Magazine features disability rights issues and focuses on the political environment, education , training, employment, assistive devices, relationships, recreation, and sports. The October issue features employment opportunities for the disabled. Federal agencies including the CIA recruit through full page display ads.

National Business Employment Weekly - P.O. Box 9100, Springfield, MA 01101; 800-562-4868, $3.95 single issue, eight-weeks $35, 6 months $112. Offers national job ads.

National Ad Search - P.O. Box 2083, Milwaukee, WI 53201; 800/992-2832, 414/351-1398, published weekly. Provides thousands of classifieds divided into 54 headings and compiled from 75 newspapers. Six weeks $40. Offers a resume job matching service free to subscribers. Federal agencies occasionally advertise for applicants in local classified sections for hard to fill vacancies and the Post Office also advertises vacancies in the classifieds for various positions.

National Employment Review - Resource Publications, 334 Knight St., Warwick, RI 02887; phone: 401-732-9850, published monthly, hundreds of job listings. Three month $14.95.

New Internships in the Federal Government - Graduate Group, 86 Norwood Rd., West Hartford, CT 06117; 203-232-3100, $27.50. Provides information on internships and a few permanent positions, published annually.

Internships in Congress - Graduate Group, 86 Norwood Rd., West Hartford, CT 06117; 203-232-3100, $27.50. Provides information on internships and a few permanent positions, published annually.

Science Education News - American Association for the Advancement of Science, 1333 H. St., NW, Washington, DC 20005; 202-326-6620, free, 10 issues/year. This newsletter often lists federal agencies that are looking for teachers and researchers.

SPOTLIGHT - College Placement Council, 62 Highland Ave., Bethlehem, PA 18042; 800-544-5272, 215-868-1421, annual subscriptions (21 issues) $65 non-members, free to members. Several positions listed under "Jobwire" for federal government career counselors and personnel directors.

The Black Collegian - Black Collegiate Services, 1240 S. Broad Ave., New Orleans, LA 70125; 504-821-5694, published quarterly, Annual jobs issue lists 150+ jobs. Subscription $10.

USA TODAY - 1000 Wilson Blvd., Arlington, VA 22229; 800-872-0001, Daily except weekends, numerous job ads. Available at most stores for 50 cents per issue. 13 weeks $32.50.

VA Practitioner - Cahners Publishing Company, 44 Cook St., Denver, CO 80206-5191; 303/388-4511, $40/year annual subscription, 14 issues. Physician and nursing positions are advertised under "Classified" for VA facilities.

JOB HOTLINES

CAREER AMERICA CONNECTION - Federal government job hotline 1-912-757-3000 stateside, Alaska 912-471-3755. **The charge is 40 cents per minute.** Operated by the Office of Personnel Management. Phone answers 24 hours a day. Provides federal employment information for most occupations. Callers can leave voice mail messages with their name, address, and phone number. Requested job announcements and applications are mailed within 24 hours. Easy to use on-line voice prompts and voice commands allow access with any touchtone or rotary dial telephone.

CU Career Connection - University of Colorado, Campus Box 133, Boulder, CO 80309-0133; 303/492-4127. The charge is $22 for affiliated members and $30 nonmembers for an access code that is good for two months. Callers must use a touchtone phone.

Federal Job Information For The Deaf - Uses Telecommunication Device for the Deaf (TDD), 202-606-0591, OPM's national job information line.

REGIONAL TDD (Telephone Device for the Deaf) Job Hotline Numbers

Washington, DC:	202-606-0591	Northeastern	617-565-8913
Southeastern:	919-790-2739	Mountain:	303-969-7047
North Central:	816-426-6022		
Southwestern States:			
Arizona	800-223-3131	Louisiana	504-589-4614
New Mexico	505-766-8662	Oklahoma	405-231-4614
Texas	214-767-8115 (Dallas/Ft. Worth)		
Texas	210-229-4000 (other locations)		
Western States:			
Alaska	800-770-8973	Nevada	800-326-6868

California	800-735-2929	Oregon	800-526-0661
Hawaii	808-643-8833	Washington	206-587-5500
Idaho	208-334-2100		

OPM Job Information Telephone Directory - Washington D.C. Federal Job Information Center Self-Service Telephone System; 202-606-2700. This telephone system contains a variety of material, ranging from general employment information of interest to applicants, to specific job opportunities in the federal government. Complete instructions on the use of the system and various options are provided upon access. Use the message codes listed below for specific information. This system is available 24 hours a day, 7 days a week. You can talk with an information specialist Monday through Friday from 8:00 a.m. to 4:00 p.m. Eastern Standard Time, by dialing message code 000 after the initial message.

1. General Job Information

101	How Jobs Are Filled
102	Competitive Service
103	Excepted Service
105	How To Apply
106	How Applications Are Rated
107	The Rule OF Three
108	Chances For Employment
110	Overseas Employment
111	Overseas Employment
112	How To Extend/Update Your Notice of Rating/Results
113	Physical Requirements
114	Age
115	Citizenship
116	Equal Employment Opportunity

2. Announcements & Forms Requests

280	To Order Forms/Announcements

3. Clerical Walk-In Test

301	Clerical Examination

4. Application Information

401	Termination of the PAC-B
402	Administrative Careers With America

Application Information (continued)

403	Other Registers/Written Tests
404	Standing Registers
405	Financial/Admin/Social Science Jobs
406	Job Vacancy Lists
407	General Notice Listings
408	SES Positions
409	Upcoming Job Fairs
410	Part Time/Job Sharing Program

5. Check On Applications Already Received

550	To Check On Applications or Tests Results

6. Veterans Information

601	Veterans Preference
602	Special Appointment Authority
603	Retired Military Hiring Information

7. Information For Current & Former Employees

701	Transfer
702	Reinstatement
703	Restoration

People With Disabilities - Special testing arrangements, call 202-606-2528

Veterans' Counseling Hotline - Provide counseling to veterans by appointment, 202-606-1848

COMPUTER BULLETIN BOARDS

These are electronic computer bulletin boards that can only be accessed with a computer, modem, and communication software, as well as a telephone line. You may scan current open examination and vacancy announcements **nationwide** while you're on line or you can download them to your computer.

National Federal Job Opportunities Bulletin Board - 24 hours a day - **912-757-3100.**

Regional Bulletin Boards:

Washington, DC Area	(202) 606-1113
Southeastern States	(404) 730-2370
Northeastern States	(215) 580-2216
North Central States	(313) 226-4423
Mountain & Southwestern States	(214) 767-0316
Western States	(818) 575-6521

PLACEMENT SERVICES

ADNET ONLINE - 8440 Woodfield Crossing Blvd., Ste. 170, Indianapolis, IN 46240; 800-682-2901, accessible through computer modem. This menu driven program lists job vacancies in 17 job categories. Each category offers an extensive selection menu. Free to Prodigy subscribers. A free online trial access is offered through computer modem dialing at 317-579-4857, 2,400 baud, 7 bits, even parity, 1 stop bit. At the prompt type guest. Call for complete details.

American Public Health Association Job Placement Service - 1015 15th St. N.W., Washington, DC 20005; 202/789-5600. This association provides numerous services to members. Call for job service application procedures and costs.

Career Placement Registry - 302 Swann Ave., Alexandria, VA 22301; 800/-368-3093, registration $15/students and $25 to $45/nonstudents depending on salary range. Entry forms available upon request. DIALOG accessible, updated weekly, over 100,000 employers use database.

Department of Veterans Affairs Physical Therapist and Occupational Therapist Placement Services - P.O. Box 24269, Richmond, VA 23224; 800-368-6008, in Virginia call 800-552-3045. These services helps you find a job in one of the more than 170 VA health care facilities throughout the United States. When you register with this free service your name and resume will be automatically referred as vacancies develop in the areas in which you want to work. Unlike most federal agencies they will accept resumes or the SF-171 Federal Employment Application.

Federal Job Matching Service - Box 594, Dept D30, NY 10546; 1-800-824-5000. This service matches your background to federal requirements. Applicants send in a federal application, SF-171. You will receive back a list of federal job titles and grade levels for which you qualify. Federal job descriptions and qualification statements are provided for every job title that the service identifies for you. The fee is $30, but only $25 with a subscription label in your name from the Federal Jobs Digest. This service matches your background to federal job requirements not to specific job openings. After you receive your reply you can submit your application direct to agencies listed in the FJD that are hiring in that occupation.

Human Resource Information Network - 9585 Valparaiso Ct., Indianapolis, IN 46268; 800/421-8884. Features the **Job Ads USA** database of up to 25,000 jobs that are compiled from over 100 newspapers. Various subscription rates apply, basic rate $95/year plus access fees for on-line time. Offers a computerized resume service.

KiNexus - Suite 560, 640 N. LaSalle St., Chicago, IL 60610; 800/828-0422, 312/335-0787, Registration fee $30/yr. This service is free if you attend a school that subscribes to this service. Over 1,900 schools currently participate. Employers access the database on line and contact applicants direct.

National Ad Search Resume Service - P.O. Box 2983, Milwaukee, WI 53201; 800/992-2832, 414/351-1398. Free to subscribers of the weekly National Ad Search newspaper. Resumes are active for six months.

Military in Transition Database (MILTRAN) - 1255 Drummers Lane, Wayne, PA 19087; 800/426-9954, 215-687-3900. Offers a resume matching service to military members leaving the armed forces. If you will soon be leaving the service or were recently discharged call for particulars.

TOPS: The Retired Officers Association - 201 N. Washington St., Alexandria, VA 22314; 800/245-8762, 703/549-2311. Offers a resume matching service for anyone who served as a commissioned officer in any branch of the service including warrants, $20/year fee.

DIRECTORIES

Congressional Staff Directory - Staff Directories, Ltd., P.O. Box 62, Mt. Vernon, VA 22121; 703-739-0900, $59/volume. Published each year to provide complete listings of Congressional members, committees, and staff. Covers over 20,000 people. This information is also available on disk for $250.

Directories In Print - Gale Research Company, Book Tower, Detroit, MI 48226; 800/877-4253, 9th edition published in 1992. This two volume set costs around $400 and is a directory of directories. It lists over 14,000 published directories worldwide. Available at most libraries.

Directory of Military Bases in the U.S. - Oryx Press, 4041 N. Central, Phoenix, AZ 85012-3997; 800 279-6799, $95, 208 pages. Provides details on over 700 bases including telephone numbers. This directory may be available at your local library.

Federal Career Directory - Superintendent of Documents, Washington, DC 20402-9325, $31.00. It will be worth your while to review this directory published by the Office of Personnel Management. It is in a notebook format, 265 pages, and loaded with specifics about federal agencies and careers. The directory hasn't been updated since 1990 and many of the contact phone numbers have changed. This valuable reference is also available at most college and high school counseling offices or you can find it at many libraries.

Government Research Directory - Gale Research, Inc., 835 Penobscot Bldg., Detroit, MI 48226; 800-877-4253, 313-961-2242, $390, 1200 pages. Over 3,700 programs and research facilities of the government are listed. Available at many libraries.

Guide to Military Installations In The U.S - Army Times Publishing Company, Springfield, VA 22159; 800-424-9335, 703-750-8900, published annually in November, $4.00 including shipping and handling. A comprehensive 100 -page guide that includes base realignment information due to base closings and other major impacts. The installations are broken down by service with detailed information on base family service centers, job training and job bank contacts and much more. A valuable guide well worth the $4.00 charge. The largest employer in the federal government is the Department of Defense with close to 1,000,000 federal civilian workers of which many are employed at or around military bases.

Encyclopedia of Associations 1992 - Gale Research Company, Book Tower, Detroit, MI 48226; 800/877-4253, three volume set, $320. Available at many libraries.

Federal Yellow Book: Who's Who in Federal Departments and Agencies - Monitor Publishing Co., 104 Fifth Ave., New York, NY 10011; 212-627-4140, Price of first subscription $215 each additional subscription $150. This is one of the most up-to-date directories of federal departments and agencies. It lists 35,000 key contacts in all branches including regional offices, 800 pages. Available at many libraries. This company also publishes the **Congressional Yellow Book**, over 700 pages of detailed information listing Congressional staff members, committees, and other valuable information.

New Careers - A directory of Jobs and Internships in Technology and Society, 1638 R. St., NW, Suite 32, Washington, DC 20009; 202/238-6555, Published every other year. Students can subscribe for $10, nonstudents $18. Provides complete details on how and where to apply for health care entry-level jobs and internships.

Washington Information Directory - Congressional Quarterly Inc., 1414 22nd St., NW, Washington, DC 20037; 800-673-2730, published June of each year, $69.95, over 1000 pages. Discusses 17 federal government subject categories and provides abundant information on federal departments and agencies.

GENERAL INFORMATION

Books, Pamphlets, & Brochures

Encyclopedia of Careers and Vocational Guidance - J. P. Ferguson Publishing Company, 111 E. Wacker Dr., Chicago, IL 60601; 312/580-5480. This three volume set features over 900 occupations and details employment trends for 71 industries. Employment information is included.

Internships 1994 - Petersons Guides, P.O. Box 2123, Princeton, NJ 08543; 800-338-3282, $28.95. This book guides interested parties to almost 50,000 internships. Available at many libraries and bookstores.

1994 Summer Employment Directory of the United States - Peterson Guides, P.O. Box 2123, Princeton, NJ 08543; 800-338-3282, $14.95. This publication along with Peterson's *Internship 1994* is updated annually. Lists over 75,000 summer job openings.

> **NOTE:** Those interested in summer employment with the federal government should also call their local FJIC or the Career America Connection and request announcement #414. This job announcement is released each year in January for the upcoming summer months and lists all agencies hiring summer help. The announcement provides information on job locations, hiring agencies, job series needed, pay, application guidance and forms.

Joyce Lain Kennedy's Career Book - VGM Career Horizons, 4255 W. Touchy Ave., Lincolnwood, IL 60646-1975; 800/323-4900, 708/679-5500. Published 1992, $17.95, paperback. This book is by far one of the most complete, informative and useful career guides on the market today. It should be added to the curriculum in every high school and college. This valuable reference and work book motivates, presents valuable tools to help one make a career selection, then propels you through the rigors of college to landing your first job.

Network Your Way to Job & Career Success - Drs. Ronald and Caryl Krannich, 147 pages, $11.95. Provides practical guidance on how to organize effective networks for job success. Shows how to prospect for new job leads, write networking letters, conduct informational interviews, and more. Available from D-Amp Publication's back-of-book catalog.

Health Care Job Explosion! Careers In The 90's - The perfect book for anyone seeking work in the health care industry. Bursting with details on over 1,000 sources of health care jobs including jobs with the federal government, this comprehensive career guide and job finder steers readers to where they can actually find job openings. Appendices include extensive guidance on health care careers with the federal government. By Dennis V. Damp, 1st edition 1993, 384 pages, $14.95, 6" x 9". D-Amp Publications, P.O. Box 1243, Coraopolis, PA 15108.

The Office of Personnel Management (Brochures & Folders) Available free from local FJICs or from school counselors. They can also be requested from OPM at 202-606-2700.

   Cooperative Education Program (S/N 006-000-01334-1) - This folder includes information on the federal cooperative education program, occupations and locations, pay and benefits, and other related information.

   Summer Employment Program (S/N 006-000-01366-0) - Answers questions for students who would like to work for the federal government during summer months.

   Job Opportunities for Persons With Disabilities (S/N 006-000-01331-7) - Includes information on selective placement procedures, special accommodations on the job, and other related information.

   Student Employment Programs (S/N 006-000-01333-3) - Includes information on the Federal Junior Fellowship program, Stay-in-School program, Summer Employment programs, advancement, and other related information.

Non-Profits' Job Finder - by Daniel Lauber, 1994, 320 pages, $16.95. Introduces readers to over 1,100 sources of jobs, internships, and grant opportunities in the non-profit field: education, teaching, social services, and many other fields. Available from D-Amp Publication's back-of-book catalog.

Government Job Finder - by Daniel Lauber, 1994, 322 pages, $16.95. Introduces readers to over 1,400 sources of vacancies for professional, labor, trade, technical, and office staff in local, state, and federal government in the U.S. and overseas. Available from D-Amp Publication's back-of-book catalog.

The Successful Job Search; A Step-by-Step Guide For a Successful Job Search In The 1990s - Roxanne S. Rogers, P.O. Box 23195, Des Moines, IA 50325;, $29.95 plus $4.55 Shipping/Handling, Iowa residents add 5% sales tax. A comprehensive 300+ page guide and workbook by Roxanne S. Rodgers host of *The Career Connection* on WHO Radio, Des Moines, Iowa and nationally known job strategist and outplacement consultant. This thorough resource includes sections that take you through each stage of job loss, including the emotional, psychological, physical,and financial hurdles that you must overcome to put the processes of the job search into action.

What Color Is Your Parachute? - by Richard N. Bolles. This classic career planning book provides comprehensive job search guidance. One of the most popular career books in print today. Available through bookstores, $14.95 paperback.

Computer Software

Federal Occupational and Career Informational System (FOCIS) - National Technical Information Services, 5285 Port Royal Rd., Springfield, VA 22161; 1-800-553-NTIS, 703-487-4650, $49.95, order # various with disk size, call for specific ordering information for your computer system. IBM-PC or compatible computers, DOS 3.0 +, 5 MB of memory required, Dbase III Plus. Developed by OPM to help job seekers obtain information about federal careers and occupations. The software is menu driven with no prior experience on a PC needed by the user. Consists of three modules: career guidance, occupational information, and tips on how to get a job. Covers 360 federal white-collar occupations and 450 federal organizations.

Quick & Easy SF-171s - Available in IBM-PC/XT/AT - 630K - DOS 3.0 or greater. Supports most printers including laser and deskjets. Customize your SF-171 federal employment application to fit the requirements of the position. Easily edit your experience and qualifications to reflect the demands of the position that you want, and keep as many versions of your SF-171 Federal Employment Application on disk. This program is not just another fill in the blanks forms program. It is a complete system specifically designed to fill in and manage the SF-171. This program generates the complete form electronically. $49.95 for the personal version. Available from D-Amp Publication's back-of-book catalog.

The Ultimate Job Finder - Brings over 4,500 of the best job sources that comprise the hidden job market into one easy-to-use search-and-retrieval software program for any IBM-compatible, MS-DOS personal computer with a hard disk drive. Users type their occupation in a box and hit the enter key. A detailed description of every job source for your specialty instantly appears on the screen. Also includes advice for resumes, cover letters, and interviewing. By Dan Lauber, author of the *Professional's Job Finder, Non-Profits' Job Finder, and Government Job Finder*. Available at national computer stores or it can be ordered direct from Planning/Communications, 7215 Oak Avenue, River Forest, IL 60305. Cost $59.95 plus $3.75 shipping. Phone orders accepted toll free at 800/829-5220.

TABLE 3-1
WASHINGTON D.C. FEDERAL PERSONNEL DEPARTMENTS (July 1993)

TDD (Telephone Device for the Deaf)
- *Telephone Hotline for Job Vacancies*

Agriculture Department	202/720-5626
Research Services	301/344-1518
•	301/344-1124
•	301/344-2288
Farmers Home Admin.	202/245-5561
Food & nutrition Service	703/756-3351
Forest Service	703/235-8145
•	703/235-2730
Soil Conservation service	202/720-4264
•	202/720-6365
Commerce Department	202/377-3827
•	202/377-5138
•	202/377-4285
TDD	202/377-5246
TDD	202/377-3706
Bureau of Census	301/763-7470
•	301/763-6064
TDD	301/763-4944
International Trade	202/482-5138
National Inst. of stds.	301/975-3007
•	301/763-4944
TDD	301/975-2039
Nat'l Oceanic & Atmospheric Admin.	301/713-0677
Office, Inspector General	202/377-4948
•	202/377-3476
TDD	202/377-5897
Patent/Trademark Office	703/305-8231
TDD	703/305-8586
Defense Department	
Air Force Depart.	703/695-4389
•	703/693-6550
Army Dept.	703/325-8840

Defense (cont.)	
One Stop Job Info.	703/780-4655
•	703/780-4677
Walter Reed Medical Ctr.	202/576-0546
Consolidated Personnel Ctr.	202/433-5370
National Naval Medical Ctr.	202/295-6800
Investigative Service	703/325-5344
Navy Department	703/697-6181
TDD	703/697-6181
Marine Corps	703/640-2048
Education	202/401-0559
TDD	202/708-5939
Energy	202/586-4333
Health & Human Services	202/619-2560
TDD	202/475-0099
Alcohol,Drug Abuse & Mental Health	301/443-4826
•	301/443-2282
TDD	301/443-5407
Food & Drug Admin.	301/443-1970
•	301/443-1969
TDD	301/463-1970
National Inst. of Health	301/496-2403
(Professional) •	301/496-9541
(Clerical) •	301/496-9452
Social Security Admin.	410/965-4506
TDD	410-965-4404
Housing & Urban Dev.	202/707-0416
Interior	
Mineral Mgmt. Service	703/787-1414
•	703/787-1402
National Parks Service	202/619-7256
•	202/619-7111
•	202/619-7364

Interior (Cont.)
U.S. Geological Survey	703/648-6131
•	703/648-7676
•	703/648-7788
Fish & Wildlife Service	703/358-1743
•	703/358-2120

Justice Dept. 202/514-6813
•	202/514-6818
TDD	202/514-7972
Bureau of Prisons	202/307-1304
•	202/514-6388
Drug Enforcement Admin.	202/307-4055
TDD	202/307-8903
Immigration/Naturalization	202/514-2530
•	202/514-4301
US Marshall Service	202/307-9629

Foreign Service 703/875-7490
•	703/516-0025

State Department 202/647-7284
•	202/647-7284
TDD	202/647-7256

Transportation 202/366-9394
TDD	202/366-9402
Federal Aviation Admin.	202/267-3870
•	202/267-3902
Urban Mass Trans. Admin.	202/366-2513

Treasury 202/377-9205
IRS	202/622-6340
•	202/622-6340
US Customs Service	202/634-5270
TDD	202/634-2069

Veterans Affairs 202/233-3771
TDD	202/233-3225

Action 202/606-5263
•	202/606-5000

Agency/Int'l Development	202/663-1401
Central Intelligence Agency	703/874-4400
•	703/351-2028
Commodity Trading Comm.	202/254-3275
Defense Logistics Agency	703/274-7088
Defense Mapping Agency	703/285-9148
District of Columbia Govt	202/727-6406
•	202/727-9726
TDD	202/347-5509
Environmental Protection	202/260-2090
•	202/260-5055

FBI	202/324-4981
Federal Deposit Ins. Corp	202/898-8890
Federal Emergency Mgmt.	202/646-3970
•	202/646-3244
Federal Energy Regulatory	202/357-0992
Federal Trade Commission	202/326-2022
TDD	202/326-2502
General Accounting Office	202/275-6092
(GS-1/12)	202/275-6017
(GS-12/Above)	202/275-6361
General Services Admin.	202/501-0370
Government Printing Office	202/512-0000

International Trade Comm.
202/205-2651
Interstate Commerce Comm.	202/275-7288
NASA	202/453-8478
•	202/755-6299
NASA Goddard Space Ctr	301/286-7918
•	301/286-5326
National Archives/Records	202/501-6100
National Endowment Arts	202/682-5405
•	202/682-5799
Ntl Endowment Humanities	202/786-0415

National Institute of Standards
& Technology	301/975-3007
National Labor Relations Bd	202/254-9044
TDD	202/634-1669
National Library of Medicine	301/496-4943
(Professionals) •	301/496-9541
(Clerical) •	301/496-9452
TDD	301/496-9452
Office of Mgmt & Budget	202/395-3765
TDD	202/395-5892
Office of Personnel Mgmt.	202/606-2424
TDD	202/606-2118
Peace Corps	202/606-3400
•	202/606-3214
•	800/424-8580
Securities & Exch. Comm.	202/272-2550
Small Business Admin.	202/653-6504
Smithsonian Institution	202/287-3100
•	202/287-3102
US Information Agency	202/619-4659
•	202/619-4539
US Postal Service	202/268-3646
•	202/268-3218
Voice of America	202/619-3117

EMPLOYMENT TYPES

The government offers *Competitive and Excepted Service jobs*. There are a multitude of employment options within these groups. Competitive Service means individuals compete for positions and the most qualified applicant is selected. Hiring is based on the applicant's knowledge, skills, and ability as compared to all other applicants. Excepted service job benefits, pay, etc. are identical in most cases to Competitive Service positions. Certain jobs are excepted by statute or by OPM. The Federal Courts, Library of Congress, the Federal Reserve System, the U.S. Foreign Service, the Tennessee Valley Authority, the FBI, the CIA, and other federal intelligence agencies are Excepted Service by statute. OPM uses the Excepted Service to fill positions that are extremely difficult to fill through normal competitive processes.

The U.S. Postal Service, Veterans Readjustment Act Appointments, attorneys, teachers in dependents' schools overseas, the CIA and FBI, Secret Service, and most positions in the Legislative and Judicial Branches are also in the Excepted Service. Foreign nationals that hold jobs overseas are excepted by Executive Order.

One disadvantage of the Excepted Service is the inability to transfer directly into a Competitive Service position. Excepted Service employees who want to apply for a Competitive Service job must go through OPM and compete for jobs with all other applicants.

For example, technicians working for the Air National Guard are in the Excepted Service. The same technician position with the Air Force Reserve is in the Competitive Service. If the Reserve base would close down the Competitive Service Technician would have first rights to any similar technician position in any competitive job around the country. The Air national Guard technician would not have this right and would have to go through OPM and get on the Federal Register to apply for competitive jobs.

Individuals do not have a choice between Competitive or Excepted Service when applying for employment. The job announcement will specify which Service the job is in. However, you should be aware of the differences and if you can choose between two jobs, it may be to your benefit to accept the competitive position. **Less than 18% of all Federal Civil Service jobs are in the Excepted Service.**

"Our business in life is not to get ahead of others,
but to get ahead of ourselves — to break our own
records, to outstrip our yesterdays by our today."

Stewart B. Johnson

TABLE 3-2
THE TYPICAL FEDERAL CIVILIAN EMPLOYEE
(NON-POSTAL EMPLOYMENT)

JOB CHARACTERISTICS	1980	1991
Pay System		
General Schedule (GS)	71%	73%
Wage Grade	21%	17%
Other	8%	10%
Occupations		
White-Collar	79%	83%
Professional	17%	22%
Blue-Collar	21%	17%
Work Schedule		
Full-Time	92%	93%
Part-Time	4%	4%
Intermittent	4%	3%
Service		
Competitive	81%	80%
Excepted & SES*	19%	20%

* - The SES is the Senior Executive Service

Source: The Federal Civilian Workforce Statistics, Employment & Trends as of June 1992, publication PSOG/OW1-2

EQUAL EMPLOYMENT OPPORTUNITY

The Federal Government is an Equal Opportunity Employer. Hiring and advancement in the Government are based on qualifications and performance regardless of your race, color, creed, religion, sex, age, national origin, or disability.

EMPLOYMENT OPTIONS

There are numerous employment paths available: full time, part time and job sharing positions, *cooperative education hiring programs, Presidential Management Internships, student employment, job opportunities for veterans and the handicapped, the Career America College Graduate Program, and summer work programs*. Military dependents and veterans can be hired under special appointment through the *Family Member Preference, Military Spouse Preference Programs, or the Veterans Readjustment Appointment (VRA) Program*. Military dependent and veteran's programs are explained in Chapter Six.

The majority of applicants will seek federal employment through announcements from FJICs or individual agencies. Another primary route is the Administrative Careers With America Examining Program. Alternate routes are categorized into special emphasis groups, such as student employment, military dependent, veteran and handicapped hiring programs.

CAREER AMERICA

The majority of college counselors are sent a comprehensive Career America promotional package. This package consists of 6 glossy brochures explaining the various college hiring programs offered by the federal government. An all new *Federal Career Directory* is also sent out to Career Planning and Placement Centers nationwide.

The Career America Connection hot line was implemented in early 1990. Individuals can now obtain timely federal employment information, 24 hours a day, 7 days a week. This OPM college hotline, 912-757-3000, costs 40 cents per minute and provides information on all aspects of federal employment including salary and benefits for entry level positions, student programs, summer employment; plus specific occupational information, such as engineering and science, health care, accounting, etc. Application packages can be requested on the hotline.

ADMINISTRATIVE CAREERS WITH AMERICA

(EXAMINING PROGRAM)

This program is a dual-track method of entry into approximately 90 professional and administrative occupations. A complete list of the 90 occupations is presented in Chapter Four. One track allows agencies to recruit and hire on-the-spot (in urgent situations) candidates who have a 3.5 grade-point average (GPA). This track is often referred to the *Outstanding Scholars Program*. The second track consists of a set of six examinations developed for each of six occupational groupings. A seventh job grouping will use ratings of education and experience rather than a written examination.

Each exam consists of two parts: An occupationally specific written test of job-relevant abilities and a biodata questionnaire called the Individual Achievement Record (IAR). The scores on each of these two parts are combined into a single score which serves as the basis for ranking candidates. Additional ACWA testing information is available in chapter four.

> You may apply for these jobs when you're within nine months of graduation, or upon completion of the qualifying academic courses <u>or</u> **THREE YEARS' WORK EXPERIENCE.**

STUDENT EMPLOYMENT OPPORTUNITIES

Numerous *Student Employment Programs* are available to attract students into the public sector. These programs offer on-the-job experience that could lead to a full time career with the government after graduation. Industry and government utilize student programs to identify prospects for future hiring. The above mentioned bulletin board and College HOTLINE provides updates on what agencies are hiring students and for which specialties.

STUDENT HIRING PROGRAMS

- Federal Junior Fellowship Program

- Federal Cooperative Education Program

- Presidential Mgmt Intern Program (PMI)

- Stay-in-School Program

- Summer Employment Program

- Student Volunteer Services

TABLE 3-3
STUDENT EMPLOYMENT PROGRAMS

Participants by Sex, 1991

PROGRAM	TOTAL	% WOMEN
Summer	34,795	53
Cooperative	16,809	50
Stay-In-School	13,088	73
Student Volunteer	6,303	53
Junior Fellowship	1,240	54

Source: The Fact Book, Federal Civilian Workforce, June 1992/PSOG/OW1-1

FEDERAL JUNIOR FELLOWSHIP PROGRAM

High school seniors can be nominated by their schools for this program. Financial-need criteria must be met and the student must be pursuing a bachelor's degree.

Students selected for this program work for agencies part-time and during summer and vacation periods while in college. Federal agencies contact high schools directly for nominations. Positions generally open in late spring. Interested high school students should contact their guidance counselors for applications and additional information.

Students that complete this program have a better chance of landing a full time position upon graduation. Agencies have an opportunity to evaluate your performance while you're working part time with them. If they were satisfied with your performance, they will steer you to appropriate job announcements if vacancies exist.

FEDERAL COOPERATIVE EDUCATION PROGRAM

The Federal Government is one of the largest employers of Co-op students. This program provides jobs for students while they are pursuing their college degree. Positions are available in over 200 occupations across the country in offices, shipyards, hospitals, laboratories, forests, parks, and in ocean and space programs. The six largest employing agencies of co-op students are the Navy, Agriculture, Army, NASA, Air Force, and Treasury.

Co-op students earn a salary based on their work experience and education. Benefits start immediately and Co-ops receive paid vacations, holidays and sick leave, major medical, life insurance, and can participate in a federal retirement plan.

ELIGIBILITY REQUIREMENTS

CO-OP STUDENTS MUST BE:

- Pursuing a professional, graduate, baccalaureate, or associate degree, undergraduate certificate or diploma, or high school diploma;

- Enrolled in the school's Cooperative Education Program;

- Maintaining good academic standing in school;

- Recommended for Co-op assignment in school;

- A U.S. citizen or a permanent resident who will be a citizen by graduation.

TABLE 3-4
MAJOR CO-OP OCCUPATIONS

Professional/Technical

Accounting & Budget
Agriculture & Forestry
Arts & Communication
Biological Sciences
Business & Industry
Computer Science
Engineering & Architecture
Investigations & Compliance
Mathematics & Statistics
Medical, Hospital
Dental & Public Health
Personnel Management
Industrial Relations
Physical Science & Psychology

Procurement Contracts
Supply
Social Science & Psychology
Transportation & Supply

Administrative & Office Support

Secretary & Clerk-Typist
Accounting Technician
Personnel Assistant
Computer Operator
Editorial Assistant
Medical Clerk
Procurement Clerk

Trade & Craft

Electronic Equipment
Installation and Maintenance
Machine Tool Work
Metal Processing
Plumbing & Pipeline
Aircraft & Pipefitting
Warehousing
Stock Handling
Industrial Equipment
Maintenance

Interested students should contact their Cooperative Education Coordinator for additional information. Also, contact Cooperative Program Managers in federal agency Personnel Offices. Agencies are listed under U.S. Government in your telephone directory.

PRESIDENTIAL MANAGEMENT INTERNSHIP (PMI) PROGRAM

This program is targeted for graduate students that would like to enter management within the federal government. Entry into this program is considered an honor and recognized throughout the government.

Professional, entry-level positions are available that provide exposure to a wide range of public management issues and offer considerable chances for career progression. PMI candidates are appointed for a two year period and most positions are located in the Washington, D.C. area. At the end of your two-year appointment you will be converted to a permanent position as long as your performance was satisfactory during your internship.

TABLE 3-5
PRESIDENTIAL MANAGEMENT INTERNSHIPS (PM1)
Top Ten Universities & Employing Agencies 1991

UNIVERSITY	NUMBER	AGENCY	NUMBER
Johns Hopkins	26	HHS	54
Columbia	22	NASA	30
George Washington	19	STATE	24
Harvard	18	JUSTICE	18
American	15	EPA	18
Georgetown	15	TREASURY	13
Texas-LBJ	14	OMB	12
Michigan	13	GAO	9
Princeton	11	OPM	9
Syracuse	10	Commerce	8

There were 247 PMI participants in 1991.

QUALIFICATIONS

Typical study areas that qualify include finance, economics, accounting, criminal justice, business administration, health administration, urban planning, social services, public administration, information systems management, law, political science, information systems management. This list is not all inclusive.

> 1. You must be scheduled to receive or have received a graduate degree.
>
> 2. During your studies you must have demonstrated an outstanding ability and personal interest in a government career in management of public policies and programs.
>
> 3. You are currently a U. S. citizen or will soon become a citizen before being appointed to a PMI.

Your Graduate School's dean, director, or chairperson must nominate you for the program. Nominations are made by the first of December of each year. Selections from each school are highly competitive and are based on skills, abilities, and knowledge.

The final selections from all nominees are made through a comprehensive individual and group interview, application assessment, writing samples, and a review of your school's recommendations.

PMI announcements are mailed in September to graduate schools nationwide. If interested, contact your career placement and guidance office. Call the Career America Hotline for additional information and specific appointment details.

STAY IN SCHOOL PROGRAM (HIGH SCHOOL & COLLEGE)

Students may qualify for the Federal Stay-in-School Program so you can continue school or resume your education. Financial-need must be established to qualify for this program. Disabled students do not have to meet financial need criteria.

Applicants must be at least 16 years of age and full-time students enrolled in any high-school, vocational school, or baccalaureate program. Students can work part time during school and full time during vacations.

Over 20,000 students nationwide participate in the Federal Stay-in-School Program. Students are paid at regular government salaries or minimum wage. Schools are contacted by agencies that offer this program and often State Employment Agencies are involved.

SUMMER EMPLOYMENT PROGRAM (HIGH SCHOOL & COLLEGE)

From May 13 to September 30 of each year training and work opportunities are created for students through the Summer Employment Program. Applicants must be at least 16 for most jobs and meet the required job qualification requirements.

Positions from general office, clerical, trade, professional, and labor occupations are offered. Regular government salaries are paid to participating students.

Look for announcement number 414 that is issued each December at most Federal Job Information Centers. Write or call your local FJIC for a job announcement. See Appendix B for a complete list of FJICs. This job announcement remains open until April 15th. Your application must be postmarked by no later than this date. A 26 page booklet is sent out with each announcement and explains the program, job locations, hiring agencies, special requirements, needed experience and education, and other pertinent information.

---

6. <u>STUDENT VOLUNTEER SERVICES</u> (HIGH SCHOOL & COLLEGE)

Students can volunteer to work with local agencies to gain valuable work experience. These jobs are not compensated. Schools coordinate participation and high school and college students are eligible for this program. A number of colleges include volunteer service internships. Interested students can contact agencies directly.

The Student Volunteer program is an excellent path for students to develop agency contacts, work experience, and gain insight into various government careers. Often, participants receive career counseling and acquire first hand information on upcoming paid student and full time openings.

All agencies are permitted to utilize this program. However, many don't participate for various reasons. Interested students should ask their career counselor for assistance when contacting agencies. Often, a counselor can persuade a manager to try out the program on a test basis. Student Volunteer Services is an excellent opportunity for aggressive students to get their foot in the door.

THE LARGEST OCCUPATIONS

White-collar workers are classified into 446 different occupations. Refer to Appendix D for a complete list of white-collar occupational groups and their descriptions. Average worldwide annual base salary for this group reached $34,664 as of September 30, 1991. Professionals earned the highest average salaries at $46,516 followed by Administrative at $41,774; Technicals at $25,677; Others at $23,254 (mostly firefighters, police, and guards); and clericals at the lowest average salary of $19,404. The following table lists the twenty white-collar occupations with at least 20,000 employees.

TABLE 3-6
WHITE-COLLAR OCCUPATIONS WITH
20,000 OR MORE EMPLOYEES

SERIES	TITLE	EMPLOYMENT 1991
318	Secretary	102,231
303	Misc. Clerk & Assistant	67,377
334	Computer Specialist	53,097
301	Misc. Administration	50,122
610	Nurse	41,082
343	Management & Program Analysis	40,809
322	Clerk-Typist	32,995
1811	Criminal Investigation	32,077
1102	Contracting	31,651
855	Electronics Engineering	30,010
2152	Air Traffic Control	26,099
802	Engineering Technicians	25,936
2005	Supply Clerical & Technician	25,553
905	General Attorney	23,953
592	Tax Examining	23,274
801	General Engineer	21,617
305	Mail and File	21,556
525	Accounting Technician	21,518
105	Social Insurance Administration	21,381
856	Electronics Technician	19,592

SOURCE: OPM Publications PB93-140804, MW 56-22

Blue-collar workers are classified into 402 different occupations and organized into 37 job family groups. Refer to Appendix D for a complete list of white-collar occupational groups and their descriptions. The average worldwide salary for this group was $28,166 as of September 30, 1991. The occupational survey for 1991 covered 359,376 full-time federal civilian employees in trades and labor occupations. From 1987 through September 30, 1991, total blue-collar employment decreased by 44,874. This is due in a large part to military downsizing efforts. The majority of blue-collar workers are employed with the Department of Defense.

The highest average salaries were in the printing family: $34,417 for men and $30,209 for women. The lowest average salaries were $19,688 for men in general services and support work and $17,886 for vessel jobs excluded from the Federal Wage System. The following table lists twelve blue-collar occupations with at least 10,000 employees.

TABLE 3-7
BLUE-COLLAR OCCUPATIONS WITH
10,000 OR MORE EMPLOYEES

SERIES	TITLE	EMPLOYMENT 1991
6907	Materials Worker	23,100
3566	Custodial Working	15,423
8852	Aircraft Mechanic	14,832
2604	Electronics Mechanics	13,816
4749	Maintenance Mechanic	12,884
5803	Heavy Mobile Equipment Mechanic	12,064
3806	Sheet Metal Mechanic	10,948
5703	Motor Vehicle Operating	10,585
7408	Food Service Working	10,433
2805	Electrician	9,715
3502	Laboring	9,573
4204	Pipefitting	8,995

SOURCE: OPM Publications PB93-140804, MW 56-22

The **Clinton/Gore National Performance Review** (NPR) proposes federal workforce reductions of 252,000 workers over the next five years. *"Most of the personnel reductions will be concentrated in the structures of overcontrol and micromanagement: supervisors, headquarters staffs, personnel specialists, accountants, and auditors."* If these cuts materialize, expect to see significant changes in Table 3-6 and 3-7 occupational rankings.

INFORMATIONAL INTERVIEWS

> Informational interviewing will become even more important when and if the **NPR's** proposals are implemented. The **NPR** report calls for decentralizing the employment system, agencies will be allowed to hire directly - without examination or rankings - under guidelines to be drafted by OPM.

Call agencies where your skills could be needed and ask to talk with a supervisor within your specialty, ie; administration, technical, computer operations, etc. Briefly explain to this individual what jobs you are interested in and if he/she would be willing to talk with you in person about future employment.

If you are uncertain your job skills are needed by an agency ask for the personnel or Human Resources Department and query them concerning positions you might qualify for. Secretaries often provide insight into what positions are utilized by the agency contacted.

If an informational interview is granted take along a signed copy of your SF-171 and a cover letter describing your desires and qualifications. The informational interview will help you investigate the many employment opportunities available to you in many diverse agencies. You will need to identify candidates to interview through the methods mentioned above. You don't have to limit your informational interviews strictly to supervisors. Any individual currently employed in a position you find attractive can provide the necessary information. The outcome of these interviews will help you make an objective career decision for specific positions. There is one key element you must stress when requesting an information interview:

> **WHEN ASKING FOR THE INTERVIEW MAKE THEM AWARE THAT YOU ARE NOT ASKING FOR A JOB AND ONLY DESIRE INFORMATION**

This should be brought to their attention immediately after requesting an interview. Many supervisors and employees are willing to talk about their job even when no vacancies exist. These interviews often provide insight into secondary careers and upcoming openings that can be more attractive than what you were originally pursuing.

Place a time limit on these interviews. When contacting supervisors, request the interview by following the above guidelines but add that you will only take 15 minutes of their time. Time is a critical resource that most of us must use sparingly. When going for the interview you should be prepared to ask specific questions that will get the information you need. The following questions will help you prepare:

INFORMATIONAL INTERVIEW QUESTIONS

EXPERIENCE AND BACKGROUND

1. What training and education is needed for this type of work?

2. How did you personally prepare for your career?

3. What experience is absolutely essential?

4. How did you get started?

5. What do you find most and least enjoyable with this work?

CREDENTIALS

Of the items listed below which do you consider most important?

1. Education
2. Special skills
3. Former work experience
4. Personality
5. Organizational knowledge
6. Other

GENERAL QUESTIONS

1. What general or specific advice would you give to someone interested in this field?

2. How do I find out more about available jobs and how are they advertised?

3. Does this agency hire directly from regional offices or do they hire through the Office of Personnel Management?

4. Does this position have career development potential and if so what is the highest grade I could achieve?

5. Is there considerable or moderate travel involved with this line of work?

6. Are you required to work shifts?

REFERRAL

1. As a result of our conversation today, are there others I should talk to?

2. May I use your name when I contact them?

If an interview is not granted ask permission to send a SF-171 for their prospective employee file. In many cases agencies cannot hire you directly unless you qualify for a direct appointment. However, if upcoming positions open they can notify you when the job will be advertised. Positions created through these methods bring aboard highly desirable employee prospects under future competitive announcements.

Certain agencies do have the authority to hire direct. To determine if an agency has this ability you must contact their regional Human Resources or Personnel Department. When agencies hire directly you must apply through their personnel office. Send direct hire agencies a cover letter and SF-171 for their prospective employment file. Regional office addresses and phone numbers can be obtained by calling local area agency offices and asking for the address and phone number of that agency's regional office. For example, the Central Intelligence Agency hires certain positions direct.

It is hard to imagine the diversity of jobs needed by most agencies. Don't exclude any agency in this process. Most agencies hire a broad spectrum of skills and professions. **When going for the interview dress appropriately for the position applied for.** You can expect numerous rejections while pursuing these methods. Don't get discouraged. A good manager in industry or the federal government is always on the lookout for talent he/she will be needing. If you present yourself in a professional manner and have a good work and educational history for the position applied for you will make a connection. Persistence pays when dealing with the government. Many promising candidates give up prematurely before giving their efforts a chance to work. It can sometimes take years to get the job you desire.

Most government job openings are first advertised within the agency and current employees have the first chance to bid for a higher paying position. If the job can't be filled in-house then it is advertised in the private sector by the Office of Personnel Management or in certain cases by the agency itself. These are the jobs you will be bidding on. The reason for going to the private sector is that no qualified in-house bidders applied for the positions.

ENGINEERING CONVERSIONS

Many professional engineering jobs are open to non degree applicants that meet the Office of Personnel Managements Engineering Conversion criteria. This is good news to those who have over 60 semester hours of college in specific areas of study. Federal regulations state that to qualify for professional engineering positions, GS-5 through GS-15, a candidate must meet basic requirements for all professional engineering positions.

ENGINEERING POSITION QUALIFICATION STANDARDS

PRIMARY PATH - There are two paths to achieving professional engineering status. The primary path consists of having an engineering degree from a 4 year accredited college. The curriculum must be accredited by the Accreditation Board for Engineering and Technology (ABET) or include the specific courses and five of the specific study areas listed in Note 1 below.

ALTERNATE PATHS - Alternate paths are available to those who don't have a four-year engineering degree but have the specific knowledge, skills, abilities, and work experience for an engineering position.

Four years of college level education, training, and/or technical experience is required and can be obtained through the following paths:

A. Professional Engineering Registration Exam
B. Engineering-in-Training-Examination
C. 60 semester hours in an accredited college
    including the courses and areas of study
    listed in Note 1 below.
D. A degree in related curriculum

The first three alternate programs require appropriate training and work experience. If an applicant has the engineering experience and completed A, B, or C above, OPM will rate them as Professional Engineers.

The fourth alternate program is a related degree. For example, applicants who have a four year degree in civil engineering and bid on a mechanical engineering job can be rated eligible if they have at least one year of experience under a mechanical professional engineer.

NOTE 1. Curriculum must include differential and integral calculus and courses (more advanced than first year physics and chemistry) in five of the seven following areas:

a. Statics: Dynamics

b. Strength of Materials

c. Fluid Mechanics, Hydraulics

d. Thermodynamics

e. Electrical Fields and Circuits

f. Nature and Properties of Materials

g. Other fundamental engineering subjects including
    Optics, Heat Transfer, Electronics

CHAPTER FOUR

CIVIL SERVICE EXAMS

Examination announcements (job opening notices) may or may not require a written test. In many cases the examination consists of a detailed evaluation of your work experiences and education listed on your employment application. Of the 446 white collar occupations, just over 90 require written tests under the new Administrative Careers With America (ACWS) program. Table 4-1 provides a complete list of occupations tested under this program. Additionally, Table 4-3 lists over 60 clerical positions that require written tests.

> With the exception of limited Direct Hire and Case Examining authority, OPM now controls the examination system for agencies and recruits and screens applicants for positions that are common to all agencies. **Al Gore's National Performance Review** proposes that agencies be given full authority to recruit and examine candidates directly, and without examination or ranking when deemed necessary. It will take years to make the transition into this configuration, if and when congress approves implementation. Currently, over 100,000 pages of personnel rules and regulations exist that define how to hire, promote, or fire federal employees. Congress must establish new rules and polices before repealing the existing law.

ADMINISTRATIVE CAREERS WITH AMERICA TESTS

About 100 job series are filled through this program, using one of two options:

- A written examination; or
- An application based on scholastic achievement, reflected by your grade point average (GPA).

Examinations consist of two parts: a written test and a multiple-choice *Individual Achievement Record* (IRA) questionnaire. The test results are combined to produce a single score which serves as the basis for ranking candidates. You must receive a score of 70 or above to be eligible.

Entry level grades are at the GS-5 and GS-7 levels with annual salaries of $18,340 and $22,717. College graduates with top grades can be hired on the spot at OPM college fairs or by agencies direct under the (ACWA) *Outstanding Scholar Program*. Applicants who meet the requirements of the Outstanding Scholar Program are not required to take a written test and they may apply directly to agencies.

Applicants who meet the requirements of the *Bilingual/Bicultural Program* may apply directly to agencies at any time, but they are required to take a written test. This program permits federal agencies to hire directly individuals who are proficient in Spanish language or have knowledge of the Hispanic culture when public interaction or job performance would be enhanced by this skill or knowledge.

To be considered under the Bilingual/Bicultural Program, you must pass the appropriate written test and have the required level of Spanish language proficiency/or the requisite knowledge of the Hispanic culture.

When applying for one of the tests, you will receive an instructional pamphlet with sample questions. Tests are administered periodically based on hiring needs.

Entry-level professional and administrative job applicants will earn eligibility by either:

- [1]Earning a college **grade point average of 3.5 or above** on a 4.0 scale or have graduated in the upper 10 percent of your class or major university subdivision and impressing agency recruiters with experience and technical abilities during an interview. This method is referred to as the *Outstanding Scholar Program*.

- Passing a job-related skills test and a new Individual Achievement Record (IAR) test. Both measure relevant personal qualities required for successful job performance.

You can test in one or all of the six occupational areas. A separate application package must be requested and completed for each test. Request *Qualification Information Statements (QIS)* from your local FJIC for the groups that interest you. This information can also be obtained by calling the Career America Connection Hotline at 912-757-3000 ($.40 per minute). Applicants must submit OPM Form 5000-B, supplied by OPM, to take the appropriate written test.

POSITIVE EDUCATION REQUIREMENTS

Several entry-level positions under the Administrative Careers With America program don't require written exams. However, they do require the completion of specific college course work. Group 7 of table 4-1 lists all 16 of these positions.

---

[1] Your GPA can be rounded in the following manner: a 3.44 is rounded down to 3.4; a 3.45 is rounded up to 3.5.

Applications should be submitted to OPM only when vacancies are announced at your FJIC for these 16 areas. You will receive a rating based on an evaluation of your education and work experience; or by meeting GPA provisions and completing the required specific course work. Federal agencies can hire you direct if you have a GPA of 3.5 or higher.

TABLE 4-1

SEVEN OCCUPATIONAL GROUPS AND RELATED OCCUPATIONS REQUIRING TESTS

Group 1-Health, Safety and Environmental Occupations

Series	Title
0018	Safety & Occupational Health Management
0023	Outdoor Recreational Planning
0028	Environmental Protection Specialist
0673	Hospital Housekeeping Management
0685	Public Health Program Specialist

Group 2-Writing and Public Information Occupations

Series	Title
1001	General Arts & Information
1035	Public Affairs
1082	Writing & Editing
1083	Technical Writing & Editing
1147	Agricultural Market Reporting
1412	Technical Information Services
1421	Archives Specialist

Group 3-Business, Finance and Management Occupations

Series	Title
0011	Bond Sales Promotions
0106	Unemployment Insurance
0120	Food Assistance Program Specialist
0346	Logistics Management
0393	Communications Specialist
0501	Financial Administration

Group 3 (Continued)

Series	Title
0560	Budget Analysis
0570	Financial Institution Examining
1101	General Business & Industry
1102	Contract Specialist
1104	Property Disposal
1130	Public Utilities
1140	Trade Specialist
1145	Agricultural Program Specialist
1146	Agricultural Marketing
1149	Wage and Hour Law Administration
1150	Industrial Specialist
1160	Financial Analysis
1163	Insurance Examining
1165	Loan Specialist
1170	Realty
1171	Appraising & Assessing
1173	Housing Management
1176	Building Management
1910	Quality Assurance Specialist
2001	General Supply
2003	Supply Program Management
2010	Inventory Management
2030	Distribution Facilities & Storage Management
2032	Packaging
2050	Supply Cataloging
2101	Transportation Specialist
2110	Transportation Industry Analysis
2125	Highway Safety Management
2130	Traffic Management
2150	Transportation

Group 4-Personnel, Administration and Computer Occupations

Series	Title
0142	Manpower Development
0201	Personnel Management
0205	Military Personnel Management
0212	Personnel Staffing
0221	Position Classification
0222	Occupational Analysis
0223	Salary & Wage Administration
0230	Employee Relations
0233	Labor Relations
0235	Employee Development
0244	Labor Management Relations Examining
0246	Contractor Industrial Relations
0301	Misc. Admin & Program
0334	Computer Specialist (Trainee)
0341	Admin Officer
0343	Management Analysis
0345	Program Analysis
1715	Vocational Rehabilitation

Group 5-Benefits Review, Tax & Legal Occupations

Series	Title
0105	Social Insurance
0187	Social Services
0526	Tax Technician
0950	Paralegal Specialist
0962	Contact Representative
0965	Land Law Examining

Group 5 (continued)		Group 6-Law Enforcement & Investigation		Group 7-Positions with Positive education requirements	
Series	**Title**	**Series**	**Grade**	**Series**	**Title**
0967	Passport & Visa Examining	0025	Park Ranger	0020	Community Planning
0987	Tax Law Specialist	0080	Security Administration	0101	Social Science
0990	General Claims Examining	0132	Intelligence	0110	Economist
		0249	Wage & Hour Compliance	0130	Foreign Affairs
0991	Worker's Compensation Claims Examining	1169	Internal Revenue Officer	0131	International Relations
		1801	Civil Aviation Security Specialist	0140	Manpower Research & Analysis
0993	Social Insurance Claims Examining	1810	General Investigator	0150	Geography
		1811	Criminal Investigator	0170	History
0994	Unemployment Compensation	1812	Game Law Enforcement	0180	Psychology
		1816	Immigration Inspector	0184	Sociology
0995	Claims Examining	1831	Securities Compliance Examining	0190	General Anthropology
0996	Veterans Claims Examining			0193	Archeology
		1854	Alcohol, Tobacco, and Firearms Inspection	1015	Museum Curator
0997	Civil Service Retirement Claims Examining			1420	Archivist
		1864	Public Health Quarantine Inspection	1701	General Education & Training
		1889	Import Specialist	1720	Education Program
		1890	Customs Inspector		

BASIC QUALIFICATIONS (ACWA)

It's important to note that a college degree isn't required to qualify for these exams. Equivalent experience is acceptable as an alternative to a college degree. For example, to qualify for a GS-5 position you would require four years of education leading to a bachelor's degree, 3 years of *responsible experience*, or an equivalent combination of education and experience.

Applicants have three avenues to explore. If you don't have three years of experience or a bachelor's degree you can use a combination of education and experience to qualify.

RESPONSIBLE EXPERIENCE

You can combine education and experience to meet the qualification requirements. One academic year of full-time study (30 semester hours or 45 quarter hours) is equivalent to 9 months of responsible experience. A bachelor's degree is equivalent to 3 years of responsible experience. To be considered as qualifying experience, your experience must be related to the position applied for.

NONACCREDITED COLLEGE COURSE WORK

COURSES TAKEN AT NONACCREDITED INSTITUTIONS ARE ACCEPTABLE IF THEY MEET THE QUALIFYING CONDITIONS:

- The courses are accepted for advanced credit at an accredited institution.
- The institution is one whose transcript is given full credit by a State University.
- The courses have been evaluated and approved by a State Department of Education.
- The course work has been evaluated by an organization recognized for accreditation by the Council of Postsecondary Accreditation.

OUTSTANDING SCHOLAR PROGRAM

If your GPA is 3.45 or higher or you graduated in the upper ten (10) percent of your class or major subdivision you can be added to OPM's referral list under their *Outstanding Scholar Program*. Applicants who meet these provisions can be placed on an OPM referral list. Agencies are authorized to make immediate offers of employment to candidates who meet the requirements of this program. Contact OPM for application forms at 202-606-2700 or call the Career America Connection at 1-912-757-3000.

SAMPLE QUESTIONS (ACWA)

The sample questions that follow are taken from the ACWA background information guides. Tests consists of:

1. VOCABULARY
2. READING
2. TABULAR COMPLETION
3. ARITHMETIC REASONING
4. THE INDIVIDUAL ACHIEVEMENT RECORD (IAR)

* NOTE: The Careers in Writing and Public Information Occupations do not have an arithmetic reasoning section.

VOCABULARY QUESTIONS:

The following questions present a key word and five suggested answers. Your task is to find the suggested answer that is closest in meaning to the key word. Wrong answers may have some connection with the word, but the meanings will be essentially different from that of the key word. Sample questions 1,2 and 3 are examples of the vocabulary questions in the test.

1. *Stipulation* means most nearly

A) essential specification
B) unnecessary addition
C) unnecessary effort
D) required training
E) required correction

The word *stipulation* refers to a required condition or item specified in a contract, treaty, or other official document. Therefore, response A, *essential specification* is the best synonym. A *stipulation* could be an addition to a contract or other document, but even without unnecessary, response B is incorrect. Response C and D are clearly unrelated to the meaning of *stipulation*. Response E, required correction, shares with *stipulation* the idea of being necessary, as well as an association with something written. However, a correction is an alteration made to remedy or remove an error or fault, so its basic meaning is completely different from that *stipulation*.

2. *Allocation* means most nearly

A) prevention
B) site
C) exchange

D) assignment
E) ointment

An *allocation* is the act of setting something apart for a particular purpose. Response D, *assignment*, refers to the act of specifying or designating something exactly or precisely, and is, therefore, the best synonym for *allocation*. Response A,C, and E are clearly unrelated to the meaning of *allocation*. Response B, site, means to put something in a location or position; however, the emphasis with site is on the physical location given to an object, rather than on the purpose of the object.

3. To *collaborate* means most nearly to work

A) rapidly
B) together
C) independently

D) overtime
E) carefully

The word *collaborate* means to work with another, especially on a project of mutual interest. Therefore, response B, *together*, is the best answer. Response A,D, and E are clearly unrelated to the meaning of *collaborate*, and response C, independently, is opposite meaning.
NOTE: Question 1 and 2 relates to the Careers in Benefit Review, Tax, and Legal Occupations. Question 3 deals with Careers in Personnel, Administrative, and Computer Occupations.

READING QUESTIONS:

In each of the questions you will be given a paragraph which contains all the information necessary to infer the correct answer. Use only the information provided in the paragraph. Do not speculate or make assumptions that go beyond this information. Also, assume that all information in the paragraph is true, even if it conflicts with some fact known to you. Only one correct answer can be validly inferred from the information contained in the paragraph.

Pay special attention to negative verbs (for example, "are <u>not</u>") and negative prefixes (for example "<u>in</u>complete" or "<u>dis</u>organized"). Also pay special attention to qualifiers, such as "all," "none," and "some." For example, from a paragraph in which it is stated that "it is not true that all contracts are legal," or that "some illegal things are contracts," but one **cannot** validly infer that "no contracts are legal" and "all contracts are two sided agreements," one can infer that "some two-sided agreements are legal," but one **cannot** validly infer that "all two-sided agreements are legal."

Bear in mind that in some tests, universal qualifiers such as "all" and "none" often give away incorrect response choices. That is not the case in these tests. Some correct answers will refer to "all" or "none" of the members of a group.

Be sure to distinguish between essential information and unessential, peripheral information. That is to say, in a real test question, the example above ("all contracts are legal" and "all contracts are two-sided agreements") would appear in a longer, full-fledged paragraph. It would be up to you to separate the essential information from its context and then to realize that a response choice that states "some two-sided agreements are legal" represents a valid inference and hence the correct answer.

4. Personnel administration begins with the process of defining the quantities of people needed to do the job. Thereafter, people must be recruited, selected, trained, directed, rewarded, transferred, promoted and perhaps released or retired. However, it is not true that all organizations are structured so that workers can be dealt with as individuals. In some organizations, employees are represented by unions, and managers bargain only with these associations.

A) no organizations are structured so that workers cannot be dealt with as individuals.
B) some working environments other than organizations are structured so that workers can be dealt with as individuals
C) all organizations are structured so that employees are represented by unions.
D) no organizations are structured so that managers bargain with unions
E) some organizations are not structured so that workers can be dealt with as individuals

The correct answer is response E. This conclusion can be derived from information contained in the third sentence of the paragraph, which states that *it is not true that all organizations are structured so that workers can be dealt with as individuals*. From this statement, it can be inferred that some organizations are not structured so that workers can be dealt with as individuals.

Note that in this question, the correct answer follows basically from one sentence in the paragraph--the third sentence. The rest of the paragraph presents additional information about personnel administration which is relevant to the discussion, but not necessary to make the inference. Part of your task in the Reading section is to understand what you read, and then discern what conclusions follow logically from statements in the paragraph. Consequently, in the test, you will find some questions in which it is necessary to use all or most of the statements presented in the paragraph, while in others, such as this one, only one statement is needed to infer the correct answer.

5) One use of wild land is the protection of certain species of wild animals or plants in wildlife refuges or in botanical reservations. Some general types of land use are activities that conflict with this stated purpose. All activities that exhibit such conflict are, of course, excluded from refuges and reservations.

A) all activities that conflict with the purpose of wildlife refuges or botanical reservations are general types of land use
B) all activities excluded from wildlife refuges and botanical reservations are those that conflict with the purpose of the refuge or reservation
C) some activities excluded from wildlife refuges and botanical reservations are general types of land use
D) no activities that conflict with the purpose of wildlife refuges and botanical reservations are general types of land use
E) some general types of land use are not excluded from wildlife refuges and botanical reservations

The correct answer is response C. The answer can be inferred from the second and third sentences in the paragraph. The second sentence tells us that *some general types of land use are activities that conflict with* the purpose of wildlife refuges and botanical reservations. The third sentence explains that *all activities that exhibit such conflict are... excluded from refuges and reservations*. Therefore, we can conclude that *some activities excluded from refuges and reservations* (the ones that conflict with the purpose of refuges an reservations) are general types of land use.

NOTE: Question 4 directly relates to the Careers in Personnel, Administrative, and Computer Occupations. Question 5 deals with the Careers in Health, Safety, and Environmental Occupations.

TABULAR COMPLETION QUESTIONS

These questions are based on information presented in tables. Only two sample questions of this type appear below, although, in the actual test, you will have to find five unknown values in each table. You must calculate these unknown values by using the known values given in the table. In some questions, the exact answer will not be given as one of the response choices. In such cases, you should select response E, "none of these." Sample questions 5 and 6, which are based on the accompanying table, are examples of the tabular completion questions in this test.

LOCAL GOVERNMENT EXPENDITURES OF FINANCES:
1979 to 1982

(In millions of dollars)

ITEM	1979	1980	1981	1982 TOTAL	1982 PERCENT*
Expenditures	(I)	432,328	485,174	520,966	100.0
Direct General Expenditures	326,024	367,340	405,576	(IV)	83.2
Utility and Liquor Stores	30,846	(II)	43,016	47,970	9.2
Water and electric	20,734	24,244	28,453	31,499	6.0
Transit and others	10,112	11,947	14,563	16,471	3.2
Insurance Trust Expenditure	23,504	28,797	36,582	39,466	(V)
Employee retirement	12,273	14,008	(III)	17,835	3.4
Unemployment compensation	11,231	14,789	20,887	21,631	4.2

Hypothetical data.

*Rounded to one decimal place.

6. What is the value of I millions of dollars?

A) 380,374
B) 377,604
C) 356,870
D) 349,528
E) none of these

The answer is A. It can be calculated by adding the values for Direct General Expenditures, Utility and Liquor Stores, and Insurance Trust Expenditure. Numerically, 326,024 + 30,846 + 23,504 = 380,374.

7. What is the value of II in millions of dollars?

    A) 338,543
    B) 64,988
    C) 53,041
    D) 40,744
    E) none of these

The answer is E. The correct value (not given as an answer) is calculated by adding the value for water and electric and the value for transit and other. Numerically, $24,244 + 11,947 = 36,191$.

NOTE: Questions 6 and 7 relate to the Careers in Benefits Review, Tax, and Legal Occupations.

ARITHMETIC REASONING QUESTIONS

In this part of the test you have to solve problems formulated in both verbal and numeric form. You will have to analyze a paragraph in order to set up the problem, and then solve it. If the exact answer is not given as one of the response choices, you should select response E, "none of these."

8. An investigator rented a car for four days and was charged $200. The car rental company charged $10 per day plus $.20 per mile driven. How many miles did the investigator drive the car?

    A) 800
    B) 950
    C) 1,000
    D) 1,200
    E) none of these

The correct answer is A. It can be obtained by computing the following: $4(10) + .20X = 200$.

9. In a large agency where mail is delivered in motorized carts, two tires were replaced on a cart at a cost of $34.00 per tire. If the agency had expected to pay $80 for a pair of tires, what percent of its expected cost did it save?

    A) 7.5%
    B) 17.6%
    C) 57.5%
    D) 75.0%
    E) none of these

The answer is E. The correct answer is not given as one of the response choices. The answer can be obtained by computing the following:

$$(80/2 - 34)/40 = X$$

$$X = 6/40 = .15$$
$$.15 \times 100 = 15\%$$

The expected $80 cost for a pair of tires would make the cost of a single tire $40. The difference between the actual cost of $34 per tire and the expected cost of $40 per tire is $6, which is 15% of the $40 expected cost.

10. It takes two typists three 8-hour work days to type a report on a word processor. How many typists would be needed to type two reports of the same length in one 8-hour work day?

    A) 4
    B) 6
    C) 8
    D) 12
    E) none of these

The correct answer is D. It can be obtained by computing the following:

$$3 \times 2 \times 2 = X.$$

The left side of the equation represents the total number of 8-hour work days of typing required for two reports: three days times two typists times two reports equals 12 8-hour work days of typing. If all of this had to be accomplished in on 8-hour work day, 12 typists would be needed to do the job.

NOTE: Question 8 deals with Careers in Law Enforcement and Investigation Occupations. Question 9 relates to the Careers in Business, Finance, and Management Occupations and question 10 relates to the Careers in Benefit Review, Tax, and Legal Occupations.

CLERICAL TESTS

The Office of Personnel Management has implemented a pilot project at the Newark, NJ area office and in the New York area which waives clerical testing. Applicants submit a SF-171 and comprehensive Supplemental Qualifications Statement and OPM rates bidders on education and/or experience. Most OPM area offices administer a multiple choice clerical test.

The written test measures the clerical and verbal abilities needed to:

■ **DESIGN, ORGANIZE, & USE A FILING SYSTEM**

■ **ORGANIZE EFFECTIVELY THE CLERICAL PROCESS IN AN OFFICE**

■ **MAKE TRAVEL, MEETING, & CONFERENCE ARRANGEMENTS**

■ **LOCATE & ASSEMBLE INFORMATION FOR REPORTS & BRIEFINGS**

■ **COMPOSE NON-TECHNICAL CORRESPONDENCE**

■ **BE EFFECTIVE IN ORAL COMMUNICATION**

■ **USE OFFICE EQUIPMENT**

TABLE 4-3
QUALIFICATION REQUIREMENTS

For Clerk Typist positions:

GRADE	GENERAL EXPERIENCE		EDUCATION	PROFICIENCY
GS-2	3 months	OR	High school or equivalent	40 wpm typing
GS-3	6 months	OR	1 year above high school	40 wpm typing
GS-4	1 year	OR	2 years above high school	40 wpm typing

For Clerk Stenographer positions:

GRADE	GENERAL EXPERIENCE		EDUCATION	PROFICIENCY
GS-3	6 months	OR	High school or equivalent	40 wpm typing
GS-4	1 year	OR	2 years above high school	40 wpm typing
GS-5	2 years	OR	4 years above high school	40 wpm typing

For all other clerical and administrative support positions covered:

GRADE	GENERAL EXPERIENCE		EDUCATION
GS-2	3 months	OR	High school or equivalent
GS-3	6 months	OR	1 year above high school
GS-4	1 year	OR	2 years above high school

Some clerical and administrative support positions also require typing and/or stenography proficiency.

GENERAL EXPERIENCE: High school graduation or the equivalent may be substituted for experience at the GS-2 level for all listed occupations except Clerk-Stenographer, where it may be substituted for experience at the GS-3 level. Equivalent combinations of successfully completed education and experience requirements may be used to meet total experience requirements at grades GS-5 and below.

Table 4-4 lists all of the positions and grades covered under the Clerical and Administrative Support Positions test. Positions at higher grade levels in listed occupations are covered under separate examinations.

TABLE 4-4
CLERICAL AND ADMINISTRATIVE SUPPORT POSITIONS
CLERK GS 2/3, CLERK TYPIST GS-2/4
CLERK STENOGRAPHER GS-3/5
SECRETARY GS-3/4

Business
Business Clerk GS-2/4
Procurement Clerk GS-2/4
Production Control Clerk GS-2/4
Property Disposal Clerk GS-2/4
Purchasing Agent GS-2/4

Communications
Communications Clerk GS-2/4
Communications Technician GS-2/4
Communications Relay Operator GS-2/4
Cryptographic Equip. Operator GS-2/4
Teletypist GS-2/4

Finance
Accounting Clerk GS-2/4
Budget Clerk GS-2/4
Cash Processing Clerk GS-2/4
Financial Clerk GS-2/4
Insurance Accounts Clerk GS-2/4
Military Pay Clerk GS-2/4
Payroll Clerk GS-2/4
Tax Accounting Clerk GS-2/4
Time & Leave Clerk GS-2/4
Voucher Examining Clerk GS-2/4

Legal
Claims Clerk GS-2/4
Legal Clerk GS-2/4
Legal Records Clerk GS-2/4

Office Clerk
Correspondence Clerk GS-2/4
Information Reception Clerk GS-2/4
Mail and File Clerk GS-2/4

Office Clerk (cont'd)
Office Equipment Operator GS-2/4
Personnel Clerk GS-2/4
Personnel (Military) Clerk GS-2/4
Printing Clerk GS-2/4
Statistical Clerk GS-2/4
Supply Clerk GS-2/4
Telephone Operator GS-2/4

Transportation
Dispatching Clerk GS-2/4
Freight Rate Clerk GS-2/4
Passenger Rate Clerk GS-2/4
Shipping Clerk GS-2/4
Transportation Clerk GS-2/4
Travel Clerk GS-2/4

Miscellaneous
Archives Clerk GS-2/4
Arts & Information Clerk GS-2/4
Coding Clerk GS-2/4
Compliance Inspection Clerk GS-2/4
Computer Clerk GS-2/4
Editorial Clerk GS-2/4
Electronic Accounting Machine Operator GS-2/4
Environmental Protection Assistant GS-2/4
Fingerprint Identification Clerk GS-2/4
Intelligence Clerk GS-2/4
Language Clerk GS-2/4
Library Clerk GS-2/4
Management Clerk GS-2/4
Messenger GS-2/4 *
Security Clerical & Assistant GS-2/4

* Under 5 U.S.C 3310, appointment to a Messenger position is restricted to persons entitled to veterans preference as long as such persons are available.

TYPING PROFICIENCY

Typing proficiency is determined one of several ways. You can present a speed certification statement from a typing course, take a typing test with OPM, or personally certify that you type 40 or more words per minute and later take a test upon reporting for duty.

TESTING PROCESS

The written clerical test consists of two parts, clerical aptitude and verbal abilities. To pass the written test, applicants must make a minimum score of 33 on the verbal abilities and a minimum combined total score of 80 on both the clerical and verbal parts. A score of 80 converts to a numerical rating of 70. In addition to written tests, applicants must complete the *Occupational Supplement for Clerical Positions* (OPM Form 1203-A1). With this form OPM will be able to determine an applicants' minimum qualifications based on a review of their education and work experience.

A final rating results from the written examination and Form 1203-A1, with 5 or 10 additional points added for veterans preference. After taking the exam and filling out the additional forms OPM will send you a (NOR) *Notice of Rating* within 5 to 10 work days of testing.

SAMPLE CLERICAL TESTS

There are several books on the market that provide sample tests for government clerical positions. You can find *ARCO* test preparation manuals at most book stores. When you apply to take an OPM test, they generally send out sample questions and explain the test in detail. The tests are multiple choice in the areas described above.

The following sample questions were provided by OPM.

SAMPLE QUESTIONS (Clerical Test)

The following sample questions show types of questions found in the written test you will take. Your answers to the questions are to be recorded on a separate answer sheet. The questions on the test may be harder or easier than those shown here, but a sample of each kind of question on the test is given.

Read these directions, then look at the sample questions and try to answer them. Each question has several suggested answers lettered A, B, C, etc. Decide which one is the best answer to the question. During the test you will be provided with an answer sheet. When taking the actual test, find the answer space that is numbered the same as the number of the question, and - darken completely the oval that is lettered the same as the letter of your answer. All questions are multiple choice. The answers to the sample questions are provided on the following pages. For some questions an explanation of the correct answer is given immediately following the sample question.

Vocabulary. For each question like 1 through 3, choose the one of the four suggested answers that means most nearly the same as the word in *italics.*

1. *Option* means most nearly
   A) use   C) value
   B) choice   D) blame

2. *Innate* means most nearly
   A) eternal   B) well-developed
   C) native   D) prospective

3. To *confine* means most nearly to
   A) restrict   C) eliminate
   B) hide   D) punish

Grammar. In questions 4, 5, and 6, decide which sentence is preferable with respect to grammar and usage suitable for a formal letter or report.

4. A) If properly addressed, the letter will reach my mother and I.
   B) The letter had been addressed to myself and my mother.
   C) I believe the letter was addressed to either my mother or I.
   D) My mother's name, as well as mine, was on the letter.

The answer to question 4 is D). The answer is not A because the word me (reach . . . me) should have been used, not the word I. The answer is not B. The expression, to myself, is sometimes used in spoken English, but it is not acceptable in a formal letter or report. The answer is not C, because the word I has been used incorrectly, just as it was in A.

5. A) Most all these statements have been supported by persons who are reliable and can be depended upon.
   B) The persons which have guaranteed these statements are reliable.
   C) Reliable persons guarantee the facts with regards to the truth of these statements.
   D) These statements can be depended on, for their truth has been guaranteed by reliable persons.

6. A) Brown's & Company employees have recently received increases in salary.
   B) Brown & Company recently increased the salaries of all its employees.
   C) Recently Brown & Company has increased their employees' salaries.
   D) Brown & Company have recently increased the salaries of all its employees.

Spelling. In questions 7 through 9, find the correct spelling of the word among the choices lettered A, B, or C and darken the proper answer space. If no suggested spelling is correct, darken space D.

7. A) athalete   C) athlete
   B) athelete   D) none of these

In question 7 an extra letter has been added to both A and B. The fourth letter in A makes that spelling of *athlete* wrong. The fourth letter in B makes that spelling of *athlete* wrong. Spelling C is correct.

8. A) predesessor   C) predecesser
   B) predecesar   D) none of these

All three spellings of the word are wrong. The correct answer, therefore, is D because none of the printed spellings of *predecessor* is right.

9. A) occassion   C) ocassion
   B) occasion   D) none of these

Correct Answers to Sample Questions

1. B   6. B
2. C   7. C
3. A   8. D
4. D   9. B
5. D

Word Relations. In questions like 10, 11, and 12 the first two words in capital letters go together in some way. The third word in capital letters is related in the same way to one of the words lettered A, B, C, or D).

10. PLUMBER is related to WRENCH as
PAINTER is related to
    A) brush   C) shop
    B) pipe   D) hammer

The relationship between the first two words in capital letters is that a PLUMBER uses the tool called the WRENCH in doing his work. A PAINTER uses the tool called the BRUSH in doing his work. Therefore, the answer to question 10 is A*. The answer is not B because a pipe is not a tool. The answer is not C for two reasons. A *shop* could be used by either a plumber or a painter and a shop is not a tool. The answer is not D. A hammer is a tool but it is not a tool used by a painter in his work.

11. BODY is related to FOOD as ENGINE is related to
    A) wheels   C) motion
    B) smoke   D) fuel.

You soon saw that the relationship between the words in question 10 does not fit the words in question 11. The relationship here is that the first runs on the second-the BODY runs on FOOD; and ENGINE runs on D) fuel.

12. ABUNDANT is related to CHEAP as SCARCE is related to
    A) ample   C) costly
    B) inexpensive   D) unobtainable

Reading. In questions like 13, 14, and 15, you will be given a paragraph, generally from 4 to 10 lines long. Read the paragraph with great care for you will have to decide which one of four statements is based on the' information in the paragraph. The statement may not be based on the main thought of the paragraph.

13. What constitutes skill in any line of work is not always easy to determine; economy of time must be carefully distinguished from economy of energy, as the quickest method may require the greatest expenditure of muscular effort and may not be essential or at all desirable.

The paragraph best supports the statement that
    A) the most efficiently executed task is not always the one done in the shortest time
    B) energy and time cannot both be conserved in performing a single task
    C) a task is well done when it is performed in the shortest time
    D) skill in performing a task should not be acquired at the expense of time

The answer is A. You can see that the paragraph points out that the task done most quickly is not necessarily the task done best. The paragraph does not compare energy and time although it mentions both, so B is not an answer. The paragraph does not support C, which is almost the opposite of the answer, A. The statement in D may be true, but it is not contained in the paragraph.

14. The secretarial profession is a very old one and has increased in importance with the passage of time. In modern times, the vast expansion of business and industry has greatly increased the need and opportunities for secretaries, and for the first time in history their number has become large.

The paragraph best supports the statement that the secretarial profession

    A) is older than business and industry
    B) did not exist in ancient times
    C) has greatly increased in size
    D) demands higher training than it did formerly

15. It is difficult to distinguish between bookkeeping and accounting. In attempts to do so, bookkeeping is called the art, and accounting the science, of recording business transactions. Bookkeeping gives the history of the business in a systematic manner; and accounting classifies, analyzes, and interprets the facts thus recorded.

The paragraph best supports the statement that

    A) accounting is less systematic than bookkeeping
    B) accounting and bookkeeping are closely related
    C) bookkeeping and accounting cannot be distinguished from one another
    D) bookkeeping has been superseded by accounting

Correct Answers to Sample Questions
10. A
11. D
12. C
13. A
14. C
15. B

Sample questions 16 through 20 require name and number comparisons. In each line across the page there are three names or numbers that are very similar. Compare the three names or numbers and decide which ones are exactly alike. On the Sample Answer Sheet, mark the answer -

A   if ALL THREE names or numbers are exactly ALIKE
B   if only the FIRST and SECOND names or numbers are exactly ALIKE
C   if only the FIRST and THIRD names or numbers are exactly ALIKE
D   if only the SECOND and THIRD names or numbers are exactly ALIKE
E   if ALL THREE names or numbers are DIFFERENT

16.	Davis Hazen	David Hozen	David Hazen
17.	Lois Appel	Lois Appel	Lois Apfel
18.	June Allan	Jane Allan	Jane Allan
19.	10235	10235	10235
20.	32614	32164	32614

In the next group of sample questions, there is a underlined name at the left, and four other names in alphabetical order at the right. Find the correct space for the underlined name so that it will be in alphabetical order with the others, and mark the letter of that space as your answer.

21. Jones, Jane

A) →
    Goodyear, G. L.
B) →
    Haddon, Harry
C) →
    Jackson, Mary
D) →
    Jenkins, Willaims
E) →

23. Olsen, C. C.

A) →
    Olsen, C. A.
B) →
    Olsen, C. D.
C) →
    Olsen, Charles
D) →
    Olsen, Christopher
E) →

22. Kessler, Neilson

A) →
    Kessel, Carl
B) →
    Kessinger, D. J.
C) →
    Keesler, Karl
D) →
    Kessner, Lewis
E) →

22. DeMattia, Jessica

A) →
    DeLong, Jesse
B) →
    DeMatteo, Jesse
C) →
    Derbie, Jessie S.
D) →
    DeShazo, L. M.
E) →

Correct Answers to Sample Questions
16. E
17. B
18. D
19. A
20. C
21. E
22. D
23. B

In questions like 25 through 28, solve each problem and see which of the suggested answers A, B, C, or D is correct. If your answer does not exactly agree with any of the first four suggested answers, darken space E.

		Answers				Answers	
25. Add:		A) 44	B) 45	27. Multiply:		A) 100	B) 115
	22	C) 54	D) 55		25	C) 125	D) 135
	+33	E) none of these			x5	E) none of these	

		Answer				Answers	
26. Subtract:		A) 20	B) 21			A) 20	B) 22
	24	C) 27	D) 29	28. Divide		C) 24	D) 26
	-3	E) none of these			6√126	E) none of these	

There is a set of 5 suggested answers for each of the groups of sample questions appearing below. Do not try to memorize these answers, because there will be a different set on each page in the test.

To find the answer to each question, find which one of the suggested answers contains numbers and letters all of which appear in that question. These numbers and letters may be in any order in the question, but all four must appear. If no suggested answers fits, mark E for that question.

29. 8 N K 9 G T 4 6

30. T 9 7 Z 6 L 3 K

31. Z 7 GK 3 98 N

32. 3 K 94 6 GZ L

33. Z N 73 8 KT 9

34. 2 3 P 6 V Z 4 L

35. T 7 4 3 P Z 9 G

36. 6 N G Z 3 9 P 7

37. 9 6 P4 N G Z 2

38. 4 9 7T L P 3 V

Suggested Answers
A = 7, 9, G, K
B = 8, 9, T, Z
C = 6, 7, K, Z
D = 6, 8, G, T
E = none of these

Suggested Answers
A = 3, 6, G, P
B = 3, 7, P, V
C = 4, 6, V, Z
D = 4, 7, G, Z
E = none of these

Correst Answeres to Sample Questions

25. D	32. E
26. B	33. B
27. C	34. C
28. E	35. D
29. D	36. A
30. C	37. E
31. A	

CHAPTER FIVE

COMPLETING YOUR SF-171

EMPLOYMENT APPLICATION

The SF-171, *"Application for Federal Employment,"* is a six page document. Forty nine (49) data blocks are provided and you must supply all requested information. Blank SF-171 forms are sent with job announcements. Pay special attention to block 24 "Work Experience". Your work experience and education will provide the OPM evaluator with the data needed to rate you eligible for a position.

Each block, 1 through 49, is listed with instructions and helpful hints. Additional information is printed on the front cover of the SF-171. Many agencies require additional supplemental application forms to document post-secondary education and certain work related skills.

> **Al Gore's NPR** proposes to eliminate standard application forms and to allow agencies to develop applications to meet their individual needs. There was some consideration given to initiating a resume format. It will not be practical for agencies to develop individual application forms until the Federal Personnel Manual (FPM) is dramatically changed or replaced with simplified personnel policies, which if tackled could take years to accomplish.

The bid package (SF-171 and associated forms) provides prospective future employers and selection officials with their first impression of the applicant. **TYPE YOUR APPLICATION AND CHECK YOUR SPELLING AND GRAMMAR.** You can use the sample SF-171 in this chapter to draft your application while waiting for the official forms from OPM. Also, use the step-by-step federal job application guide printed in Appendix A to organize your job search.

This document is the key to all federal employment. I have personally seen excellent, highly qualified job applicants not rate eligible for positions simply because they neglected to thoroughly complete their 171 application.

A SF-171 can be duplicated and used for bidding on similar announcements within the same job series. If you intend to bid on several different job series, then develop new experience blocks that are relevant to that specific job series. If you should duplicate your application, don't fill in the position or signature and date block. You will need an original signature on each SF-171 copy sent in. After duplicating your SF-171, sign and date each copy.

COMPUTER GENERATED APPLICATIONS

DataTech sells an excellent and comprehensive SF-171 computer program called *Quick & Easy 171's* for $49.95 (personal version). *Quick & Easy* is designed to be easy to use ... even for the person with little or no computer experience. You enter your information into the computer using a series of screens that look just like the SF-171. This program is completely menu driven with advanced help at the touch of a key and it comes with an internal word processor and spell checker. The application, form and all, can be printed on hundreds of printers including inkjet and laserjets. The program requires an IBM-PC/XT/AT - 640K - DOS 3.0 or greater, one floppy and one hard drive. Also available for windows. This program is available from the publisher. Ordering information is printed in the back of this book.

RANKING FACTORS

The Vacancy Announcement is the key to developing your SF-171 application. Each announcement lists the required knowledge, skills, and abilities required for the position. Pay special attention to the instruction in this chapter on filling out block 24 (EXPERIENCE). Also education, self-development, and awards are important rating areas that require you to list detailed information.

SF-171 APPLICATION INSTRUCTIONS

BLOCK 1 -   WHAT KIND OF JOB ARE YOU APPLYING FOR?

Place the title of the position you are applying for and the announcement number (if known) in this block. The announcement number is generally located in the upper right hand corner of the bid with the closing date listed below.

BLOCK 2 -   SOCIAL SECURITY NUMBER

BLOCK 3 - SEX

Place a check mark in the appropriate block.

BLOCK 4 - BIRTH DATE

Birth date must be in month/day/year format. For example, if you were born on May 1, 1955, put 5/1/55 in the block.

BLOCK 5 - BIRTHPLACE

City, State, or Country.

BLOCK 6 - NAME (Last, First, Middle)

BLOCK 7 - OTHER NAMES EVER USED (e.g., maiden name, nickname, etc.)

BLOCK 8 - HOME PHONE NUMBER

BLOCK 9 - WORK PHONE NUMBER

BLOCK 10 - PRIOR FEDERAL EMPLOYMENT

List federal employment periods including student program participation.

BLOCK 11 - WHEN CAN YOU START WORK?

Month & Year

BLOCK 12 - WHAT IS THE LOWEST PAY YOU WILL ACCEPT?

Before placing a dollar amount in this block, check the pay offered in the advertisement. If you place a dollar amount in this block that is greater than what the bid offers, your package will not be rated. If the bid is advertised at a GS-7/9, then put GS-7 (if a GS-7 pay is acceptable to you) as the lowest pay that you will accept. Even if you place GS-7 as the lowest pay acceptable on a Multi-grade bid, such as the GS-7/9, you will generally be hired at the highest grade that you rate out at up to the GS-9 in this example. If you list GS-9 for a GS-7/9 bid and you only qualified for a GS-7 you will not be considered for the job.

BLOCK 13 - IN WHAT GEOGRAPHIC AREA(s) ARE YOU WILLING TO WORK?

Any restrictions you place on yourself will reduce your employment opportunities. List the broadest option possible. For example; anywhere in the United States or all areas (no restrictions). However, if you can't relocate, then place the city and state that are acceptable. Better yet, list a section of a state, such as Southwestern Pennsylvania. Job announcements are advertised to fill vacancies throughout the FJICs territory. This can take in several states. If you list just one city you won't be called for jobs in cities within commuting distance.

NOTE: If you indicate anywhere in the United States for an announcement issued through a FJIC your bid will in most cases only be good for the geographic area covered by that FJIC. If you truly want to work anywhere in the country, in most cases, you will have to apply through each FJIC. You may wish to subscribe to the *Federal Jobs Digest* or similar publication, refer to the resources listed in Chapter Three. This publication lists national jobs from all FJICs and individual agencies.

BLOCK 14 - ARE YOU WILLING TO WORK:

If you are only available for full time work check yes in block 15A. Check whatever is acceptable to you, full time, part time, etc. A part time position can lead to full time employment. Check yes in block 14F if you are available for weekends or rotating shifts. The more options you accept the greater your chances.

NOTE: If the hiring agency needs shift workers and you check no to block 14 (F) - weekends, shifts, or rotating shifts - your application will not be considered for that position.

BLOCK 15 - ARE YOU WILLING TO TAKE A TEMPORARY JOB LASTING:

Select YES or NO to option A, B or C.

BLOCK 16 - ARE YOU WILLING TO TRAVEL AWAY FROM HOME FOR:

Many jobs require at least some travel. Check whatever you find acceptable.

BLOCK (17 - 18) -   MILITARY SERVICE AND VETERANS PREFERENCE

For military service and veterans preference. List requested information and check yes or no to all blocks. See chapter 6 to determine if you can elect 5 or 10 point veterans preference. You must provide discharge papers (Form DD-214) when hired.

BLOCK 23 - MAY WE ASK YOUR PRESENT EMPLOYER ABOUT YOUR CHARACTER, QUALIFICATIONS, AND WORK RECORD?

Check yes or no.

BLOCK 24 - WORK EXPERIENCE

In block 24A list the name and address of your current employer and provide all of the requested information. Block 24 B is used for your previous employer and so on. Use additional blocks for all past employment that is skill related. **THIS INCLUDES MILITARY TIME.** Go back as many years as needed to capture all work experience that is related to the job you're bidding on.

Block 24 asks you to describe the **DUTIES, RESPONSIBILITIES, AND ACCOMPLISHMENTS** of your present and past employment.
The more detail you provide the higher score you can receive.

EXAMPLES

DUTY:

TECHNICAL EXAMPLE: "I maintained electronic control equipment." (Mention the specific equipment, subassemblies, etc. that you maintained.) Include test equipment used for troubleshooting, soldering techniques, completion of modifications, schematic review, etc. Capture all of your duties including administrative.

ADMINISTRATIVE EXAMPLE: "I typed correspondence, maintained our office filing system, made travel arrangements for the staff, answered the phone, and worked with wordperfect and Dbase III Plus." Include all office equipment, hardware, and software that you worked with; copy machines, dictaphone, computer systems.

★ **A DUTY** is defined as an action or conduct required by one's profession or position. Most of what we do at work are duties.

RESPONSIBILITY:

TECHNICAL EXAMPLE: "I certified system operation and decided when to remove certification on marginally performing systems." (Mention specific systems, etc.) Explain the certification process.

ADMINISTRATIVE EXAMPLE: "I issued travel orders upon receipt of training requests and made travel arrangements for all participants. Prior to travel order completion, I consulted with Budget and Resource Planning to confirm that travel funds were assigned for this training."

★ **A RESPONSIBILITY** is defined as an ability to meet obligations or to act without superior authority or guidance.

ACCOMPLISHMENT:

TECHNICAL EXAMPLE: "I developed a new procedure for scheduling preventative maintenance that was adopted company wide."

ADMINISTRATIVE EXAMPLE: " I developed a dbase system for our administrative numerical files. This new system sorts files alphabetically by file subject name."

★ **AN ACCOMPLISHMENT** is defined as something contributed by you to your job of considerable value to the company but not a normal part of your job.

The SF-171 provides ten (10) lines to describe past work experience. **Expand and do not shorten your work experience descriptions to fit into the available ten lines.** Use 8 1/2" x 11" supplement sheets attached to the SF-171. In the upper left hand corner of each supplement sheet type your name, Social Security Number, the SF-171's block you are continuing from, and announcement number. Number the attachments. On the last line of the respective block 24A-X, put continued on Supplement sheet and use the page number for reference. The greater detail provided to the OPM rater the better chance you have of making the list of eligibles and achieving a higher rating score. Only the highest rated candidates are referred to a selecting official.

BLOCK 25 - DID YOU GRADUATE FROM HIGH SCHOOL?

A GED certificate is acceptable. Check yes in this block if you graduated high school or will graduate or receive a GED within the next nine months.

BLOCK 26 - NAME AND LOCATION OF YOUR HIGH SCHOOL.

BLOCK 27 - HAVE YOU EVER ATTENDED COLLEGE OR GRADUATE SCHOOL?

Check Yes or No. If you check yes continue on to blocks 28 through 31.

BLOCK 28 - NAME AND LOCATION OF COLLEGE OR UNIVERSITIES ATTENDED.

BLOCK 29 & 30 -   CHIEF UNDERGRADUATE AND GRADUATE SUBJECTS.

Start with your major and list semester or quarter hours for each major subject area.

BLOCK 31 - OTHER JOB RELATED TRAINING COURSES.

List the name and address of each school or course that you attended that is related to the jobs you are applying for. List the dates attended, classroom hours, subject and training completion. Go back as far as the related training goes and include military schools, etc..

BLOCK (32 - 35)   SPECIAL SKILLS, ACCOMPLISHMENTS AND AWARDS.

You will receive points for special skills, accomplishments, and awards. Include special licenses, certificates, computer skills, special machine skills, publications, public speaking and writing experience, membership in professional or scientific societies, patents or inventions.

These blocks also provide space to list foreign languages and typing skills. Go back as far as necessary to capture all related items. Include military accomplishments.

BLOCK 36 - REFERENCES

Three references are required. The references you list must know of your fitness for the work you are applying for and they cannot be previous supervisors.

BLOCKS (37 - 47)   BACKGROUND INFORMATION

Each background data question must be answered truthfully. In question 45 you must provide details for questions answered YES in numbers 38-44. If your application is fraudulent immediate dismissal is authorized and sanctioned. Answering yes to these questions does not mean your application will be rejected. The circumstances will be considered in most cases.

BLOCKS (48 - 49)   SIGNATURE, CERTIFICATION, & RELEASE OF INFORMATION.

An original signature is required when submitting this application. Copies of your SF-171 can be used. Leave blocks 1, 48, and 49 blank until you copy your application. After you run off copies, sign each copy and complete blocks 1 and 49. This permits the use of the same SF-171 for various open job announcements.

CAUTION:

Bids for different job series must be tailored to the bid specifications. It is unwise to use the same SF-171 for job announcements in different job series. Be sure each bid sent in covers the required experience and revise SF-171 data to reflect these differences. **Quick & Easy 171's is** well suited for this purpose. This computer program offers editing of your application to tailor it as needed for various jobs.

The extra time and care devoted to the preparation of your SF-171 employment application is time well spent. Your SF-171 is your future employer's first contact with you. Its appearance and detail reflect your character and professionalism. A distinctive and well prepared application can weigh the tables in your favor long before the final selection is made. A well prepared, typed, application saves the reviewer time. If you personally received five applications, four handwritten and poorly constructed, which one would you concentrate on? Keep this in mind when you complete your application.

Application for Federal Employment—SF 171

Read the instructions before you complete this application. *Type or print clearly in dark ink.*

Form Approved
OMB No. 3206-0012

GENERAL INFORMATION

1 What kind of job are you applying for? *Give title and announcement no. (if any)*

2 Social Security Number

3 Sex
☐ Male   ☐ Female

4 Birth date *(Month, Day, Year)*

5 Birthplace *(City and State or Country)*

6 Name *(Last, First, Middle)*

Mailing address *(include apartment number, if any)*

City   State   ZIP Code

7 Other names ever used *(e.g., maiden name, nickname, etc.)*

8 Home Phone
Area Code | Number

9 Work Phone
Area Code | Number | Extension

10 Were you ever employed as a civilian by the Federal Government? If **"NO"**, go to Item 11. If **"YES"**, mark each type of job you held with an**"X"**.

☐ Temporary ☐ Career-Conditional ☐ Career ☐ Excepted

What is your **highest** grade, classification series and job title?

Dates at **highest** grade: FROM   TO

FOR USE OF EXAMINING OFFICE ONLY

Date entered register

Form reviewed:
Form approved:

Option	Grade	Earned Rating	Veteran Preference	Augmented Rating
			☐ No Preference Claimed	
			☐ 5 Points (Tentative)	
			☐ 10 Pts. (30% Or More Comp. Dis.)	
			☐ 10 Pts. (Less Than 30% Comp. Dis.)	
			☐ Other 10 Points	

Initials and Date

☐ Disallowed ☐ Being Investigated

FOR USE OF APPOINTING OFFICE ONLY

Preference has been verified through proof that the separation was under honorable conditions, and other proof as required.

☐ 5-Point ☐ 10-Point--30% or More Compensable Disability ☐ 10-Point--Less Than 30% Compensable Disability ☐ 10-Point--Other

Signature and Title

Agency   Date

AVAILABILITY

11 When can you start work? *(Month and Year)*

12 What is the **lowest** pay you will accept? *(You will not be considered for jobs which pay less than you indicate.)*
Pay $ _____ per _____ OR Grade _____

13 In what geographic area(s) are you willing to work?

14 Are you willing to work: | YES | NO
A. 40 hours per week *(full-time)?*
B. 25-32 hours per week *(part-time)?*
C. 17-24 hours per week *(part-time)?*
D. 16 or fewer hours per week *(part-time)?*
E. An intermittent job *(on-call/seasonal)?*
F. Weekends, shifts, or rotating shifts?

15 Are you willing to take a temporary job lasting:
A. 5 to 12 months *(sometimes longer)?*
B. 1 to 4 months?
C. Less than 1 month?

16 Are you willing to travel away from home for:
A. 1 to 5 nights each month?
B. 6 to 10 nights each month?
C. 11 or more nights each month?

MILITARY SERVICE AND VETERAN PREFERENCE

17 Have you served in the United States Military Service? *If your only active duty was training in the Reserves or National Guard, answer "NO". If "NO", go to item 22.* | YES | NO

18 Did you or will you retire at or above the rank of major or lieutenant commander? |

MILITARY SERVICE AND VETERAN PREFERENCE *(Cont.)*

19 Were you discharged from the military service under honorable conditions? *(If your discharge was changed to "honorable" or "general" by a Discharge Review Board, answer "YES". If you received a clemency discharge, answer "NO".)* If **"NO"**, provide below the date and type of discharge you received. | YES | NO

Discharge Date *(Month, Day, Year)* | Type of Discharge

20 List the dates *(Month, Day, Year)*, and branch for all **active duty** military service.
From | To | Branch of Service

21 If all your active military duty was after October 14, 1976, list the full names and dates of all campaign badges or expeditionary medals you received or were entitled to receive.

22 Read the instructions that came with this form before completing this item. When you have determined your eligibility for veteran preference from the instructions, place an **"X"** in the box next to your veteran preference claim.

☐ NO PREFERENCE
☐ 5-POINT PREFERENCE -- You must show proof when you are hired.

10-POINT PREFERENCE -- If you claim 10-point preference, place an **"X"** in the box below next to the basis for your claim. **To receive 10-point preference you must also complete a Standard Form 15, Application for 10-Point Veteran Preference, which is available from any Federal Job Information Center. ATTACH THE COMPLETED SF 15 AND REQUESTED PROOF TO THIS APPLICATION.**

☐ Non-compensably disabled or Purple Heart recipient.
☐ Compensably disabled, less than 30 percent.
☐ Spouse, widow(er), or mother of a deceased or disabled veteran.
☐ Compensably disabled, 30 percent or more.

THE FEDERAL GOVERNMENT IS AN EQUAL OPPORTUNITY EMPLOYER
PREVIOUS EDITION USABLE UNTIL 12-31-90

NSN 7540-00-935-7150   171-110   Standard Form 171 (Rev. 6-88)
U.S. Office of Personnel Management
FPM Chapter 295

WORK EXPERIENCE *If you have no work experience, write "NONE" in A below and go to 25 on page 3.*

23 May we ask your present employer about your character, qualifications, and work record? *A "NO" will not affect our review of your qualifications. If you answer "NO" and we need to contact your present employer before we can offer you a job, we will contact you first. . . . .* | YES | NO |

24 READ **WORK EXPERIENCE** IN THE INSTRUCTIONS BEFORE YOU BEGIN.

- Describe your current or most recent job in Block **A** and work backwards, describing each job you held **during the past 10 years**. If you were **unemployed** for longer than **3 months** within the past 10 years, list the dates and your address(es) in an experience block.

- You may sum up in one block work that you did **more than 10 years ago.** But if that work **is related** to the type of job you are applying for, describe each related job in a separate block.

- INCLUDE VOLUNTEER WORK *(non-paid work)--***If the work** *(or a part of the work)* **is like the job you are applying for,** complete **all** parts of the experience block just as you would for a paying job. You may receive credit for work experience with religious, community, welfare, service, and other organizations.

- INCLUDE MILITARY SERVICE--You should complete **all** parts of the experience block just as you would for a non-military job, including all supervisory experience. Describe each major change of duties or responsibilities in a separate experience block.

- IF YOU NEED MORE SPACE TO DESCRIBE A JOB--Use sheets of paper the same size as this page (be sure to include **all** information we ask for in **A** and **B** below). On **each** sheet show your name, Social Security Number, and the announcement number or job title.

- IF YOU NEED MORE EXPERIENCE BLOCKS, use the SF 171-A or a sheet of paper.

- IF YOU NEED TO UPDATE (ADD MORE RECENT JOBS), use the SF 172 or a sheet of paper as described above.

A | Name and address of employer's organization *(include ZIP Code, if known)* | Dates employed *(give month, day and year)* | Average number of hours per week | Number of employees you supervise |
| From: | To: |
| Salary or earnings | Your reason for wanting to leave |
| Starting $ per |
| Ending $ per |

| Your immediate supervisor | | | Exact title of your job | If Federal employment *(civilian or military)* list series, grade or rank, and, if promoted in this job, the date of your last promotion |
| Name | Area Code | Telephone No. | | |

Description of work: Describe your specific duties, responsibilities and accomplishments in this job, **including** the job title(s) of any employees you supervise. *If you describe more than one type of work (for example, carpentry and painting, or personnel and budget), write the approximate percentage of time you spent doing each.*

For Agency Use (skill codes, etc.)

B | Name and address of employer's organization *(include ZIP Code, if known)* | Dates employed *(give month, day and year)* | Average number of hours per week | Number of employees you supervised |
| From: | To: |
| Salary or earnings | Your reason for leaving |
| Starting $ per |
| Ending $ per |

| Your immediate supervisor | | | Exact title of your job | If Federal employment *(civilian or military)* list series, grade or rank, and, if promoted in this job, the date of your last promotion |
| Name | Area Code | Telephone No. | | |

Description of work: Describe your specific duties, responsibilities and accomplishments in this job, **including** the job title(s) of any employees you supervised. *If you describe more than one type of work (for example, carpentry and painting, or personnel and budget), write the approximate percentage of time you spent doing each.*

For Agency Use (skill codes, etc.)

— ← —————— **ATTACH ANY ADDITIONAL FORMS AND SHEETS HERE**

EDUCATION

25 Did you graduate from high school? *If you have a GED high school equivalency or will graduate within the next nine months, answer "YES".*

YES	If **"YES"**, give month and year graduated or received GED equivalency: . . . . _____
NO	If **NO"**, give the highest grade you completed: . _____

26 Write the name and location *(city and state)* of the last high school you attended or where you obtained your GED high school equivalency.

27 Have you ever attended college or graduate school?   YES   If **"YES"**, continue with **28**.   NO   If **NO"**, go to **31**.

28 NAME AND LOCATION *(city, state and ZIP Code)* OF COLLEGE OR UNIVERSITY. *If you expect to graduate within nine months, give the* **month** *and* **year** *you expect to receive your degree:*

	Name	City	State	ZIP Code	MONTH AND YEAR ATTENDED From	To	NUMBER OF CREDIT HOURS COMPLETED Semester	Quarter	TYPE OF DEGREE *(e.g. B.A., M.A.)*	MONTH AND YEAR OF DEGREE
1)										
2)										
3)										

29 CHIEF UNDERGRADUATE SUBJECTS *Show major on the first line*

	NUMBER OF CREDIT HOURS COMPLETED Semester	Quarter
1)		
2)		
3)		

30 CHIEF GRADUATE SUBJECTS *Show major on the first line*

	NUMBER OF CREDIT HOURS COMPLETED Semester	Quarter
1)		
2)		
3)		

31 If you have completed any **other courses or training related to the kind of jobs you are applying for** *(trade, vocational, Armed Forces, business)* give information below.

NAME AND LOCATION *(city, state and ZIP Code)* OF SCHOOL	MONTH AND YEAR ATTENDED From	To	CLASS-ROOM HOURS	SUBJECT(S)	TRAINING COMPLETED YES	NO
School Name 1)						
City State ZIP Code						
School Name 2)						
City State ZIP Code						

SPECIAL SKILLS, ACCOMPLISHMENTS AND AWARDS

32 Give the title and year of any honors, awards or fellowships you have received. List your special qualifications, skills or accomplishments that may help you get a job. *Some examples are: skills with computers or other machines; most important publications (do not submit copies); public speaking and writing experience; membership in professional or scientific societies; patents or inventions; etc.*

33 How many words per minute can you: TYPE? TAKE DICTATION?

Agencies may test your skills before hiring you.

34 List **job-related** licenses or certificates that you have, such as: *registered nurse; lawyer; radio operator; driver's; pilot's; etc.*

	LICENSE OR CERTIFICATE	DATE OF LATEST LICENSE OR CERTIFICATE	STATE OR OTHER LICENSING AGENCY
1)			
2)			

35 Do you speak or read a language other than English *(include sign language)?* **Applicants for jobs that require a language other than English may be given an interview conducted solely in that language.**   YES   NO

If **"YES"**, list each language and place an **"X"** in each column that applies to you. If **"NO"**, go to **36**.

LANGUAGE(S)	CAN PREPARE AND GIVE LECTURES Fluently	With Difficulty	CAN SPEAK AND UNDERSTAND Fluently	Passably	CAN TRANSLATE ARTICLES Into English	From English	CAN READ ARTICLES FOR OWN USE Easily	With Difficulty
1)								
2)								

REFERENCES

36 List three people who are not related to you and are not supervisors you listed under **24** who know your qualifications and fitness for the kind of job for which you are applying. At least **one** should know you well on a personal basis.

FULL NAME OF REFERENCE	TELEPHONE NUMBER(S) *(Include Area Code)*	PRESENT BUSINESS OR HOME ADDRESS *(Number, street and city)*	STATE	ZIP CODE
1)				
2)				
3)				

BACKGROUND INFORMATION-- *You must answer each question in this section before we can process your application.*

37 Are you a citizen of the United States? *(In most cases you must be a U.S. citizen to be hired. You will be required to submit proof of identity and citizenship at the time you are hired.)* If **"NO"**, give the country or countries you are a citizen of: _____ | YES | NO |

NOTE: It is important that you give complete and truthful answers to questions **38 through 44.** If you answer "YES" to any of them, provide your explanation(s) in **Item 45. Include** convictions resulting from a plea of nolo contendere *(no contest).* **Omit:** 1) traffic fines of $100.00 or less; 2) any violation of law committed before your 16th birthday; 3) any violation of law committed before your 18th birthday, if finally decided in juvenile court or under a Youth Offender law; 4) any conviction set aside under the Federal Youth Corrections Act or similar State law; 5) any conviction whose record was expunged under Federal or State law. We will consider the date, facts, and circumstances of each event you list. In most cases you can still be considered for Federal jobs. However, **if you fail to tell the truth or fail to list all relevant** events or circumstances, this may be grounds for not hiring you, for firing you after you begin work, or for criminal prosecution (18 USC 1001).

	YES	NO
38 During the last **10 years**, were you **fired from any job** for any reason, did you **quit after being told that you would be fired**, or did you leave by mutual agreement because of specific problems?.		
39 Have you **ever** been convicted of, or forfeited collateral for **any felony violation?** *(Generally, a felony is defined as any violation of law punishable by imprisonment of longer than one year, except for violations called misdemeanors under State law which are punishable by imprisonment of two years or less.)*		
40 Have you **ever** been convicted of, or forfeited collateral for **any firearms or explosives violation?**		
41 Are you **now** under charges for **any** violation of law?		
42 During the **last 10 years** have you forfeited collateral, been convicted, been imprisoned, been on probation, or been on parole? Do **not** include violations reported in 39, 40, or 41, above.		
43 Have you **ever** been convicted by a military **court-martial?** If no military service, answer **"NO"**.		
44 Are you **delinquent** on any Federal debt? *(Include delinquencies arising from Federal taxes, loans, overpayment of benefits, and other debts to the U.S. Government **plus** defaults on Federally guaranteed or insured loans such as student and home mortgage loans.)*		

45 If "YES" in: **38** - Explain for each job the problem(s) and your reason(s) for leaving. Give the employer's name and address.
39 through 43 - Explain each violation. Give place of occurrence and name/address of police or court involved.
44 - Explain the type, length and amount of the delinquency or default, and steps you are taking to correct errors or repay the debt. Give any identification number associated with the debt and the address of the Federal agency involved.
NOTE: If you need more space, use a sheet of paper, and include the item number.

Item No.	Date (Mo./Yr.)	Explanation	Mailing Address
			Name of Employer, Police, Court, or Federal Agency
			City State ZIP Code
			Name of Employer, Police, Court, or Federal Agency
			City State ZIP Code

	YES	NO
46 Do you receive, or have you ever applied for retirement pay, pension, or other pay based on military, Federal civilian, or District of Columbia Government service?		
47 Do any of your relatives work for the United States Government or the United States Armed Forces? Include: *father; mother; husband; wife; son; daughter; brother; sister; uncle; aunt; first cousin; nephew; niece; father-in-law; mother-in-law; son-in-law; daughter-in-law; brother-in-law; sister-in-law; stepfather; stepmother; stepson; stepdaughter; stepbrother; stepsister; half brother; and half sister.*		

If **"YES"**, provide details below. If you need more space, use a sheet of paper.

Name	Relationship	Department, Agency or Branch of Armed Forces

SIGNATURE, CERTIFICATION, AND RELEASE OF INFORMATION

YOU MUST SIGN THIS APPLICATION. Read the following carefully before you sign.

- A false statement on any part of your application may be grounds for not hiring you, or for firing you after you begin work. Also, you may be punished by fine or imprisonment (U.S. Code, title 18, section 1001).
- If you are a male born after December 31, 1959 you must be registered with the Selective Service System or have a valid exemption in order to be eligible for Federal employment. You will be required to certify as to your status at the time of appointment.
- I **understand** that any information I give may be investigated as allowed by law or Presidential order.
- I **consent** to the release of information about my ability and fitness for Federal employment by *employers, schools, law enforcement agencies and other individuals and organizations, to investigators, personnel staffing specialists, and other authorized employees of the Federal Government.*
- I **certify** that, to the best of my knowledge and belief, **all** of my statements are true, correct, complete, and made in good faith.

48 SIGNATURE *(Sign each application in dark ink)*	**49** DATE SIGNED *(Month, day, year)*

☆ U.S. GOVERNMENT PRINTING OFFICE: 1992 312-071/50114

CHAPTER SIX

VETERANS & MILITARY DEPENDENT HIRING PROGRAMS

There are several special emphasis civil service employment programs available to veterans. *Veterans Preference*, and the *Veterans Readjustment Act (VRA)* are two of the better known programs. Unknown to many, military dependents and spouses of active duty personnel receive hiring preference for government jobs under the *Military Spouse Preference Program and the Family Member Preference Program.*

[1]WHEN VACANCIES ARE ANNOUNCED BY AN AGENCY, THE SELECTING OFFICIAL CAN FILL THE POSITION BY:

- Internal promotions or reassignments of existing federal workers;
- Reemploying former employees;
- Using approved special purpose noncompetitive appointments such as the VRA, Spouse Preference, and Military Dependent programs; and,
- Appointing a new employee who has successfully completed an examination. The examination can be either written or an extensive examination of your past work experience and education as listed on a Federal Employment Application.

---

[1] Publication WEE-2 (Veterans Preference)

VETERANS PREFERENCE

When an agency advertises job vacancies through the Office of Personnel Management or locally through direct hire authority the agency must select from the top rated eligible applicants. Government publication WEE-2 states; *"The official may not pass over a Veterans' Preference eligible, however, and appoint a nonpreference eligible lower on the list unless the reasons for passing over the veteran are sufficient."*

Veterans preference gives special consideration to eligible veterans looking for federal employment. Veterans who are disabled or who served on active duty in the United States Armed Forces during certain specified time periods or in military campaigns are entitled to preference over nonveterans both in hiring into the federal civil service and in retention during *reductions in force*. There are two classes of preference for honorably discharged veterans:

FIVE-POINT PREFERENCE IS GIVEN TO VETERANS WHO SERVED ON ACTIVE DUTY:

- During the period 12/7/41, to 7/1/55; or

- For more than 180 consecutive days, any part of which occurred after 1/31/55 and before 10/15/76.

- Served in a campaign or expedition for which a campaign metal has been authorized, including Lebanon, Grenada, Panama, and Southwest Asia (Desert Shield/Storm). Medal holders who enlisted after September 7, 1980, or entered active duty on or after October 14, 1982, must have served continuously for 24 months or the full period called or ordered to active duty. This service requirement does not apply to veterans with compensable service-connected disabilities, or to veterans separated for disability in the line of duty, or for hardship.

TEN-POINT PREFERENCE

Ten-point preference is given to disabled veterans - **WITH A 30% RATED DISABILITY** - who served on active duty at any time. The disability must be service-connected. Wives, husbands, widows, widowers and mothers of disabled veterans also receive preference in certain cases.

Ten points are added to the passing examination score of:

- A veteran who served at any time and who (1) has a present service-connected disability or (2) is receiving compensation, disability retirement benefits, or pension form the military or the Department of Veteran Affairs.

- An unmarried spouse of certain deceased veterans, a spouse of a veteran unable to work because of a service-connected disability, and a mother of a veteran who died in service or who is permanently and totally disabled.

Ten-point preference eligibles may apply for any job for which (1) a list of exam eligibles is (or is about to be) established, or (2) a non-temporary appointment was made in the last 3 years.

> **PURPLE HEART RECIPIENTS ARE CONSIDERED TO HAVE A SERVICE CONNECTED DISABILITY**

WHAT DOES IT MEAN?

If you apply for a federal job, your knowledge, skills and abilities will be rated on a point system. You will receive points for related education, experience, special skills, awards, and written tests if required. The maximum points anyone can accumulate is 100. If an eligible five-point preference candidate accumulates 90 points, five additional points are awarded on preference for a total score of 95. Therefore, the preference veteran, in most cases, must be hired before an agency can hire anyone with less than 95 points in this example. A 10 point preference vet would have a total score of 100.

Hiring preference in civil service examinations is awarded regardless of scores. Qualified veterans with a compensable service-connected disability of 10 percent or more are placed at the top of most civil service examination registers, except for scientific and professional jobs at GS-9 or higher.

A federal agency hiring candidates from an examination list must consider the top three available candidates for each vacancy. An agency may not pass over a candidate with preference and select an individual without preference who has the same or lower score, unless OPM approves the agency's reasons.

SPECIAL CONSIDERATION

Veterans can file application with the Office of Personnel Management after an examination has closed. *If a current list of eligibles exists the veteran can apply within 120 days before or after separation. Ten-point preference veterans can apply anytime to be placed on an existing eligibles list.*

Announcements are open for limited times. Your bid package must be returned and post-marked by no later than the closing date of the announcement. There are several exceptions to this:

ALL VETERANS, regardless of when they served on active duty, may file application for any examination which was open while he or she was in the armed forces or which was announced within 120 days before or after his or her separation, provided the veteran makes application within 120 days after an honorable discharge. A disabled veteran receives 10 points preference and may file an application at any time for any position for which there is a list of eligibles, for which a list is about to be established, or for which a non-temporary appointment has been made in the preceding three years.

ADDITIONAL INFORMATION

You can obtain the following publications from FJICs or through OPMs telephone directory listed in Chapter Three:

- CE-5   Reduction In Force (RIF) for Veterans Preference Appointments
- CE-62   Rights of federal employees who perform military duty
- CE-100 Veterans Readjustment Appointment Program

VETERANS READJUSTMENT APPOINTMENTS (VRAs)

> **BETWEEN 1982 & 1991 THE FEDERAL GOVERNMENT HIRED OVER 136,000 VETERANS UNDER VRA APPOINTMENTS.**

There are over 3,113,000 government employees and 28% (over 840,000) are VETERANS. **The average salary is $34,664** and many veterans start with 4 weeks vacation per year because military time counts towards benefits. **Veterans have an edge...** and the pay and benefits are outstanding.

VRA appointments were originally limited to Vietnam Era Vets. *Public Law 102-568 - OCT. 29, 1992* greatly expanded VRA appointments to millions of Post Vietnam Era Vets. You may be eligible for a non-competitive federal government job appointment. By law, federal agencies may hire qualified veterans of the Armed Forces directly under the Veteran's Readjustment Appointment (VRA) program. VRA appointees initially are hired for a 2-year period in the excepted service. Successful completion of the VRA program leads to a permanent civil service appointment in the competitive service. The features of the new law are:

- If you served on active duty between August 5, 1964, and May 7, 1975, you have either 10 years after the date of your last separation from active duty, or until December 31, 1995, whichever is later.

- If you first entered active duty <u>after</u> May 7, 1975, you have 10 years after the date of your last separation from active duty, or until December 31, 1999, whichever is later.

- Education restrictions were removed.

- Extension of the VRA program through December 31, 1999.

WHAT IS A VRA APPOINTMENT?

A vet can be hired by any federal agency without going through the Office of Personnel Management (OPM). An agency that identifies a hiring need can pick up a VRA candidate immediately. If an agency has to advertise an opening through OPM it can take up to six months before the position can be filled.

Appointments are for two years. If the VRA employee maintains satisfactory performance for this two year period he or she must be converted to a career appointment. This means if you pass required training courses and perform well on the job you will be converted to a full time government position.

VRA appointees can be hired at grades up to a GS-11, starting at $33,623 per year, depending on their VRA status, experience, background, and position applied for.

HOW TO APPLY

Complete a Federal Employment Application, SF-171, and forward it to selected agencies. Refer to the resources listed in Chapter Three and the Appendices for specific agency addresses and telephone numbers. **A blank SF-171 is printed in Chapter Five and provides complete line by line instructions**. You can also request blank forms from any local federal government office.

Send a cover letter with your application explaining that you are a VRA candidate and would like to be considered for an appointment with that agency. If the employer likes your qualifications and has an opening he/she can hire you direct.

Follow up each application with a phone call. Often it helps to call an agency first and obtain a name and address to which you can send an application. Send applications to every office and department that interests you. You can send copies of your application. However, each copy must be personally signed.

Agencies **DO NOT HAVE TO HIRE THROUGH THE VRA PROGRAM**. Only if your education and work experience meets their requirements, they have openings, and like what they see will they make you an offer. Be tactful and don't be demanding.

ELIGIBILITY

You are an eligible veteran if you (A) served on active duty for a period of more than 180 days, all or part of which occurred after August 4, 1964, and have other than a dishonorable discharge, or (B) was discharged or released from active duty because of a service-connected disability.

The requirement for more than 180 days active service does not apply to (1) veterans separated from active duty because of a service-connected disability, or (2) reserve and guard members who served on active duty (under 10 U.S.C. 672 a,d, or g; 673 or 673 b) during a period of war, such as the Persian Gulf War, or in a military operation for which a campaign or expeditionary medal is authorized.

AUTHORIZED CAMPAIGN BADGE FOR VIETNAM ERA SERVICE

Documentation of the Vietnam veteran's eligibility for an authorized campaign badge should be shown on the Form DD-214, Certificate of Release from Active Duty. The Federal Personnel Manual Supplement 296-33, Subchapter 7, lists campaign badges and expeditionary medals authorized for operations during the Vietnam era. This manual is available at many Depository Libraries.

The Department of Defense (DOD) established the dates of service medals and campaign badges. It is noted that the Vietnam Service Medal is authorized for the period July 3, 1965 to March 28, 1973, which is a narrower period than the Vietnam era of August 5, 1964 to May 7, 1975.

> Compared to other sectors, the federal government employs two times the number of veterans and three times the number of disabled veterans. In 1990, 12% of all federal employees hired were veterans. The Department of Veterans Affairs, Army, Air Force, and Navy were the top employing agencies. Approximately 60% of all federal employees who retired from 1984 through 1990 were veterans.

NOTE: Call OPM in Washington, D.C. or your local FJIC to request publication CE-100 titled *Veterans' Readjustment Appointments*. Page two of this publication provides an updated list of U.S. Personnel Management veterans representatives for VRA inquires by state. They update this list quarterly.

MILITARY DEPENDENT HIRING PROGRAMS

Dependents of military and civilian sponsors and spouses of active duty military personnel receive hiring preference when applying for civilian employment with Department of Defense Agencies. The Military Family Act of 1985 expanded hiring preference to many jobs previously not available to this program and for jobs within the States, Territories, and U. S. Possessions.

The U.S. Army in Europe alone hires the majority of civilian employees. Most are either residents of the host country or family members of military and civilians officially stationed in Europe. The largest number of European vacancies were in Germany with additional vacancies in Belgium, Italy, Saudi Arabia, the Mid-East, and Africa. The majority of jobs in the Pacific region are in Korea, Japan, and the Philippines. A limited number of positions are also available in the States.

Family Member Employment Assistance Programs are available at most large bases. These programs are sponsored by local Civilian Employment Offices and Family Support Centers to provide employment information, career assistance and counseling, job skills training, and personal development workshops.

MILITARY SPOUSE PREFERENCE PROGRAM

Military Spouse Preference Programs concentrate on placement into competitive civil service vacancies in the 50 states, the Territories, the Possessions, the District of Columbia, and in foreign areas. Noncompetitive positions for Spouse Preference are generally Excepted Service and *Nonappropriated Fund Instrumentality (NAFI)* positions. NAFI jobs are in service clubs, exchanges, retail stores, snack bars, base services, and related activities.

Preference is given for employment in Department of Defense (DOD) civilian positions for which a military spouse is *best-qualified* at pay grades GS-1 through GS-15 or equivalent.

Best qualified doesn't mean the highest rated candidate. This term is used to identify anyone who meets the basic requirements for the position. Generally, the only candidates with a higher preference are veterans and career civil service employees displaced from their jobs through a reduction in force.

COMPETITIVE POSITIONS

NONSTATUS applicants are those who have never worked for the government and must establish eligibility with an OPM area office. Individuals can also establish eligibility at overseas Department of Defense (DOD) locations that have direct hire authority.

Previous federal employees, called *STATUS* applicants, are individuals who have previous federal employment and reinstatement eligibility. They must submit a current SF-171 or the Standard Form (SF) 50, Notification of Personnel Action, which indicates status, and a copy of their last government performance appraisal to the appropriate *Civilian Personnel Office* (CPO).

EXCEPTED SERVICE AND NAFI POSITIONS

The majority of overseas positions are *Excepted Service* and do not require OPM eligibility. Each employing CPO maintains a list of qualified and available candidates. Excepted Service applicants must complete a SF-171 application and supplemental forms required by the CPO. Applicants for NAFI positions require a service application form such as the Army's DA-3433. All required forms are provided by local CPOs.

ELIGIBILITY

A spouses' eligibility begins 30 days before the military sponsor's overseas reporting date. A spouse with less than six months time remaining in the area may be non-selected for permanent continuous positions. Also, preference entitlement ends when the spouse accepts or declines (whichever occurs first) any position expected to last longer than 12 months at any acceptable grade level. Preference is limited to positions in the same commuting area as that of the new duty station. However, a spouse may compete for positions, without preference, outside the commuting area. Spouse preference can be exercised only once for each permanent relocation of the military member.

HOW TO APPLY

Spouses can apply for preference at any armed forces or defense agency facility within the commuting area of the military member's duty station. You can apply at any service branch in your area. Contact your local CPO for employment information and application forms.

■ The National Security Agency and Defense Intelligence Agencies do not participate in spouse and family member preference programs.

FAMILY MEMBER PREFERENCE

Most family member positions are clerical. However, family members are eligible to apply for any position for which they qualify. Family members of both military and civilian sponsors are given equal preference for positions designated for U. S. citizen occupancy, after military spouse and veteran's preference, for employment in nonsupervisory positions at pay grades of GS-8 or below.

Normally, family members are appointed under Excepted appointments which cannot extend longer than 2 months beyond the sponsor's departure or separation date. Family members hired under this program do not acquire competitive civil service status, but may gain eligibility for Federal Civil Service re-employment when returning to the States under Executive Order 12362.

EXECUTIVE ORDER 12362

Eligible family members may be noncompetitively appointed - they would not need to apply through OPM to any position in the United States for which they meet all qualification requirements and time-in-grade restrictions. They also need to be U.S. citizens, and to have: worked 18 months in a family member position under overseas local hire appointment, within any ten year period beginning 1 January 1980; received a fully successful supervisory performance rating; been a family member of an appropriate sponsor officially assigned overseas; and accompanied or joined the military or civilian on official assignment.

APPLICATION PROCEDURES

Most Excepted Service and NAFI stateside and overseas vacancies are filled by local CPOs. Stateside competitive positions are controlled by OPM in most cases while overseas competitive positions are often handled by CPOs that have direct hire authority.

Army, Air Force, Navy and Marine installation Family Support Centers work with local CPOs to offer family members employment assistance, career counseling and in some cases skills training. Family Support Centers have slightly different names within each military branch. In the Army they are called Army Community Service (AWS) offices. Contact your local Support Center for additional information.

If a military sponsor is relocating to a new duty station, family members should contact the CPO or Family Support Center at the new location and request employment information. CPOs provide detailed job information and often provide the names of other federal agencies in the commuting area, as well as non-federal personnel offices.

Family member counseling is provided by local CPO Recruitment and Placement offices upon request and at least thirty days prior to departing an area. These counseling sessions provide information on eligibility for special programs, what to hand carry to the new location, and briefings on what needs to be done prior to departing an area.

SPOUSE PREFERENCE APPLICATION PROCEDURES

Spouse preference applicants must submit a SF-171 employment application along with a detailed statement. The statement must include:

■ Your name,

■ The name of the installation or activity at which you are applying,

■ A statement that you have not been offered and declined a position for which you applied under spousal preference during your current PCS,

■ The position title or number for which you are applying; and

■ A copy of the service member's official orders, attached to the statement and application.

According to John J. Ford, Chief of the Staffing Branch, Department of the Army, Alexandria, Virginia; "Neither program is a guarantee of employment. Whether a family member or military spouse is hired depends on (1) the number of positions available in the area to which the military sponsor is being assigned; (2) the number of (other) military spouses available for employment in the area; (3) the applicant's ability to meet the work experience and/or education requirements of the position being filled; and (4) the number of military veterans available for employment in the area."

CHAPTER SEVEN

OVERSEAS EMPLOYMENT OPPORTUNITIES

Thousands of United States citizens work for the federal government in foreign countries, in the United States territories, Alaska, and Hawaii. [1]The positions that are most often available are administrative (technical and professional), accountants, auditors, budget and program officers, management analysts, nurses, procurement officers, shorthand reporters, equipment specialists, engineers, social workers, housing officers, teachers, and alcohol and drug abuse specialists. Clerical (clerk-typist, stenographer) and secretary positions are normally filled locally overseas.

> The Defense Department, the largest employer of civilians overseas, announced in July of 1993 that 92 overseas U.S. military sites will close or have their operations reduced. European troop strength will drop to 100,000 by September 30, 1996. The number of positions with the DOD may drop considerably when the base closings occur.

Positions are filled in several ways. In the U.S. territories, Hawaii, and Alaska most positions are filled through competitive civil service announcements. Various positions overseas are filled through Excepted Service and Nonappropriated Fund Instrumentality (NAFI) hiring programs. Excepted Service positions are described in Chapter Two. Nonappropriated Fund positions are paid using money generated within the Department of the Army and other military branches through sales revenues. These positions are primarily governed by military regulations.

---

[1]Publication titled Jobs in Europe, published by AEAGA-CRC.

When positions are filled locally overseas, U.S. citizens living abroad, dependents of citizens employed or stationed overseas, or foreign nationals, can be hired. Most countries have agreements with United States installations that require the hiring of local nationals whenever possible to bolster the local economy. All positions held by foreign nationals are in the Excepted Service. Excepted Service positions are not subject to OPM's competitive hiring requirements.

[1]There are 115,734 overseas civilian federal employees, of which 72,733 are U.S. citizens as of March 1993. Total overseas federal civilian employment dropped 20% from 143,513 in 1989, 27,779 positions, to 115,734. However, the majority (approximately 19,000) of the lost jobs were occupied by foreign nationals. During this same period federal civilian employment of U.S. citizens fell 9.6%, from 80,395 to 72,733.

The drop in total overseas employment can be attributed to military downsizing. The Department of Defense is the largest employer of civilians overseas. Consequently, the majority of lost jobs were associated with military base closings, especially in Germany.

Most of the upper and mid level positions are filled through internal placement. Internal placement allows government employees wanting to work overseas to first apply for the positions in-house. If there are no in-house bidders, agencies then advertise through competitive announcements at FJICs. Overseas applicants should contact the following two FJICs for open job announcements and then consult the detailed resource listings that follow:

■ **Pacific overseas areas:**

Federal Job Information Center
Federal Bldg. Room 5316
300 Ala Moana Blvd.
Honolulu, HI 96850
Overseas Jobs - (808) 541-2784
Hawaii Jobs - (808) 546-2791

■ **Atlantic overseas areas:**

Federal Job Information Center
Overseas Job Opportunities (Atlantic Areas)
Federal Bldg. Room 1416
1900 E. Street NW
Washington, DC 20415
(202) 606-2700

CONDITIONS OF EMPLOYMENT

Overseas workers must meet various requirements: physical, security, qualifications, tour of duty, etc. Announcements list specific restrictions, conditions, and special qualifications.

PHYSICAL EXAMINATIONS

Individuals wanting to work overseas must meet certain stringent requirements. Thorough physical exams for both the applicant and, in many cases, accompanying dependents require physicals. You must be able to physically adapt to the conditions at various locations that may not have adequate health care facilities. Individuals on medication or who require special care will not be considered for certain positions. Any physical impairment that would create a hazard to others or to yourself, or would reduce performance level will disqualify the applicant.

---

[1]Federal Publication PWI 9305, Federal Civilian Workforce Statistics, March 1993.

SECURITY CLEARANCE CHECKS

All applicants considered for appointment must pass a comprehensive security clearance, character and suitability check. These investigations take from a few weeks to several months to complete. If you are selected for a position you will be appointed conditionally, pending the results of the investigation.

TRANSPORTATION AGREEMENTS

Individuals selected for overseas assignment are generally required to sign a transportation agreement. Typically, overseas tours last from twelve to thirty-six months.

FOREIGN LANGUAGE REQUIREMENTS

A foreign language that would not be a position requirement in the States may be required for certain overseas positions. The job announcement will specify if a language is required. Several agencies appoint candidates without the required language skill and give them a period of time to develop acceptable language proficiency.

DEPENDENTS

Most agencies permit professional employees to take dependents with them. Professional positions are generally considered to be mid-level positions and above. Other employees can often arrange for dependents to follow them at a later date.

> **Government employees' dependents are often given priority employment consideration at U.S. overseas facilities. Your spouse may receive hiring preference.**

PAY AND BENEFITS

Pay is generally the same overseas for the comparable Stateside position. Additional allowances such as a post differential, cost-of-living and quarters allowance, are provided where conditions warrant. Military base privileges are authorized in many circumstances and Department of Defense schools are available for dependent children through grade 12.

Basic benefits are the same for all civil service employees. Overseas employees also receive free travel, transportation and storage of household goods, and extra vacation with free transportation to stateside homes between tours of duty.

COMPETITION

There are a limited number of overseas positions and competition is keen. However, if you are well qualified in an occupation and available for most locations, your opportunity to be selected is good. The normal rotation of current employees back to the United States creates a large number of recurring vacancies.

CITIZENSHIP

Applications are accepted only from U.S. citizens and American Samoans.

APPLYING FOR AN OVERSEAS JOB

Apply early. It pays to apply for federal jobs well in advance of the time you will be available for employment. Applications usually take six to eight weeks for processing. It may take longer if written tests are required, especially in overseas areas. Many jobs limit the number of applications available and the time allowed for filing. Applications are given out until the limit is reached or until the closing date of the announcement. Refer to Chapter Five for detailed Federal Employment Application (SF-171) guidance.

TEMPORARY EMPLOYMENT

Federal agencies often hire temporary employees. You may be considered for both temporary and permanent positions. If you accept a temporary appointment, your name will remain on the register for consideration for permanent positions. Temporary employment is usually for one year or less, but may be extended for up to four years.

OTHER JOBS

A number of jobs with Department of Defense agencies are not in the competitive civil service system. These include *Non Appropriated Fund Instrumentalities (NAFI)* jobs in post exchanges, military clubs and recreation services. Teachers in DOD Dependent Schools overseas are not civil service employees, but are hired on yearly contracts. Applications for these jobs must be submitted to the individual agencies or personnel offices. Jobs with the U.S. Postal Service are also excluded from the competitive civil service. These resources also will assist you in locating NAFI jobs:

NAFI Jobs

U.S. Army Civilian Personnel Center
ATTN: PECC-NAF
Hoffman II Bldg., 200 Stovall St.
Alexandria, VA 22322

Commissary Management Positions

HQ, Defense Commissary Agency
Directorate of Personnel & Training
Fort Lee, VA 23801-6300

Club Managers Worldwide

HQDA (DACF-NFS-R)
2461 Eisenhower Avenue
Hoffman Bldg., 1, Rm. 1222
Alexandria, VA 22331-0523

Community & Family Support Positions

HQDA (CFSA-HR-PS-R) U.S. Army
Community/Family Support Center
2461 Eisenhower Ave.
Alexandria, VA 22331-0523

OVERSEAS FEDERAL JOB SOURCES

This section presents resources that can be used to locate federal job announcements for overseas jobs. Refer to Chapter Three's Common Job Source lists for additional resources. Appendix D provides a complete list of federal occupations. Also refer to Appendix C for detailed descriptions of government agencies and departments.

A number of the periodicals and books listed in this chapter are available at libraries. Many publishers will send complimentary review copies of periodicals upon request.

Resource headings include job openings, placement services, *Hiring Agency Directory*, and general information. The Hiring Agency Directory lists addresses of many agencies that offer overseas employment. Job openings include publications with job ads, job hotlines, and computer bulletin board resources. The general information section lists related books, pamphlets, brochures, and computer software. All job sources are listed alphabetically with the <u>larger publications underlined</u>.

JOB OPENINGS

PERIODICALS WITH FEDERAL OVERSEAS JOB ADS

Federal Career Opportunities - Federal Research Service, 243 Church St., NW, Vienna, VA 22180; 703-281-0200, bi-weekly, $38/three month subscription. Provides approximately 4,000 federal job vacancies in each issue.

Federal Jobs Digest - Breakthrough Publications, P.O. Box 594, Dept D30, Millwood, NY 10546; 1-800-824-5000, published bi-weekly, $29 for 3 month subscription, $54/six-month subscription. Up to 30,000 federal job vacancies listed per issue. The Federal Jobs Digest compiles vacancies from OPM, regional announcements, overseas vacancies, and schedules for U.S. Postal exams. This publication provides comprehensive federal career articles with each issue and lists updated personnel office contacts.

Federal Times - 6883 Commercial Dr., Springfield, VA 22159; 703-750-8920, weekly; $48/year subscription rate, $24 for six months. Publishes several hundred vacancies with brief descriptions under "Jobs" starting at the GS-7 level.

International Employment Hotline - Worldwise Books, P.O. Box 3030, Oakton, VA 22124, monthly, $36 for a one-year subscription, $25 for six months. Published since 1980, this newsletter lists current job openings around the world each month and features advice and information of concern to the international job hunter. Announces new job vacancies in the government, private, and non-profit sectors under country of assignment with job title, description and method of application, along with the employer's address and other contact information. Approximately 30% of each issue is devoted to editorial coverage of the international job market. Articles explore topics as diverse as hiring practices of international organizations, how to create a better resume, how to identify and avoid scams aimed at job hunters, and how Americans currently working overseas got their jobs. This a comprehensive and worthwhile publication for the serious overseas job hunter.

JOB HOTLINES

Career America Connection - Federal government job hotline 1-912-757-3000 stateside, Alaska 912-471-3755. **The charge is 40 cents per minute.** Operated by the Office of Personnel Management. Phone answers 24 hours a day. Provides federal employment information for most occupations. Callers can leave voice-mail messages with their name, address, and phone number. Requested job announcements and applications are mailed within 24 hours. Easy to use on-line voice prompts and voice commands allow access with any touchtone or rotary dial telephone.

OPM Job Information Telephone Directory - Washington D.C. Federal Job Information Center Self-Service Telephone System; 202-606-2700, Code 110 for overseas employment. This telephone system contains a variety of material, ranging from general employment information of interest to applicants, to specific job opportunities in the federal government. Complete instructions on the use of the system and various options are provided upon access. Use the 35 message codes listed in Chapter Three's Resources for specific information on subjects other than overseas jobs. This system is available 24 hours a day. You can talk with an information specialist Monday through Friday from 8:00 a.m. to 4:00 p.m. Eastern Standard Time.

Peace Corps Recruiting Contacts - The Peace Corps has numerous university programs including; *The Peace Corps Preparatory Program, The Master's Internationalist Program, The Community College Model, Campus Compact Internships, Student Internships, Cooperative Education, Volunteer Partners*, and *Research Collaboration* programs. For specific information on university programs contact University Program Coordinators, Peace Corps of the United States, 1990 K St., N.W., 7th Floor, Washington, D.C. 20526, phone 1-800-424-8580, ext 2214.

U.S. Department of State Jobs - 703-875-7109 Call this number for current Foreign Service Specialist job openings. The State Department employs 25,992 employees of which approximately 9,500 workers are *Foreign Service Officers* and 5,000 are civil service members. Around 1,000 Americans are employed overseas by this agency.

U.S. Information Agency (USIA) - 202-619-0909 (Voice of America), 202-619-4539 (USIA Job Recording). USIA employs, 8,291 of which the majority of overseas workers are *Foreign Service Officers*. Around 1,000 Americans are employed overseas by this agency.

COMPUTER BULLETIN BOARDS

These are electronic computer bulletin boards that can only be accessed with a computer, modem, and communication software, as well as a telephone line. You may scan current open examination and vacancy announcements **nationwide** while you're on line or you can download them to your computer.

National Federal Job Opportunities Bulletin Board - 24 hours a day - **912-757-3100.**

Regional Bulletin Boards:

    Washington, DC Area   (202) 606-1113

PLACEMENT SERVICES

ADNET ONLINE - 8440 Woodfield Crossing Blvd., Ste. 170, Indianapolis, IN 46240; 800-682-2901, accessible through computer modem. This menu driven program lists job vacancies in 17 categories. Each category offers an extensive selection menu. Free to Prodigy subscribers. A free online trial access is offered through computer modem dialing at 317-579-4857, 2,400 baud, 7 bits, even parity, 1 stop bit. At the prompt type guest. Call for complete details.

Career Placement Registry - 302 Swann Ave., Alexandria, VA 22301; 800-368-3093, registration is $15/students and $25 to $45/nonstudents depending on salary range. Entry forms are available upon request. DIALOG accessible, updated weekly, over 100,000 employers use database.

Federal Job Matching Service - Box 594, Dept D30, NY 10546; 1-800-824-5000. This service matches your background to federal requirements. Applicants send in a federal application, SF-171. You will receive back a list of federal job titles and grade levels for which you qualify. Federal job descriptions and qualification statements are provided for every job title that the service identifies for you. The fee is $30, but only $25 with a subscription label in your name from the Federal Jobs Digest. This service matches your background to federal job requirements not to specific job openings. After you receive your reply you can submit your application direct to agencies listed in the FJD that are hiring in that occupation.

KiNexus - Suite 560, 640 N. LaSalle St., Chicago, IL 60610; 800-828-0422, 312-335-0787, Registration fee $30/yr. This service is free if you attend a school that subscribes to this service. Over 1,900 schools currently participate. Employers access the database on line and contact applicants direct.

Military in Transition Database (MILTRAN) - 1255 Drummers Lane, Wayne, PA 19087; 800-426-9954, 215-687-3900. Offers a resume matching service to military members leaving the armed forces. If you will soon be leaving the service or were recently discharged call for particulars.

TOPS: The Retired Officers Association - 201 N. Washington St., Alexandria, VA 22314; 800-245-8762, 703-549-2311. Offers a resume matching service for anyone who served as a commissioned officer in any branch of the service including warrants, $20/year fee.

HIRING AGENCY DIRECTORY

The following list of agency personnel offices that hire overseas is not complete. Some agencies employ small numbers of workers for overseas assignments and they may not be listed. This listing is comprised of the agencies that offer a large number of position overseas and therefore provide the greatest opportunities for job seekers. Some of the key occupations are listed for each agency. Other occupations may also be hired overseas by these agencies. Write to the addresses listed for additional information including complete occupational lists.

How to Find an Overseas Job with the U.S. Government, by Will Cantrell and Francine Modderno, is an excellent resource for detailed job descriptions for each listed agency. This valuable guide describes the actual jobs available with each agency and provides additional information on the application process, minimum qualifications, etc. Available from the publishers' back-of-book catalog, or look this title up at your local library. Write for additional information to Worldwise Books, P.O. Box 3030, Oakton, VA 22124-9030.

Agency for International Development (AID) - Recruitment Division, Human Resources Department, Rm. 50, SA-2, Washington, D.C. 20523-0222. Overseas employment approximately 1250.

>Accountants, auditors, contract officers, agricultural specialists, economists, engineers, housing/urban planning specialists, project officers, public health/nutrition specialists, lawyers, family planners, and private enterprise advisors. They also employ Foreign Service Specialists that are not affiliated with the regular U.S. Foreign Service Corps. Participates in many of the federal student employment programs.

Central Intelligence Agency (CIA) - Central Intelligence Agency, Office of Personnel, P.O. Box 12727, Arlington, VA 22209-8727. This agency is the second largest employer of U.S. civilians overseas behind the Department of Defense. Its total employment is estimated at over 30,000, worldwide. This agency by law does not reveal employment statistics.

>Employees work in hundreds of occupations including many professional and technical categories. Areas include intelligence, operations, science and technology, and administration.

Department of Transportation (DOT) - Central Employment Information M-18.1, 400 7th St., SW Room 9113, Washington, DC 20590.

>Employees work in hundreds of occupations including many professional and technical categories. Employs a large number of electronics technicians.

Federal Highway Administration, Office of International Programs, HP1-10, Rm. 3327, Washington, D.C. 20509.

>Civil engineers

Federal Aviation Administration, Human Resource Management Division, Headquarters, Rm. 516, 800 Independence Ave., S.W., Washington, D.C. 20591.
Aviation safety inspectors, pilots, electronics technicians.

Drug Enforcement Administration (DEA) - 700 Army-Navy Drive, Arlington, VA 22202. Employs about 200 workers overseas.
Drug enforcement agents, administrative, clerical

General Accounting Office (GAO) - Office of Recruitment, GAO, 441 G. St., N.W., Washington, D.C. 20548. Employs a small number of evaluators in Germany.
Accounting program evaluators

Library of Congress - The Library of Congress, Human Resources Operations Office, 101 Independence Ave., S.E., Rm. 107, Washington, D.C. 20540.
Administrative librarians

National Security Agency (NSA) - Recruitment Program, National Security Agency, ATTN: M322, Fort George G. Meade, MD 20755-6000.
Engineering, computer science, languages, mathematics, cryptography, intelligence research, traffic analysis, communications security, signals analysis, and administrative and management.

Peace Corps - Peace Corps Personnel, 1990 K St., N.W., Rm. 4100, Washington, D.C. 20526. The primary purpose of the professional staff is to support volunteers.
Programming and training, administration, training, agriculture, education, rural development, and health.

Radio Free Europe - RFE/RL, Inc., Personnel Department, 1201 Connecticut Avenue, N.W., Washington, D.C. 20036 or RFE/RL Inc., Employment Office, Oettingensir. 67, D-8000 Munich 22, Germany. Employs over 1700 workers worldwide.
Broadcasting, broadcast analysis, research, electronic engineering, news writing, administration, and computer systems.

U.S. Customs Service - Personnel Department, 1301 Constitution Avenue NW., Washington, D.C. 20229.
Criminal investigators, inspectors, administrative

U.S. Department of State - Recruitment Division, P.O. Box 9317, Arlington, VA 22210. Foreign service employees include approximately 4,200 Foreign Service Officers and 3400 Foreign Service Specialists who serve in more than 140 countries and in the United States.
Foreign service officers, enforcement specialists, technical specialists, medical care specialists, administrative specialists, advisors, building operations, and internships.

U.S. Information Agency - Personnel Office, Rm 518, 301 4th Street, S.W., Washington, D.C. 20547. Also write to Voice of America, Office of Personnel, Rm. 1543, 330 Independence Avenue, S.W., Washington, D.C. 20547.

Foreign service officers, broadcasting, programs, educations, and cultural affairs, administrative positions, and the U.S. speakers program.

U.S. Department of Commerce - Office of Foreign Service Personnel, ATTN: Recruitment, U.S. Department of Commerce, Rm 3226, Washington, D.C. 20230.

Foreign commercial service officers (FCSOs), Foreign service secretaries/ administrative assistants, and related occupations.

National Oceanic & Atmospheric Administration (NOAA) - Career Resource Center, 1335 East-West Hwy, Room 2262, Silver Springs, MD 20910.

Professional trained in engineering, oceanography, earth sciences, meteorology, fisheries science, and related occupations.

U.S. Department of Agriculture (Foreign Agricultural Service) - FAS Personnel Division, Recruitment Officer, Rm. 5627 South Bldg., U.S. Dept. of Agriculture, 14th and Independence Ave., S.W., Washington, D.C. 20250-1000.

Agricultural economists (about 100 stationed abroad)

U.S. Department of Defense (DOD) - The Department of Defense is the largest employer of civilian federal workers stateside and abroad and they hire in most job series including technical, professional, and administrative. Refer to the detailed listings of military headquarters civilian personnel offices listed later in this chapter and in Appendix C, which includes a comprehensive list of military installations. To locate overseas jobs with the DOD, contact military headquarters personnel offices or OPM FJICs.

> **Department of Defense Dependent Schools** - Refer to *Overseas Employment Opportunities for Educators* (Department of Defense Dependent Schools) in the next section. This program is further explained under the Department of Defense summary later in this chapter.

> **Defense Intelligence Agency (DIA)** - Defense Intelligence Agency, Civilian Personnel Office, RPM-1 (Recruitment), Washington, D.C. 20301.
> Intelligence specialists, bilingual research technicians, and secretaries.

GENERAL INFORMATION

Books, Pamphlets, & Brochures

Foreign Service Career (U.S. Department of State) - The State Department publishes a free comprehensive, 40-page *Foreign Service Booklet*. Sample tests are included, plus a complete description of available jobs, benefits, applications and more. Request a free copy from U.S. Department of State, Recruitment Division, P.O. Box 12226, Arlington, VA 22219.

How to Find Overseas Job with the U.S. Government - Worldwise Books, 421 pages, $28.95. This comprehensive guide provides detailed information on overseas opportunities with 17 separate government agencies and the specialized agencies of the United Nations. This reference offers 70 chapters of detailed information for most federal agencies and departments that hire civilian workers for overseas jobs. A thorough job description is presented for each occupation with details on how to qualify, application specifications including required forms, minimum qualifications, and contact addresses. The most comprehensive and thorough federal overseas job resource available and a must for the serious overseas job seeker. Available from D-Amp Publications' back-of-book catalog or for additional information, write to Worldwise Books, P.O. Box 3030, Oakton, VA 22124-9030.

International Internships and Volunteer Programs - Worldwise Books, 233 pages, $18.95. Find dozens of exciting international opportunities in this comprehensive guide. This book provides application procedures and program descriptions for organizations that sponsor internships and volunteer opportunities of international scope, including public and private sectors. The lack of pertinent work experience is the most formidable obstacle to an international career. Internship and volunteer opportunities featured in this book can help you overcome that obstacle by providing work experience in the international arena, or even in a foreign setting. Many of the organizations you can work for as an intern or volunteer will offer you a salaried position, once you've proved yourself. Available from D-Amp Publications' back-of-book catalog or for additional information, write to Worldwise Books, P.O. Box 3030, Oakton, VA 22124-9030.

Overseas Employment Opportunities for Educators (Department of Defense Dependent Schools) - Recruitment and Assignment Section, Hoffman Building I, 2461 Eisenhower Avenue, Alexandria, VA 22331-1100, 703-696-3067. This complete employment package is free for the asking. It covers eligibility, position categories and special requirements, application procedures, program information and entitlement, housing, living/working conditions, shipment of household goods, and complete application forms and guidance. Refer to Department of Defense descriptions in this chapter and appendix C for additional information on this subject.
The Complete Guide To International Jobs & Careers - by Drs. Ronald and Caryl Krannich. Impact Publications, 337 pages, $13.95. This revealing book helps job seekers better understand the what, where, and how of working in one of today's fastest growing job markets.

Provides frank answers to the most important questions about this fascinating employment arena. Discover what is the outlook for international jobs in the 1990's, how one should best prepare for an international job, what is the best approach to finding a job, what types of organizations "public or private" are hiring abroad, and where are the jobs. Available from D-Amp Publications' back-of-book catalog.

<u>**Computer Software**</u>

Federal Occupational and Career Informational System (FOCIS) - National Technical Information Services, 5285 Port Royal Rd., Springfield, VA 22161; 1-800-553-NTIS, 703-487-4650, $49.95, order # various with disk size, call for specific ordering information for your computer system. IBM-PC or compatible computers, DOS 3.0 +, 5 MB of memory required, Dbase III Plus. Developed by OPM to help job seekers obtain information about federal careers and occupations. The software is menu-driven, with no prior experience on a PC needed by the user. Consists of three modules: career guidance, occupational information, and tips on how to get a job. Covers 360 federal white-collar occupations and 450 federal organizations.

Refer to Chapter Three for additional software for SF-171 preparation and more.

PACIFIC OPPORTUNITIES

There are federal civil service employees in Hawaii, Guam, Japan, Korea, the Philippines, and American Samoa. The outlook for jobs is for continued hiring by Department of Defense agencies and very limited hiring by other agencies.

Most federal jobs in the Pacific overseas areas are with the Department of Defense. Many positions in DOD agencies are currently filled under a special appointment authority for hiring family members of U.S. military or civilian personnel stationed in foreign areas. Jobs not filled by the special appointment authority are frequently filled by federal employees that transfer overseas or are filled by U.S. citizens living in the local areas on a temporary or time-limited basis. Generally, the greatest demand is for experienced engineering, administrative, educational, technical, and scientific occupations.

[1]Federal employees in Hawaii and Guam receive cost-of-living allowances (COLAs) in addition to their basic pay. The COLAs are 22.5% on Oahu, 17.5% on Kauai, 20% on Maui, Lanai, and Molokai, and 15% on Hawaii. Other areas in the Pacific pay COLA ranging from 10% to 20% above standard pay.

For information about job vacancies and recruitment, including vacancy lists, write or call the following military *Job Information Centers* (JICs):

---

[1]WORKING FOR US IN HAWAII AND THE PACIFIC, Published by the OPM's FJIC in Honolulu.

ADDITIONAL AGENCY OVERSEAS JICs

PACIFIC AREA

Hawaii

Human Resources Office (Code 170.3)
Pearl Harbor Naval Shipyard, Box 400
Pearl Harbor, Hawaii 96860-5352
(808) 474-5170, Hours: M-F 7:00 a.m. - 3:30 p.m.

U.S. Army Support Command, Hawaii
Civilian Personnel Office
Bldg. T-1500 (Attn: APZV-PAC-R)
Fort Shafter, HI 96858-5002
(808) 438-9301 (Recording)
(808) 438-9302 (Information)
(808) 437-9556 (Recording NAFI Jobs)
Hours: M-F, 10:30 a.m. - 1:00 p.m.

Central Civilian Personnel Office
15th MSSQ/MSC
Hickam AFB, Hawaii 96853-5000
(808) 449-6733 (Recording)
(808) 449-2903 (Information)
Hours: M-F 8:00 a.m. - 3:00 p.m.

Human Resource Office
Navy Public Works Center, Pearl Harbor
4300 Radford Drive
Honolulu, HI 96818-3298
(808) 471-0850 (Recording)
(808) 471-0566 (Information)
Hours: M-F 8:00 a.m. - 3:00 p.m.

Japan

Camp Zama CPO
17th Area Support Group
ATTN: AJGH-PA-PORP
APO AP 96343-0082

Yokosuka
Commander Flt. Act. CPO
PSC 473, Box 22
FPO AP 96349-0009

Guam

Consolidated CPO (NAVY)
PSC 455, Box 182
FPO AP 96540
(671) 339-2102 (International Call)

Andersen Air Force Base
Civilian Personnel Office
633 MSSQ/MSC
APO AP 96543-5000
(671) 366-7123 (International Call)

Okinawa

Camp Butler CPO
Camp Smedley D. Butler, Okinawa
Marine Corp Base
FPO AP 96373-5000

Kadena Air Base
Civilian Personnel Office
18th MSSQ/MSC
APO AP 96368-5134

Korea

Osan Air Base, CPO
51 MSSQ/MSC
APO AP 96278-5000

Seoul and Yongsan, CPO
EANC-SA-CPR
Unit # 15333
APO AP 96205-0177

Pusan CPO
Attn: SES Branch
20th Area Support Group, Pusan
Unit # 15181
APO AP 96259-0270

ATLANTIC OPPORTUNITIES

The majority of positions are in Germany, Belgium, Italy, and Africa. Germany, the largest employer, has 26,312 federal civilian employees. The majority of these jobs are filled by residents of the host country or by family members of military and civilians officially stationed in Europe. Approximately 5% are U.S. citizens who were recruited outside of Europe.

Local Army Civilian Personnel Offices (CPOs) have primary responsibility within Europe for most noncareer, technical and administrative positions.

If you seek employment with the Department of the Army, Navy or Air Force, or any other federal agency in the Atlantic region, the U.S. Army, Europe and Seventh Army (USAREUR), located in Leiman, Germany, has been delegated the examining authority by the Office of Personnel Management for certain positions above the GS-7 grade level.

Status and Nonstatus applicants, who are seeking employment in the Atlantic Overseas Area for GS-7 and above positions, should write to: The **Civilian Recruitment Center, USAREUR & 7th Army, Unit 29150, APO AE 09100**. Telephone, 011 49 6221 577258

A status applicant is one who previously worked for the federal government and obtained career status. Nonstatus applicants have never worked for the federal government and must establish eligibility with the Office of Personnel Management or with an agency that has been delegated examining authority, such as the USAREUR.

USAREUR publishes a booklet titled, *"Jobs in Europe"* which covers status and nonstatus applicants. The booklet provides a list of jobs for which USAREUR is accepting applications and provides minimum qualification requirements for positions for which they recruit. Write USAREUR at the above address for this free booklet. It is updated several times each year.

LARGEST OVERSEAS AGENCIES

DEPARTMENT OF DEFENSE (DOD)

The DOD is the largest overseas employer and provides hiring support to other federal agencies, including the Department of the Air Force and Navy, through its Overseas Employment Program (OEP). The OEP gives first consideration to qualified employees currently working at federal installations overseas. Former employees with reinstatement rights and current government employees should contact DOD Civilian Personnel Offices (CPOs) at DOD installations. When positions can't be filled in-house, OPM opens a competitive register to fill the position. Contact FJICs in the area in which you desire employment.

DEPARTMENT OF DEFENSE SCHOOLS (DoDDS)

Elementary and secondary schools have been operating on U.S. military bases overseas since 1946 for children of military and civilian personnel. The DoDDS provides educational opportunities comparable to those offered in the better school systems in the United States. This segment of U.S. public education consists of around 200 elementary, middle, junior high, and high schools and a community college. [1]The schools are located in 19 countries around the world, with an enrollment of approximately 112,706 students, and are staffed with approximately 15,000 employees. In comparison with the largest school systems in the United States, the overseas school system enrollment is among the top ten.

SCHOOL LOCATIONS:

> **Atlantic Region** - Belgium, England, Iceland, Netherlands, Norway, Scotland
> **Germany Region**
> **Mediterranean Region** - Azores, Bahrain, Greece, Italy, Spain, Turkey
> **Pacific Region** - Japan, Korea, Okinawa (Japan)
> **Panama/Island Region** - Bermuda, Canada (Newfoundland), Cuba, Panama

SALARY:

Overseas salaries are comparable to the average of the range of rates for similar positions in urban school jurisdictions in the U.S. having a population of 100,000 or more. The range of the school year 1991-92 entry level salary rates for teachers was from $23,130 to $39,250.   The school year consists of 190 duty days, with a minimum of 175 days of classroom instruction. Teachers are presently paid on several different pay lanes (bachelor's degree, bachelor's degree plus 15 semester hours, master's degree plus 30 semester hours, and doctor's degree).

HOUSING AND LIVING CONDITIONS:

In some areas, living quarters are provided by the United States government. These quarters may be in dormitories, apartments, old hotels, converted office buildings, or new modern facilities. These U.S. government quarters are usually provided without charge.

Write to the following address for a complete informational employment package: Department of Defense Dependents Schools, Recruitment and Assignment Section, Hoffman Building I, 2461 Eisenhower Avenue, Alexandria, VA 22331-1100.

DEPARTMENT OF THE ARMY

The Department of the Army generally hires locals for trades, laborers, equipment operators, crafts and clerical positions. Dependents of military and civilian U.S. citizens assigned abroad receive hiring preference for many of these positions. Contact CPOs at local Army posts for a current list of vacancies.

---

[1]Reference DODDS Pamphlet "Overseas Employment Opportunities for Educators" 1993-94 edition.

FOREIGN AGRICULTURAL SERVICE

The Foreign Agricultural Service (FAS) was established in 1953 to encourage foreign countries to import American farm products. Over 500 employees work at the Washington, D.C., headquarters. Another 275 employees are stationed at posts throughout the world.

This agency staffs 75 foreign posts covering 110 countries to maintain a worldwide agricultural intelligence and reporting service. Most overseas employees are members of the Foreign Service. They are selected from among agricultural economists in FAS who have passed a rigorous examination process for entry into the Foreign Service. FAS Foreign Officers are rotated between Washington assignments and 2-to-4-year assignments at overseas locations.

Positions are generally filled from the Professional and Administrative Career Examination and various agricultural occupations:

Agricultural Program Specialist	**GS-1145**
Agricultural Marketing Series	**GS-1146**
Agricultural Market Reporting	**GS-1147**
Agricultural Engineering	**GS- 890**

Economists start at the GS-9 pay grade and have promotion potential to the GS-12 grade ($27,789 - $52,385 per year). For additional information write to: Recruitment Officer FAS Personnel Division, Room 5627 South Building, 14th and Independence Avenue, S.W. Washington, D.C. 20250-1000.

U.S. DEPARTMENT OF COMMERCE

The National Oceanic and Atmospheric Administration hires persons with meteorological and electronic backgrounds to man weather observation posts. The U.S. and Foreign Commercial Service has another 165 officers serving abroad and in Washington, D.C. Some 3,400 Foreign Service Specialists serve as secretaries, communications technicians, financial and personnel managers, and physicians and nurses. For information write to: **Department of Commerce, Personnel Office, Room 5001, Washington, D.C. 20526.**

DEPARTMENT OF TRANSPORTATION (DOT)

Several agencies within the DOT hire for overseas assignments. The Federal Highway Administration provides assistance to foreign countries. Write to: **Office of Personnel, Federal Highway Administration, 400 7th NW, Washington D.C. 20590.**

The Federal Aviation Administration stations pilots, inspectors, and electronic technicians overseas. Most positions are filled in-house through a competitive bidding process. When vacancies can't be filled in-house, competitive announcements are advertised through OPM. Write to: **DOT, Employment Office, Personnel, Room 9113, 400 7th St. SW, Washington, D.C. 20590**

DEPARTMENT OF STATE

The Foreign Service of the United States is America's diplomatic, commercial, and overseas cultural and information service. This agency assists the President and Secretary of State in planning and carrying out American foreign policy at home and abroad. Some 4,200 Foreign Service Officers of the Department of State serve as administrative, consular, economic, and political officers in more than 240 American Embassies and Consulates in over 140 countries.

The United States Information Agency (USIA) deploys 950 Foreign Service Officers abroad as public affairs, information, and cultural affairs officers.

Personnel in this agency spend an average of 60% of their careers abroad, moving at 2 to 4 year intervals. Many overseas posts are in small or remote countries where harsh climates, health hazards, and other discomforts exist, and where American-style amenities frequently are unavailable.

ENGLISH LANGUAGE SKILLS:

The Foreign Service requires all employees to have a strong command of the English language. All Foreign Service Officers must be able to speak and write clearly, concisely, and correctly. The Departments of State and Commerce and USIA give high priority to English-language skills in selecting officers and evaluating their performance.

FOREIGN LANGUAGE SKILLS:

Knowledge of a foreign language is not required for appointment. Candidates without such knowledge are appointed as language probationers and must acquire acceptable competency in at least one foreign language before tenure can be granted. Officers can attend classes at the *National Foreign Affairs Training Institute*, which offers training in over 40 languages. These agencies seek particularly persons with knowledge of Arabic, Chinese, Japanese, or Russian.

SALARY SCHEDULE:

New entry-level officers are appointed at classes 6, 5, or 4, depending on their qualifications, experience, and salary record. Level 6 is approximately equivalent to the GS 8/9 grade or $25,670 - $37,697 per year. Top administrators are level 1 and receive between $66,609 and $86,589 per year in accordance with 1994 pay schedules. Cost Of Living Adjustments (COLA) are authorized for certain overseas areas.

The U.S. Department of State offers a free, comprehensive, 40-page *Foreign Service Booklet*. Sample tests are included, plus a complete description of available jobs, benefits, applications and more. Write to: **U. S. Department of State, Recruitment Division, P.O. Box 9317 Rosslyn Station Arlington, VA 22219.**

CHAPTER EIGHT

THE U. S. POSTAL SERVICE

The U. S. Postal Service (USPS) employs 781,438 workers in 300 job categories for positions at over 40,000 post offices, branches, stations, and community post offices throughout the United States. Approximately 40,000 postal workers are hired each year to backfill for retirements, transfers, deaths and employees who choose to leave the Postal Service.

Vacancies are advertised internally by the USPS and not by the Office of Personnel Management. In 1971, the Postal Service became independent. Pay scales are determined by the Postal Pay Act and are not a part of the General Pay Schedule.

Pay starts at $19,407 per year for full time career employees at the PS-1A pay grade and increases to $39,381 at the PS-10-O top pay grade. The average postal worker's salary is approximately $29,000 per year. The PS pay scale is the largest pay system in the USPS and is predominately for bargaining unit employees. There is also Executive and Administrative Schedules for nonbargaining unit employees that ranges earn from $41,993 up to $143,800 for the Postmaster General. Postal employees receive the same benefits provided to federal employees. Chapter one explains these benefits in detail. However, postal workers pay considerably less for their health benefits than competitive federal civil service employees.

EMPLOYEE CLASSIFICATIONS

Initial appointments are either casual (temporary) or Part-Time Flexible (Career). Hourly rates for Part-Time Flexible employees varies depending upon the position's rate schedule. Some positions are filled full-time such as the Maintenance (Custodial) classification.

Full-Time and Part-Time Flexible (career) employees comprise the *Regular Work Force*. This category includes security guards. Part-Time Flexible employees are scheduled to work fewer than 40 hours per week and they must be available for flexible work hours as assigned. Part-Time Flexible employees are paid by the hour. A typical hourly rate is $10.45 per hour.

A *Supplemental Work Force* is needed by the Postal Service for peak mail periods and offers casual (temporary) employees two 89-day employment terms in a calendar year. During Christmas an additional 21 days of employment can be offered to Supplemental Work Force employees.

College students may be considered for casual (temporary) employment with the Postal Service during the summer months. The rate of pay is $7.00 per hour. Tests are not required and appointments cannot lead to a career position. Apply early for summer work. Contact Post Offices in your area by no later than February for summer employment applications.

QUALIFICATION REQUIREMENTS

Various standards from age restrictions to physical requirements must be met before you can take one of the Postal Service exams.

AGE LIMIT

You must be eighteen to apply. Certain conditions allow applicants as young as sixteen to apply. Carrier positions, requiring driving, are limited to age 18 or older. High school graduates or individuals that terminated high school education for sufficient reason are permitted to apply at age 16.

ENTRANCE EXAMS

Clerk, carrier and other specific postal job applicants must pass an entrance exam. Specialties such as mechanic, electronic technician, machinist, and trades must pass a written test. The overall rating is based on the test results and your qualifying work experience and education. Professionals don't require an entrance exam or written test. They are rated and hired strictly on their prior work experience and education.

CITIZENSHIP

Applicants do not have to be U.S. citizens. If you have permanent alien resident status in the United States of America or owe allegiance to the United States of America you can apply for Postal Service jobs.

PHYSICAL REQUIREMENTS

Physical requirements are determined by the job. Carriers must be able to lift a 70 pound mail sack and all applicants must be able to efficiently perform assigned duties. Eyesight and hearing tests are required. Applicants must have at least 20/40 vision in the good eye and no worse than 20/100 in the other eye. Eyeglasses are permitted.

STATE DRIVERS LICENSE

Applicants must have a valid state driver's license for positions that require motor vehicle operation. A safe driving record is required and a Postal Service road test is administered for the type of vehicle that you will operate.

DRUG TESTING (SUBSTANCE ABUSE)

A Post Office for a major eastern city recently went through over 800 applicants to hire 100 new employees. At least 700 that were on the register tested positive for various illegal substances or didn't show up for the mandatory urine test. Many federal agencies now require pre-employment physicals that include urine testing for illegal substances.

APPLICATION PROCEDURES

Applicants for many postal careers must pass the Postal Service entrance exam with a score of 70 percent or better. Exams for Mailhandler, Clerk/Carrier, Clerk-Typist, Automated Mark-Up Clerk, Rural Carrier, Distribution Clerk, Motor Vehicle Operator, Auto Mechanic, and others are available.

To apply for postal positions you must contact a Management Sectional Center (MSC), Bulk Mail Center, General Mail Facilities or a Sectional Center Facility to register for the postal workers civil service exam. Contact your local post office to find out where the tests are administered in your area.

A passing score of 70 percent or better will place the applicant's name on an eligible register for a period of two years. Applicants can write to the Postal Examination office for a one-year extension. Requests for extension must be received between the eighteenth-and twenty-fourth month of eligibility. Most people hired have a score of between 90% and 100%. There is a separate register for each position. To improve your chances, test for as many different positions that you can qualify for.

VETERANS PREFERENCE

Veterans receive 5 or 10 point preference. Those with a 10% or greater compensable service-connected disability are placed at the top of the register in the order of their scores. All other eligibles are listed below the disabled veterans group in rank order. The Veterans Preference Act applies to all Postal Service positions. Refer to Chapter 6 for a complete review of Veteran's hiring programs.

Custodial exams for the position of cleaner, custodian, and custodial laborer are exclusively for veterans and present employees. This exam is open only to veterans preference candidates.

POSTAL CLERKS AND MAIL CARRIERS
- THE LARGEST USPS OCCUPATIONS -

Nature of the Work

Each day, the United States Postal Service receives, sorts, and delivers millions of letters, bills, advertisements, and packages. To do this, it employs about 781,438 workers. Almost 9 out of 10 of these workers are postal clerks, who sort mail and serve customers in post offices, or mail carriers, who deliver the mail.[1]

Clerks and carriers are distinguished by the type of work they do. Clerks are usually classified by the mail processing function they perform, whereas carriers are classified by their type of route, city or rural.

About 440 mail processing centers throughout the country service post offices in surrounding areas and are staffed primarily by postal clerks. Some clerks, more commonly referred to as mail handlers, unload the sacks of incoming mail; separate letters, parcel post, magazines, and newspapers; and transport these to the proper sorting and processing area. In addition, they may perform simple canceling operations and rewrap packages damaged in processing after letters have been put through stamp-canceling machines. They are taken to other workrooms to be sorted according to destination. Clerks operating electronic letter-sorting machines push keys corresponding to the ZIP code of the local post office to which each letter will be delivered; the machine then drops the letters into the proper slots. A growing proportion of clerks operate optical character readers (OCRs) and bar code sorters, machines that can "read" the address and sort a letter according to a code printed on the envelope. Others sort odd-sized letters, magazines, and newspapers by hand. Finally, the mail is sent to local post offices for sorting according to delivery route and delivered.

Postal clerks at local post offices sort local mail for delivery to individual customers and provide retail services such as selling stamps and money orders, weighing packages to determine postage, and checking that packages are in satisfactory condition for mailing. Clerks also register, certify, and insure mail and answer questions about postage rates, post office boxes, mailing restrictions, and other postal matters. Occasionally, they may help a customer file a claim for a damaged package.

Once the mail has been processed and sorted, it is ready to be delivered by mail carriers. Duties of city and rural carriers are very similar. Most travel established routes delivering and collecting mail. Mail carriers start work at the post office early in the morning, where they spend a few hours arranging their mail for delivery and taking care of other details.

---

[1]Occupational Outlook Handbook, 1992-93, U.S. Department of Labor

Carriers may cover the route on foot, by vehicle, or a combination of both. On foot, they carry a heavy load of mail in a satchel or push it in a cart. In some urban and most rural areas, they use a car or small truck. Although the Postal Service provides vehicles to city carriers, most rural carriers use their own automobiles. Deliveries are made house-to-house, to roadside mailboxes, and to large buildings. such as offices or apartments, which generally have all the mailboxes on the first floor.

Besides delivering and collecting mail, carriers collect money for postage-due and c.o.d. (cash on delivery) fees and obtain signed receipts for registered, certified, and insured mail. If a customer is not home, the carrier leaves a notice that tells where special mail is being held.

After completing their routes, carriers return to the post office with mail gathered from street collection boxes, homes, and businesses. They turn in the mail receipts and money collected during the day and may separate letters and parcels for further processing by clerks.

The duties of some city carriers may be very specialized; some deliver only parcel post while others collect mail from street boxes and receiving boxes in office buildings. In contrast, rural carriers provide a wide range of postal services. In addition to delivering and picking up mail, they sell stamps and money orders and accept parcels, letters, and items to be registered, certified, or insured.

All carriers answer customers' questions about postal regulations and services and provide change-of-address cards and other postal forms when requested. In addition to their regularly scheduled duties, carriers often participate in neighborhood service programs in which they check on elderly or shut-in patrons or notify the police of any suspicious activities along their route.

Postal clerks and mail carriers are classified as casual, part-time flexible, part-time regular, or full time. Casual workers help process and deliver mail during peak mailing or vacation periods. Part-time flexible workers do not have a regular work schedule or weekly guarantee of hours; they replace absent workers and help with extra work as the need arises. Part-time regulars have a set work schedule of less than 40 hours per week. Full-time postal employees work a 40-hour week over a 5-day period.

Working Conditions

Postal clerks usually work in clean, well-ventilated, and well-lit buildings. However, other conditions vary according to work assignments and the type of laborsaving machinery available. In small post offices, mail handlers use handtrucks to move heavy mail sacks from one part of the building to another and clerks may sort mail by hand. In large post offices and mail processing centers, chutes and conveyors move the mail, and much of the sorting is done by machines. Despite the use of automated equipment, the work of mail handlers and postal clerks can be physically demanding. These workers are usually on their feet, reaching for sacks and trays of mail or placing packages and bundles into sacks and trays.

Mail handlers and distribution clerks may become bored with the routine of moving and sorting mail. Many work at night or on weekends because most large post offices process mail around the clock, and the largest volume of mail is sorted during the evening and night shifts.

Window clerks, on the other hand, have a greater variety of duties, frequent contact with the public, and rarely have to work at night. However, they may have to deal with upset customers, and they are held accountable for the assigned stock of stamps and for postal funds.

Most carriers begin work early in the morning, in some cases as early as 4 a.m. if they have routes in the business district. A carrier's schedule has its advantages, however: Carriers who begin work early in the morning are through by early afternoon, and they spend most of the day on their own, relatively free from direct supervision.

Carriers spend most of their time outdoors, and deliver mail in all kinds of weather. Even those who drive often must walk when making deliveries and must lift heavy sacks of parcel post items when loading their vehicles. In addition, carriers always must be cautious of potential hazards on their routes. Wet roads and sidewalks can be treacherous, and each year numerous carriers are bitten by unfriendly dogs.

Employment

The U.S. Postal Service employed 302,000 postal clerks and 305,000 mail carriers in 1990. Three-fourths of them worked full time. Most postal clerks worked at mail processing centers, although some clerks provided window service and sorted mail at local post offices. Although most mail carriers worked in cities and suburban communities, 42,000 were rural carriers.

Training, Other Qualifications, and Advancement

Postal clerks and mail carriers must be U.S. citizens or have been granted permanent resident-alien status in the United States. They must be at least 18 years old (or 16, if they have a high school diploma). Qualification is based on a written examination that measures speed and accuracy at checking names and numbers and ability to memorize mail distribution procedures. Applicants must pass a physical examination as well, and may be asked to show that they can lift and handle mail sacks weighing up to 70 pounds. Applicants for jobs as postal clerks operating electronic sorting machines must pass a special examination that includes a machine aptitude test. Applicants for mail carrier positions must have a driver's license, a good driving record, and a passing grade on a road test.

Applicants should apply at the post office or mail processing center where they wish to work in order to determine when an exam will be given. Applicants' names are listed in order of their examination scores. Five points are added to the score of an honorably discharged veteran, and 10 points to the score of a veteran wounded in combat or disabled. When a vacancy occurs, the appointing officer chooses one of the top three applicants; the rest of the names remain on the list to be considered for future openings until their eligibility expires, usually 2 years from the examination date.

Relatively few people under the age of 25 are hired as career postal clerks or mail carriers, a result of keen competition for these jobs and the customary waiting period of 1-2 years or more after passing the examination. It is not surprising, therefore, that most entrants transfer from other occupations.

New postal clerks and mail carriers are trained on the job by experienced workers. Many post offices offer classroom instruction. Workers receive additional instruction when new equipment or procedures are introduced. They usually are trained by another postal employee or, sometimes, a training specialist hired under contract by the Postal Service.

A good memory, good coordination, and the ability to read rapidly and accurately are important. In addition, mail handlers should be in good physical condition. Mail handlers and distribution clerks work closely with other clerks, frequently under the tension and strain of meeting dispatch transportation deadlines. Window clerks and mail carriers must be courteous and tactful when dealing with the public, especially when answering questions or receiving complaints.

Postal clerks and mail carriers often begin on a part-time flexible basis and become regular or full time in order of seniority as vacancies occur. Full-time clerks may bid for preferred assignments such as the day shift, a window job, or a higher level nonsupervisory position as expediter or window service technician. Carriers can look forward to obtaining preferred routes as their seniority increases, or to higher level jobs such as carrier technician. Both clerks and carriers can advance to supervisory positions.

Job Outlook

Those seeking a job in the Postal Service can expect to encounter keen competition. The number of applicants for postal clerk and mail carrier positions is expected to continue to far exceed the number of openings. Job opportunities will vary by occupation and duties performed.

Overall employment of postal clerks is expected to grow more slowly than the average through the year 2005. In spite of the anticipated increase in the total volume of mail, automation will continue to increase the productivity of postal clerks. Increasingly, mail will be moved using automated materials-handling equipment and sorted using optical character readers, bar code sorters, and other automated sorting equipment. In addition, demand for window clerks will be moderated by the increased sales of stamps and other postal products by grocery and department stores and other retail outlets.

Conflicting factors also are expected to influence demand for mail carriers. Despite competition from alternative delivery systems and new forms of electronic communication, the volume of mail handled by the Postal Service is expected to continue to grow. Population growth and the formation of new households, coupled with an increase in the volume of third class mail, will stimulate demand for mail delivery. However, increased use of the "ZIP + 4" system, which is used to sort mail to the carrier route, should decrease the amount of time carriers spend sorting their mail. In addition, the Postal Service is moving toward more centralized mail delivery, such as the use of more cluster boxes, to cut down on the number of door-to-door deliveries. Although these trends are expected to increase carrier productivity, they will not significantly offset the growth in mail volume, and employment of mail carriers is expected to grow about as fast as the average for all occupations.

In addition to jobs created by growth in demand for postal services, some jobs will become available because of the need to replace postal clerks and mail carriers who retire or stop working for other reasons. The factors that make entry to these occupations highly competitive-attractive salaries, a good pension plan, steady work, and modest educational requirements-contribute to a high degree of job attachment, so that replacement needs produce relatively fewer job openings than in other occupations of this size. In contrast to the typical pattern, postal workers generally remain in their jobs until they retire; relatively few transfer to other occupations.

Although the volume of mail to be processed and delivered rises and falls with the level of business activity, as well as with the season of the year, full-time postal clerks and mail carriers have, to date, never been laid off. When mail volume is high, full-time clerks and carriers work overtime, part-time clerks and carriers work additional hours, and casual clerks and carriers may be hired. When mail volume is low, overtime is curtailed, part-timers work fewer hours, and casual workers are discharged.

Earnings

In 1990, base pay for beginning full-time carriers and postal clerks was $23,640 a year, rising to a maximum of $29,440 after 10 1/2 years of service. For those working between 6 p.m. and 6 a.m, a supplement is paid. Experienced, full-time, city delivery mail carriers earn an average salary of $29,100 a year. Postal clerks and carriers working part-time flexible schedules begin at $11.75 an hour and, based on the number of years of service, increase to a maximum of $15.30 an hour.

Rural delivery carriers had average base salaries of $27,300 in 1990. Their earnings are determined through an evaluation of the amount of work required to service their routes. Carriers with heavier workloads generally earn more than those with lighter workloads. Rural carriers also receive a maintenance allowance when required to use their own vehicles. In early 1991, this was approximately 30 cents per mile.

Postal workers enjoy a variety of employer-provided benefits. These include health and life insurance, vacation and sick leave, and a pension plan.

In addition to their hourly wage and benefits package, some postal workers receive a uniform allowance. This group includes those workers who are in the public view for 4 or more hours each day and various maintenance workers. The amount of the allowance depends on the job performed some workers are only required to wear a partial uniform, and their allowance is lower. In 1990, for example, the allowance for a letter carrier was $229 per year, compared to $98 for a window clerk.

Most of these workers belong to one of four unions: American Postal Workers Union, National Association of Letter Carriers, National Postal Mail Handlers Union, and National Rural Letter Carriers Association.

Related Occupations

Other workers whose duties are related to those of postal clerks include mail clerks, file clerks, routing clerks, sorters, material moving equipment operators, clerk typists, cashiers, data entry operators, and ticket sellers. Others with duties related to those of mail carriers include messengers, merchandise deliverers, and delivery-route truck drivers.

Sources of Additional Information

Local post offices and State employment service offices can supply details about entrance examinations and specific employment opportunities for postal clerks and mail carriers.

ADDITIONAL REFERENCE MATERIAL

The books listed below are excellent resources for individuals actively seeking employment with the U.S. Postal Service. Together they provide a directory for all postal jobs, sample tests, and comprehensive information on exactly what you need to do to land the job of your choice. Your local library may carry these books. If not, you can obtain copies direct from the publisher. Complete ordering information is provided on the last page of this book.

**The Book of
$16,000 - $60,000 Post Office Jobs**   **$14.95**
Where they are, What they Pay,   by Veltisezar Bautista
and How to Get Them
ISBN: 0-931613-04-3, trade paper, 186 pages (8 1/2 x 11)

This book will show you how to get a high-paying postal job, whether you are a high school graduate, a student, a college dropout, a mechanic, an engineer, or a computer programmer. The author shows you where the jobs are and how to land one. Nearly 300 specific postal job classifications are presented with full details.

The Book of U.S. Postal Exams   **$13.95**
How to score 95%-100% and get   by Veltisezar B. Bautista
a $20,000-a-year job
ISBN: 0-931613-02-7, trade paper, 230 pages (8 1/2 x 11)

This guide includes the most commonly-given exams for the majority of job classifications. Acclaimed as the most comprehensive postal exam book ever published, it's enabling men and women nationwide to score between 95%-100% on postal job exams. Provides unique test taking tips, sample exams, and sage advice.

OCCUPATIONS LIST
(Partial Listing)

Craft & Wage per hour positions:

Administrative Clerk
Building Equipment Mechanic
Data Conversion Operator
Electronic Technician
Garageman-Driver
Letter Carrier
Maintenance Mechanic
Motor Vehicle Operator

Auto Mechanic
Clerk Stenographer
Distribution Clerk
Engineman
General Mechanic
Mail Handler
Mark Up Clerk
Security Guard

Professional

Accounting Technician
Budget Assistant
Computer System Analyst
Transportation Specialist
Technical Writer

Architect/Engineer
Computer Programmer
Electronic Engineer
Industrial Engineer

Management

Foreman of Mail
Labor Relations Representative
Manager Bulk-Mail
Manager-Station/Branch
Schemes Routing Officer
Supervisor-Customer Service
Tour Superintendent

General Foreman
Administrative Manager
Manager-Distribution
Postmaster-Branch
Safety Officer
Supervisor-Accounting
System Liaison Specialist

CHAPTER NINE

EMPLOYMENT OPPORTUNITIES FOR
PEOPLE WITH DISABILITIES

Over 212,900 people with disabilities - 7 percent of the total federal civilian workforce - work for the federal government.[1] Opportunities exist at all levels of government and in hundreds of occupations. Total disabled federal employment has remained constant at 7 percent since 1980. The enactment of The *Americans With Disabilities Act* (ADA) and increased awareness of hiring options by federal managers should expand total disabled employment opportunities throughout government.

The federal government offers several special noncompetitive appointments (special emphasis hiring options) for people with physical or mental disabilities. There are distinct advantages for managers to hire individuals under special emphasis hiring appointments. Managers are able to hire individuals under special appointments within days where it may take as long as three to six months to fill positions under OPMs competitive process. Secondly, federal managers are tasked with specific performance targets, called *"critical job elements (CJEs)"*, for maintaining workforce diversity. All agencies are required by law to develop outreach efforts to identify qualified candidates to meet agency workforce diversity goals.

This chapter explains the various hiring options for people with disabilities. Individuals seeking appointments with the federal government must be proactive and begin networking with local agencies, contacting listed resources, and aggressively seeking out all available federal employment opportunities. Agencies have direct hire authority for Schedule A and 700-hour

---

[1]Reported by the Office of Workforce Information

trial appointments presented in this chapter. Therefore interested parties must contact individual agencies to determine what's available. Refer to the agency lists in Appendix C and the common resources listed in Chapter Three. Additional special hiring programs exist for disabled veterans. Refer to Chapter Six for complete details.

HIRING OPTIONS

The federal government provides opportunities for qualified persons with physical and mental disabilities. Applicants with handicaps must be considered fairly for all jobs in which they are able to perform the job duties efficiently and safely.[2]

The Office of Personnel Management (OPM) conducts a nationwide program for applicants who are handicapped and individual agencies are required by law to develop and implement plans for hiring, placement, promotion, and retention of handicapped individuals. Federal agencies may also take advantage of either competitive hiring or special appointing authority.

Agency Human Resource Management departments encourage federal managers to give people with disabilities full and fair consideration, and to make accommodations when necessary. Although the majority of employees with handicaps obtain their jobs through competitive procedures, there are some for whom ordinary procedures do not function fairly or accurately. The competitive process is explained in Chapters Two and Three. To meet the needs of those with severe impairments, agencies may use the following special appointing techniques:

- A 700-hour trial appointment which gives individuals an opportunity to demonstrate their ability to perform the duties of a position. Applicants must either meet the minimum qualifications standards or be certified by a state vocational or VA rehabilitation (VR) counselor as being capable of performing the duties of the position.

- Excepted Schedule A appointments are available for people that are severely physically handicapped who have: (1) successfully completed a 700-hour trial appointment, (2) been certified to a position by a State VR or VA counselor.

- Excepted Schedule A appointments are available for persons that are mentally impaired and are certified to a position by a State VR counselor as being capable of performing the duties of the position satisfactorily.

Individuals appointed under Schedule A may be non-competitively converted to a competitive appointment on the recommendation of his/her supervisor. The requirement for conversion is successful completion of trial periods, and satisfactory performance must have been maintained over a two year period.

---

[2]Reference EEOC Federal Register 29 CFR Parts 1602, 1627, and 1630.

COMPETITIVE VERSES EXCEPTED SERVICE

A good number of people with disabilities start their federal career in the excepted service while most federal jobs are in the competitive service.

Congress excepted certain jobs and groups from the competitive service. In the competitive service individuals must compete for positions through examination. The end result is that individuals are placed on a competitive register in rank order of their rating. Agencies then can select from the top three candidates on the list when vacancies arise.

The excepted service includes a number of agencies such as the CIA, FBI, National Security Agency, and about a dozen or so others. Specific jobs are also excepted and include the Stay-in-school program, student interns, veterans readjustment appointments, and the physically and mentally impaired programs discussed above. Excepted service employees on permanent excepted appointments are eligible for all benefits including health insurance, life insurance, leave, retirement, and they are eligible for promotion and reassignment just like those in the competitive service. The first year of employment is a trial period similar to the one-year probationary period for the competitive service.

There are some differences between these two appointments. First, excepted service employees are not eligible for transfer to other agencies or for noncompetitive reinstatement that is afforded to competitive service employees. Excepted service employees are also placed in a separate category when agencies go through a reduction in force, typically referred to as layoffs in private industry.

These differences cease to exist after the two year period of acceptable performance is achieved. Workers with physical or mental impairments may be converted to the competitive service upon supervisory recommendation.

UNPAID WORK EXPERIENCE

Most rehabilitation organizations include on-the-job training and job placement programs for participants. Vocational rehabilitation centers work with federal agencies to place people with disabilities in jobs that provide meaningful work experience. Agencies benefit from the services provided by these workers and they get an opportunity to evaluate a prospective employee before offering a special trial 700-hour appointment.

Federal regulations limit unpaid services from a person with disabilities to those who are clients of a State *Office of Vocational Rehabilitation* (OVR). Applicants must be enrolled in one of the OVR programs. A signed agreement must be initiated between the rehabilitation center and the federal agency. Agencies have the authority to negotiate these agreements individually with Vocational Rehabilitation Facilities within their area. Once an agreement is initiated the agreement covers all participants. Individuals accepted into these programs don't receive any compensation from the government; however, many sponsors provide a small stipend to the worker.

SPECIAL ACCOMMODATIONS

When appropriate, OPM uses special examination (testing) procedures for applicants who are physically handicapped to assure that their abilities are properly and fairly assessed.[3] Special testing arrangements are determined on an individual basis depending on the applicant's disability. For example: readers, examinations in Braille, tape, or large print for visually impaired competitors; and interpreters for test instructions and modifications of parts of tests for hearing impaired competitors.

Accommodations on the job

When federal agencies hire a person with disabilities, efforts are made to accommodate the individual to remove or modify barriers to their ability to effectively perform the essential duties of the position. Agencies may, for example: (1) provide interpreter service for the hearing impaired, (2) use readers for the visually impaired, (3) modify job duties, (4) restructure work sites, (5) alter work schedules, and (6) obtain special equipment or furniture.

APPOINTMENT CRITERIA

These procedures apply to those with severe disabling conditions or to those who have a number of minor conditions. All others are subject to the usual competitive hiring process.

Applicants establish eligibility by:

- Meeting the experience and/or education requirements in the qualification standards, including any written test requirement, or:

- Certification by state Office of Vocational Rehabilitation (OVR) or the Veterans Administration.

---

[3]U.S. OPM, Office of Affirmative Employment Programs, ES-5 (GPO 0-157-269).

The OVR certification option permits agencies to waive the established qualification requirements. Employment usually begins with a 700-hour temporary trial appointment which lasts approximately four months. If the applicant doesn't meet the qualification requirements, agencies need a certification letter from an OVR or the VA and a report of medical examination. If the applicant meets the qualification requirements, including any applicable exam, a medical report is the only requirement.

When the trial period performance is satisfactory the agency may convert the trial appointment to a permanent excepted appointment. No further documentation is needed, except agency personnel actions are required to initiate this change.

In the event an agency chooses to permanently appoint a person with disabilities without a trial period, OVR or VA certification is mandatory regardless of whether the applicant meets the qualification standards. A certification letter contains the following:

1. A statement from the applicant's counselor indicating that he/she is familiar with the duties of the position, and certification that the applicant, in the counselor's judgment, is capable of performing the duties without hazard to him or herself or others.

2. A medical examination report or summary of one which fully describes the extent and nature of the disability.

OVR counselors should also describe any limitations, suggest job or worksite modifications, and provide any other information which could help in accommodating the applicant and making a sound judgment. Agency selective placement coordinators will assist the counselor, explain the agency's requirements.

Individuals seeking 700-hour trial appointment or unpaid work experience must work with an OVR or VA rehabilitation counselor. Consult local phone directories and use the resources listed below to locate centers in your area.

COMMON JOB SOURCES

This section presents resources that can be used to locate federal job announcements for people with disabilities. After reviewing the listed resources refer to Appendix D for a complete list of federal occupations. A number of the periodicals and directories listed in this chapter are available at libraries. Others, such as *Career Woman*, are free to women within two years of graduation. Many newsletter and periodical publishers will send complimentary review copies of their publications upon request.

Resource headings include job openings, placement services, directories, and general information. Job openings include publications with job ads, job hotlines, and computer bulletin boards. The general information section lists related books, pamphlets, brochures, and computer software. All job sources are listed alphabetically with the <u>larger publications underlined</u>.

JOB OPENINGS

<u>KEY PERIODICALS & NEWSPAPERS WITH FEDERAL JOB ADS</u>

Ability Magazine - Jobs Information Business Service, 1682 Langley, Irvine, CA 92714; 714-854-8700 or 800-453-453-JOBS. Offers an electronic classified system which allows employers to recruit qualified individuals with disabilities, and people with disabilities to locate employment opportunities.

Affirmative Action Register for Effective Equal Opportunity Recruitment - AAR, Inc., 8356 Olive Blvd., St. Louis, MO 63132; 800-537-0665, 314-991-1335, Monthly magazine, $15 annual subscription rates. Lists university, state, federal, and other publicly-funded positions for veterans, women, minorities, and handicapped job seekers.

CAREERS & The DisAbled (Equal Opportunity Publications) - 150 Motor Parkway, Ste. 420, Hauppauge, NY 11788; 516-273-0066. This company publishes a number of excellent target audience publications including **CAREERS & The DisAbled, Career Woman, Minority Engineer, Woman Engineer, Equal Opportunity, and Independent Living** magazines.

Display ads feature national employers including the federal government seeking applicants for many varied fields. Each issue offers a dozen to sixty or more display job ads. Call for subscription rates. A resume matching service is also available to subscribers.

Mainstream - Magazine of the Able Disabled - Exploding Myths, Inc., 2973 Beech St., San Diego, CA 92102; 619-234-3138, $24/year, $3.50 for single copies, monthly. Magazine features disability rights issues and focuses on the political environment, education, training, employment, assistive devices, relationships, recreation, and sports. The October issues features employment opportunities for the disabled. Federal agencies including the CIA recruit through full page display ads. Examples of articles include; Get a Job!, Employing Good Sense, Telecommuting, Vox Populi - Machines that speak your language. This very informative magazine is an excellent resource.

JOB HOTLINES

CAREER AMERICA CONNECTION - Federal government job hotline 1-912-757-3000 stateside, Alaska 912-471-3755. **The charge is 40 cents per minute.** Operated by the Office of Personnel Management. Phone answers 24 hours a day. Provides federal employment information for most occupations. Callers can leave voice-mail messages with their name, address, and phone number. Requested job announcements and applications are mailed within 24 hours. Easy to use on-line voice prompts and voice commands allow access with any touchtone or rotary dial telephone.

CU Career Connection - University of Colorado, Campus Box 133, Boulder, CO 80309-0133; 303/492-4127. The charge is $22 for affiliated members and $30 nonmembers for an access code that is good for two months. Callers must use a touchtone phone.

Federal Job Information For The Deaf - Uses Telecommunication Device for the Deaf (TDD), 202-606-0591, OPM's national job information line.

REGIONAL TDD (Telephone Device for the Deaf) Job Hotline Numbers

Washington, DC:	202-606-0591	Northeastern	617-565-8913
Southeastern:	919-790-2739	Mountain:	303-969-7047
North Central:	816-426-6022		
Southwestern States:			

Arizona	800-223-3131	Louisiana	504-589-4614
New Mexico	505-766-8662	Oklahoma	405-231-4614
Texas (Dallas)	214-767-8115		
Texas (Other)	210-229-4000		

Western States:

Alaska	800-770-8973	Nevada	800-326-6868
California	800-735-2929	Oregon	800-526-0661
Hawaii	808-643-8833	Washington	206-587-5500
Idaho	208-334-2100		

OPM Job Information Telephone Directory - Washington D.C. Federal Job Information Center Self-Service Telephone System; 202-606-2700. This telephone system contains a variety of material, ranging from general employment information of interest to applicants, to specific job opportunities in the federal government. Complete instructions on the use of the system and various options are provided upon access. Use the message codes listed below for specific information. This system is available 24 hours a day, 7 days a week. You can talk with an information specialist Monday through Friday from 8:00 a.m. to 4:00 p.m. Eastern Standard Time, by dialing message code 000 after the initial message. A complete listing is provided in Chapter Three.

People With Disabilities - Special testing arrangements - Washington D.C. area, 202-606-2528.

Temple University Computer Institute - Temple University, Computer Institute, 301 Ritter Hall, Philadelphia, PA 19122; 215-787-5632. Publishes a comprehensive Information Access: Technology Resources to Support the Employment of People with Disabilities guide. Lists hundreds of on-line direct access data bases and electronic bulletin boards of which a number of services provide job placement and career guidance information for people with disabilities. Write or call to obtain a copy of this valuable networking resource. Also request a copy of their On-Line Services Reference Manual for The Assistive Technology Data Base, The Computer Institute Bulletin Board System, Electronic Mail and their VAX Phone system.

COMPUTER BULLETIN BOARDS featuring FEDERAL JOB OPPORTUNITIES

These are electronic computer bulletin boards that can only be accessed with a computer, modem, and communication software, as well as a telephone line. You may scan current open examination and vacancy announcements **nationwide** while you're on line or you can download them to your computer.

National Federal Job Opportunities Bulletin Board - 24 hours a day - **912-757-3100.**

Regional Bulletin Boards:

Washington, DC Area	(202) 606-1113
Southeastern States	(404) 730-2370
Northeastern States	(215) 580-2216
North Central States	(313) 226-4423
Mountain & Southwestern States	(214) 767-0316
Western States	(818) 575-6521

PLACEMENT SERVICES

ADNET ONLINE - 8440 Woodfield Crossing Blvd., Ste. 170, Indianapolis, IN 46240; 800-682-2901, accessible through computer modem. This menu driven program lists job vacancies in 17 job categories. Each category offers an extensive selection menu. Free to Prodigy subscribers. A free online trial access is offered through computer modem dialing at 317-579-4857, 2,400 baud, 7 bits, even parity, 1 stop bit. At the prompt type guest. Call for complete details.

American Public Health Association Job Placement Service - 1015 15th St. N.W., Washington, DC 20005; 202/789-5600. This association provides numerous services to members. Call for job service application procedures and costs.

Career Placement Registry - 302 Swann Ave., Alexandria, VA 22301; 800/-368-3093, registration $15/students and $25 to $45/nonstudents depending on salary range. Entry forms available upon request. DIALOG accessible, updated weekly; over 100,000 employers use database.

Federal Job Matching Service - Box 594, Dept D30, NY 10546; 1-800-824-5000. This service matches your background to federal requirements. Applicants send in a federal application, SF-171. You will receive back a list of federal job titles and grade levels for which you qualify. Federal job descriptions and qualification statements are provided for every job title that the service identifies for you. The fee is $30, but only $25 with a subscription label in your name from the Federal Jobs Digest. This service matches your background to federal job requirements not to specific job openings. After you receive your reply you can submit your application direct to agencies listed in the FJD that are hiring in that occupation.

NOTE: Many of the OVR and VA rehabilitation centers offer job placement services. Many associations also offer valuable services including job placement to their members. Refer to the associations lists that follow and contact local OVR and VA facilities in your area to identify available job placement services.

DIRECTORIES

Americans With Disabilities Act Resource Directory - U.S. Equal Employment Opportunity Commission, 1801 L St., N.W., Washington, D.C. 20507; 800-669-EEOC (Voice) or 800-800-3302 (TDD), 209 pages, first copy free. One of the most comprehensive resource guides available. Offers information on federal agencies that enforce ADA provisions, national non-government technical assistance resources, regional and state locations of federal programs, and telecommunications relay services.

Encyclopedia of Associations 1992 - Gale Research, Inc., 835 Penobscot Bldg., Detroit, MI 48226; 800-877-4253. The complete set costs $320 and includes approximately 22,000 associations. Available at many libraries. Use this resource to identify associations for your specific disability. This resource is also available in two additional formats including CD ROM and the DIALOG online computer system. For information on how to subscribe to online services contact DIALOG Information Services - 3460 Hillview Ave., Palo Alto, CA 94304; 800-334-2564.

Telecommunications For The Deaf, Inc. - Publishes a directory listing of businesses with TDD numbers.

GENERAL INFORMATION

Associations & Organizations

The following list of associations and organizations offer numerous services to people with physical or mental impairments. Many offer job placement services, provide on-site accessibility surveys, job analysis and offer advice and support to the group represented. Contact individual listings for details of services provided.

American Cancer Society - 1599 Clifton Rd., Atlanta, GA 30329; 404-320-3333. Refers employers to organizations offering help in recruiting qualified individuals with disabilities, and community programs offering consultation and technical assistance to cancer patients, survivors, and their families. Publishes information on the employment of cancer patients and survivors.

American Council of the Blind - 1155 15th St., N.W., Ste. 720, Washington, D.C. 20005; 202-467-5081 or 800-424-8666. Provides information on topics affecting the employment of individuals who are blind, including job seeking strategies, job accommodations, electronic aids, and employment discrimination. Provides information on job openings for individuals who are blind and visually impaired. Offers free legal assistance in employment discrimination cases.

American Foundation For The Blind - 15 West 16th St., New York, NY 10011; 212-620-2000 (Voice) or 212-620-2158. Promotes networking and mentorship opportunities by matching individuals who are blind and visually impaired through a national database.

American Speech-Language-Hearing Association - 10801 Rockville Pike, Rockville, MD 20852; 301-897-5700 (Voice), **Helpline** 800-638-8255 (Voice/TDD). Provides information and technical assistance on overcoming communication barriers.

The ARC (Formerly Association for Retarded Citizens) - 500 East Border St., Ste. 300, Arlington, TX 76010; 817-261-6003 (Voice) or 817-277-0553 (TDD). Aids the employment of people with mental retardation by providing information and on-site technical assistance to employers who hire, train, and retain mentally retarded workers.

Arthritis Foundation - 1314 Spring St., N.W., Atlanta, GA 30309; 404-872-7100 or 800-283-7800. Helps people with arthritis and lupus obtain and retain employment.

Direct Link For The Disabled - P.O. Box 1036, Solvang, CA 93464; 805-688-1603. Provides technical assistance for making job accommodations and worksite adaptations for individuals with disabilities. Offers a job placement service.

Disabled American Veterans - 807 Maine Ave., SW, Washington, DC 20024; 202-554-3501 (Voice/TDD). Provides information on recruitment sources for veterans with disabilities. Offers a broad range of services to disabled veterans.

Epilepsy Foundation of America - 4351 Garden City Dr., Landover, MD 20785; 301-459-3700 or 800 EFA-1000 (Voice/TDD). Maintains a network of local employment assistance programs, which provide education and support to employers on epilepsy and employment issues including employment referrals.

Goodwill Industries of America - 9200 Wisconsin Ave., Bethesda, MD 20814-3896; 301-530-6500 (Voice) or 301-530-0836 (TDD). Works cooperatively with employers to place qualified individuals with disabilities in jobs, and offers job seeking skills training and placement services to individuals with disabilities.

Helen Keller National Center for Deaf-Blind Youths and Adults - 111 Middle Neck Rd., Sands Point, NY 11050; 516-944-8900 (Voice/TDD). Provides job placement for deaf-blind individuals, and on-site support services for employers and employees.

Mainstream, Inc. - 3 Bethesda Metro Center, Ste. 830, Bethesda, MD 20814; 301-654-2400 (Voice/TDD) or 301-654-2401 (Voice/TDD). Provides career counseling, job seeking skills training, job placement, and job development for individuals with disabilities.

National Center For Learning Disabilities - 99 Park Ave., New York, NY 10016; 212-687-7211. Provides information, referral, public education and education and outreach programs on learning disabled. Offers job placement and publishes a quarterly newsletter.

National Diabetes Information Clearinghouse - Box NDIC, 9000 Rockville Pike, Bethesda, MD 20892; 301-468-2162.

National Downs Syndrome Congress - 1800 Dempster St., Park Ridge, IL 60068; 800-232-6372. Provides general information on Down Syndrome and the employment of individuals with Down Syndrome. Provides supported employment programs for individuals with Down Syndrome.

National Mental Health Association - 1021 Prince St., Alexandria, VA 22314; 703-684-7722.

National Multiple Sclerosis Society - 733 Third Avenue., New York, NY 10017; 212-986-3240.

National Spinal Cord Injury Association - 600 West Cummings Park, Ste. 2000, Woburn, MA 01801; 617-935-2722 or 800-962-9629.

Spina Bifida Association of America - 1700 Rockville Pike, Ste. 250, Rockville, MD 20852; 301-770-7222 and 800-621-3141 (Voice).

United Cerebral Palsy Association, Inc. - 1522 K St., N.W., Washington, DC 20005; 202-842-1266 (Voice/TDD) or 800-872-5827 (Voice/TDD).

Books, Pamphlets, & Brochures

Accent On Information - P.O. Box 700, Bloomington, IL 61702; 309-378-2961. Send for their free guide on obtaining employment for people with disabilities.

JAN (Job Accommodation Network) - They will send out an informational brochure upon request. Call 1-800-JAN-7234 for free consulting and information about job accommodations and the employability of people with disabilities. A service of the President's Committee on Employment of People with Disabilities.

Ready Willing & Available (A Business Guide For Hiring People With Disabilities) - Free from The Presidents Committee, 1331 F Street, NW, Washington, D.C. 20004-1107; 202-376-6200, 202-376-6205 (TDD).

Technical Assistance Manual on the Employment Provisions of ADA - U.S. Equal Employment Opportunity Commission, 1801 L St., N.W., Washington, D.C. 20507; 800-669-EEOC (Voice) or 800-800-3302 (TDD), over 200 pages, $25 per year includes basic manual and annual supplements for the next two years. Assists employers, and persons with disabilities learn about their obligations and rights under the ADA Act Title I.

Worklife - The Presidents Committee, Senior Editor, PCEPD, 1331 F Street, NW, Washington, D.C. 20004; 202-376-6200, 202-376-6205 (TDD). A limited number of free complimentary subscriptions are available from the President's Committee. A publication on employment and people with disabilities, focusing on employment information that is vital to both employers and persons with disabilities seeking employment.

Computer Software

Federal Occupational and Career Informational System (FOCIS) - National Technical Information Services, 5285 Port Royal Rd., Springfield, VA 22161; 1-800-553-NTIS, 703-487-4650, $49.95, order # various with disk size, call for specific ordering information for your computer system. IBM-PC or compatible computers, DOS 3.0 +, 5 MB of memory required, Dbase III Plus. Developed by OPM to help job seekers obtain information about federal careers and occupations. The software is menu driven with no prior experience on a PC needed by the user. Consists of three modules: career guidance, occupational information, and tips on how to get a job. Covers 360 federal white-collar occupations and 450 federal organizations.

Quick & Easy SF-171s - Available in IBM-PC/XT/AT - 630K - DOS 3.0 or greater. Supports most printers including laser and deskjets. Customize your SF-171 federal employment application to fit the requirements of the position. Easily edit your experience and qualifications to reflect the demands of the position that you want, and keep as many versions of your SF-171 Federal Employment Application on disk. This program is not just another fill in the blanks forms program. It is a complete system specifically designed to fill in and manage the SF-171. This program generates the complete form electronically. $49.95 for the personal version. Available from D-Amp Publication's back-of-book catalog.

CHAPTER TEN

EMPLOYMENT SECRETS

Many talented job seekers are frustrated by the required paperwork and give up prematurely. If you take the time to thoroughly complete your application and seek out all available job vacancies your chances will increase substantially.

APPLY EARLY

It pays to start your employment search early for federal jobs, well in advance of the time you will be available for employment. Applications usually take six to eight weeks for processing. It may take longer if written tests are required. From the time you first identify an opening to actual interviews and hiring can take from 2 to 4 months or longer.

All individuals interested in federal employment should start researching the system, identifying jobs, and preparing for tests - if required - months in advance.

> The **NPR** reported that significant problems exist with the over-regulated federal personnel system. The Clinton administration plans to submit proposals to congress that, if enacted, will streamline the federal hiring process. Eventually, many of the aggravations associated with the federal job search will either be eliminated or the process simplified.

APPLY FREQUENTLY

Most job hunters send in an application for only one announcement. Seek out all available bids and continue to send in applications with every opportunity. The more bids sent in the greater your chances. Review Appendices to identify all of the job series that you can possibly qualify for. If you are having difficulty identifying job series that fit your training, experience and abilities you may wish to take advantage of the "Federal Job Matching Service" provided by Federal Jobs Digest. Refer to Chapter Three's "Placement Services" resources for complete details. You will find that you can qualify for several to twenty or more job series. Don't overlook Wage Grade (WG) positions. When requesting bids from the FJIC ask for announcements related to all of the identified job series. You will be surprised by just how many you qualify for.

Consider the electronics technician field for example. All of the following job series require basic electronic technician skills:[1]

GS-856 Electronics Technician

GS-802 Electronics Engineering Technician

WG-2500 Wire Communications Equipment Installation & Maintenance Family

WG-2600 Electronic Equipment Installation & Maintenance Family

WG-2602	Electronic Measurement Equipment Mechanic
WG-2604	Electronic Mechanic
WG-2606	Electronic Industrial Controls
WG-2698	Electronic Digital Computer Mechanic
WG-2610	Electronic Integrated Systems Mechanic

WG-2800 Electrical Installation Maintenance Family (4 occupations)

WG-3000 Instrument Work Family (5 occupations)

OVER 40 ELECTRONIC RELATED JOBS ARE LISTED UNDER VARIOUS WAGE GRADE FAMILIES

[1]Publication TS-56, March 1990, Part 3, Definitions of Trades and Labor Job Families and Occupations.

GETTING IN THE FRONT DOOR

"There are two things to aim at in life: first, to get what you want; and after that to enjoy it. Only the wisest of people achieve the second."

LOGAN PEARSALL SMITH

A BIRD IN THE HAND IS WORTH TWO IN THE BUSH

Getting in is half the battle. If you want to enter a certain field with a particular agency and there are currently no openings, apply for other jobs with that agency. For instance, if you qualify for a logistics/supply position and they only have clerk openings it may be to your benefit to apply and get on board. Agencies generally advertise in-house first to offer qualified workers opportunities for advancement. You will have a good chance to bid on other jobs if you have the qualifications and a good track record.

MOBILITY - CONTACT MULTIPLE FJICs

Request bids from several FJICs. Even if you wouldn't consider relocating you will at least receive a rating for a specific job series. Once rated send copies of your rating notification and SF-171 to agencies in your area. Always send a short cover letter explaining what job you are interested in and furnish some personal background. Each year additional agencies apply for and receive direct hire or the new Case Examining authority for specific job skills. The more contacts you make the better.

If you are willing to relocate, send to all FJICs within your area of consideration and subscribe to one of the federal job newsletters such as the *Federal Jobs Digest*. **The larger the area of consideration the better your chances.** Choice jobs with certain agencies often require an applicant to accept a job in a not so desirable location. Often, agencies have to advertise through OPM because the area isn't desirable and they can't get in-house bidders. Once hired, you will have an opportunity to bid to better locations after you are trained and have the required agency experience.

During my early government career I accepted a job with an agency in a remote little town of 7,000 inhabitants. After completing the required initial training and receiving what the agency calls system certification I was able to successfully bid to the area of my choice. It took me three years to gain the training and experience needed to bid out to other areas. When I did relocate the agency paid for the complete move including real estate expenses.

One important fact to remember: In most cases **your first move is at your expense**. If you are willing to relocate you will be responsible for the cost of the move. However, if you bid out to other locations after your first year of employment the government picks up the tab. The moving allowances are generous. Agencies often buy your house from you at close to market rates, pay for the move of your household goods, and pay real estate sales commissions and closing costs at your new location. On top of this you will receive 60 days of temporary quarters expenses at your new location, 60 hours of leave for the move, and a free house hunting trip may be authorized.

CAUTION

Don't jump blindly at an employment offer. Many agencies have difficulty filling jobs in high-cost living areas such as New York, L.A., and Washington D.C. Investigate the cost of living in the area you are selected for before saying yes. If you can't afford to live in the area you may have to turn down the initial offer.

"LOOK BEFORE YOU LEAP"

TRAINING AND EXPERIENCE

Often, applicants neglect to add valuable work experience and training to their bid package. Go back as many years as the related education and experience goes. For example, if you were a supply specialist in the military in 1965, and you are applying for a supply/logistics position, then by all means add your military experience and training to block 24 of the SF-171.

Many agencies require supplemental application qualification forms. If you are applying for an electronics position these forms often capture your math, electronics training and specific experience background. List all of your math training back through high school. Trigonometry and algebra are required for many electronic positions. If you only had these subjects in high school and you don't list them you won't be rated eligible for the position.

"THE SECRET TO SUCCESS IS THAT THE HARDER

YOU WORK THE LUCKIER YOU GET."

KEYS TO SUCCESS

There are three basic ingredients to successfully finding federal employment for qualified applicants:

- **Invest the time and energy needed to seek out all openings.**

- **Correctly fill out all required application forms.**

- **Don't give up when you receive your first rejection.**

You can learn from rejections by contacting the selecting official. Ask what training and/or experience would enhance your bid package for future positions. If they specify certain training or experience, then work to achieve the desired skills.

You may discover that you did have the specific skills needed. However, you either neglected to put these facts in your bid or considered them unimportant for the job applied for. This happens frequently. It doesn't pay to debate your qualifications over spilled milk. The job has already been filled. Thank the selecting official for his candor and time then **revise your bid for the next opening.**

Write the selecting official a BRIEF letter of thanks and explain that you neglected to incorporate the recommended skills in the original application. Send him a copy of your revised SF-171 for future reference. **Managers appreciate dealing with rational and mature individuals and you will be remembered.**

It took me two years to land my first competitive federal civil service job. I was not aware of the employment options available at that time and I simply sent written requests for bids every two weeks to the local FJIC. Today there are many options available through special emphasis hiring, case and direct hire authority, Outstanding Scholar Programs, student employment, Administrative Careers With America and internships, to name a few. Add to this list the over 1,000 job resources provided throughout this book. Take advantage of as many of the programs that you qualify for to expedite your career search. Don't give up or get overly frustrated with the paperwork mill surrounding federal employment. There are software programs available today to soften the SF-171 Employment Application process. If you can't afford a copy many counselors from larger schools purchase these programs. Finally, I must add that it is unwise to get angry with the process; instead of getting mad, **GET INVOLVED**.

NETWORKING

Networking is a term used to define the establishment of a group of individuals that assist one another for mutual benefit. You can establish your own network by talking to personnel specialists, contacting regional agency employment departments, conducting informational interviews, and by bidding on all applicable job announcements. By following the guidelines outlined in the book and using your innate common sense your chances of success are magnified ten fold.

Use the over 1,000 contacts presented in this book to begin your personal employment network. Add to this information individual contacts that you make with local agencies.

We grow great by dreams. All big men are dreamers. They see things in the soft haze of a spring day or in the red fire of a long winter's evening. Some of us let these dreams die, but others nourish and protect them, nurse them to the sunshine and light which come always to those who sincerely hope that their dreams will come true.

WOODROW WILSON

APPENDIX A

JOB HUNTERS CHECKLIST
"Your Career Calendar"

WHAT TO DO NOW

☐ Review the Federal Occupations Lists in Appendix D. This appendix will provide a list of specific Federal jobs that you may qualify for.

☐ Call or write the Federal Job Information Center (FJIC) in the area you are seeking employment. SEE APPENDIX B for a complete national listing. Request the following information:

A. Announcements for specific job series. SEE APPENDIX D
B. A list of local government agencies.   SEE APPENDIX C
C. Application form, SF-171.

☐ Contact regional and local agency personnel offices. See Appendix C for regional office addresses and phone numbers. This appendix also provides a summary of most agencies and departments and provides employment contact phone numbers and addresses.

A. Request agency career opportunities brochures.
B. Talk with agency personnel offices and request job announcements and information on special hiring programs.
C. Obtain local government field office phone numbers from your phone directory. Look under U.S. Government in the Blue Pages.

> *Applications will only be accepted for current announcements. If you're a Clerk Typist and the government doesn't have typist openings, they will not accept your application.*

☐ **CALL THE CAREER AMERICA CONNECTION. 1-912-757-3000.** This service costs $.40 per minute. Callers receive updates on what jobs are available and you can leave voice messages to request open job announcements. **THIS SERVICE IS NOT ONLY FOR COLLEGE GRADUATES.** IT ALSO PROVIDES INFORMATION ON STUDENT HIRING PROGRAMS. IF YOU HAVE AT LEAST THREE YEARS OF EXPERIENCE IN A FIELD YOU MAY ALSO QUALIFY FOR COLLEGE HOT LINE JOB ANNOUNCEMENTS. DETAILS IN CHAPTER THREE.

☐ Review Chapter Three's listings to identify job announcement resources. Also review:

    ☐ Chapter Three for Student Hiring Programs.

    ☐ Chapter Six for Veteran's Hiring programs.

    ☐ Chapter Seven for overseas job resources.

    ☐ Chapter Eight for U.S. Postal Service jobs.

    ☐ Chapter Nine for job resources for people with disabilities.

☐ Locate your high school and college transcripts, military records, awards, and professional licenses. Collect past employment history; salary, addresses, phone numbers, dates employed, etc.

☐ Visit your local library and review these publications;

A. *The United States Government Manual.* This book provides agency descriptions, addresses, contacts and basic employment information.

B. *The Federal Career Directory.* If your library doesn't have this publication check with a local college placement office. This directory provides an agency description, lists typical entry level positions, agency contacts, student employment programs, etc.

Note: Books A & B are published by OPM.

C. *The Occupational Outlook Quarterly*, published by the U.S. Department of Labor, Bureau of Labor Statistics. This is a highly informative quarterly publication that highlights employment trends and features interesting career articles.

WHAT's AVAILABLE

☐ Call local agencies listed in the phone directory. Also visit local Federal Buildings. **REQUEST INFORMATIONAL INTERVIEWS** per instructions in chapter three.

☐ Research agencies in Appendix C of this book, the United States Government Manual, and the Federal Career Directory.

☐ Review Appendix D for occupational listings of federal jobs by title and series. **Identify all job series that you could possibly qualify for**.

☐ Review Chapters Three, Six, Seven, Eight and Nine.

APPLYING FOR A JOB

☐ You will receive requested job announcements within a week. Each announcement will be accompanied by all required application forms. You can use the blank SF-171 form in Chapter Four to draft your application while waiting for forms from OPM.

☐ If no vacancies exist for your specialty, call or write the FJIC frequently to find out about new openings. FJICs <u>WILL NOT</u> place your name on a list for automatic notification when jobs do become available.

☐ Contact other FJICs and Individual agencies. The more contacted the greater chance of finding open announcements.

☐   Complete and sign ALL application forms received with the bid. (Type them if possible). Follow SF-171 instruction presented in Chapter 4.

☐   Retain a copy of your SF-171 and all other forms required in the announcement. These copies can be used for other bids. However, an original signature must be on all copies sent.

☐   Send in the completed forms to the address specified on the announcement.

CAUTION

APPLICATIONS MUST ARRIVE BY NO LATER THAN THE CLOSING DATE OF THE ANNOUNCEMENT FOR YOUR APPLICATION TO BE CONSIDERED.

TEST RESULTS

Your application will be processed and results returned to you within several weeks. You will receive a *Notice of Rating or Notice of Results* informing you of your eligibility by mail. If rated eligible, your name will be placed on the Federal Register for that position along with all other eligible applicants. Your name and application will be forwarded to a selecting official as positions become available.

APPENDIX B

FEDERAL JOB INFORMATION CENTERS

ALABAMA
Huntsville: Bldg. 600, Ste. 341, 3322 Memorial Pkwy. South 35801-5311, (205) 544-5803, Self Service: M-F/7-4

ALASKA
Anchorage: 222 W. 7th Ave., Box 22, 99513 (907) 271-5821, Staff on Duty: T-Th/11-1

ARIZONA
Pheonix: Century Plaza Bldg., Rm 1415 3225 N. Central Ave., 85012 (602) 640-5800, Self Service: M-F/9-3:30

ARKANSAS
See San Antonio, TX (405) 231-4948

CALIFORNIA
Los Angeles: 9650 Flair Dr., Ste. 100A, El Monte, 91731, (818) 575-6510, Staff on Duty: M-F/9-3

Sacramento: Federal Bldg., 1029 J. St., 2nd Floor 95814, (916) 551-1464 Staff on Duty: M-F/9-12

San Francisco: 211 Main St. 2nd Floor, Rm. 235, 94120, (415) 744-5627, Staff on Duty: M-F/9-12

COLORADO
Denver: P.O. Box 25167, 80225, (303) 969-7050. Located at 12345 W. Alameda Pkwy., Lakewood, CO Request forms from (303) 969-7065, Staff on Duty: M-F/12-3:45, Self Service: M-F/9-12

CONNECTICUT
See Massachusetts FJIC

DELAWARE
See Philadelphia, PA FJIC

DISTRICT OF COLUMBIA
Metro Area: 1900 E Street, N.W., Rm 1416, 20415, (202) 606-2700, Staff on Duty: M-F/8-4

FLORIDA
Orlando: 3444 McCrory Pl., Suite 125 32803-3701, (407) 648-6148, Staff on Duty: MWF/9-3, Self Service: TTh/8-4

GEORGIA
Atlanta: Richard B. Russell Federal Bldg., Rm, 940A, 75 Spring St., SW 30303, (404) 331-4315, Staff on Duty: M-F/9-4

GUAM
Agana: Pacific Daily News Bldg., Rm. 902 96910, (671) 472-7451

HAWAII
Honolulu (Plus Overseas), Fed. Bldg., Rm. 5316, 300 Ala Moana Blvd. 96850, (808) 541-2791; Overseas jobs (808) 541-2784, Staff on Duty: M-F/9-12

IDAHO
See Washington Listing

ILLINOIS
Chicago: 175 W. Jackson, Rm. 530, 60604, (313) 353-6192, Self Service: M-F/7-4:45 (For Madison & St. Clair Counties, see St. Louis, MO FJIC)

INDIANA
Indianapolis: Minton-Capehart Fed. Bldg., 575 N. Pennsylvania St. 46204, (317) 226-7161, Self-Service: M-F/7-6 (For Clark, Dearborn, & Floyd counties, see Ohio FJIC)

IOWA
See Kansas City, MO listing (816) 426-7757 (For Scott County see Illinois FJIC) (For Pottawatamie County see Kansas FJIC)

KANSAS
Wichita: One-Twenty Bldg., Rm. 101, 120 S. Market St. 67202, (316) 269-0552; Self Service: M-F/8-4 (Johnson, Leavenworth and Wyandotte Counties, see Kansas City, MO)

KENTUCKY
See Ohio FJIC (For Henderson County, see Indiana)

LOUISIANA
New Orleans: 1515 Poydras St., Suite 608 70112, (504) 589-2764, Self-Service: M-F/9-4

MAINE
See Massachusetts FJIC

MARYLAND
Baltimore: Rm. 101, 300 West Pratt St., 21201, (410) 962-3822, Staff on Duty: M-F/1-3, Self Service: M-F/9-4

MASSACHUSETTS
Boston: Thos. P O'Neill Fed Bldg., 10 Causeway St. 02222-1031, (671) 565-5900, Staff on Duty: M-F/9-2

MICHIGAN
Detroit: 477 Michigan Ave., Rm. 565, 48226, (313) 226-6950, Self-Service: M-F/8-4:30

MINNESOTA
Twin Cities: 1 Federal Drive, Rm. 501, Bishop Henry Whipple Federal Bldg.,

Ft. Snelling, 55111, (612) 725-3430, Self Service: M-F/7:30-4:30

MISSISSIPPI
See Alabama FJIC

MISSOURI
Kansas City: Federal Bldg. Rm. 134, 601 E. 12th St. 64106, (816) 426-5702, Self Service: M-F/8-4 (For counties west of and including Mercer, Grundy, Livingston, Carroll, Saline, Pettis, Benton, Hickory, Dallas, Webster, Douglas, and Ozark.)

St. Louis: 400 Old Post Office Bldg., Rm., 815 Olive St. 63101, (314) 539-2285, Self Service: M-F/8-4 (For all other Missouri Counties not listed under Kansas City)

MONTANA
See Colorado FJIC Listing

NEBRASKA
See Kansas FJIC Listing

NEVADA
See Sacramento or Los Angeles FJIC

NEW HAMPSHIRE
See Massachusetts FJIC

NEW JERSEY
(For Bergan, Essex, Hudson, Hunterdon, Middlesex, Morris, Passaic, Somerset, Sussex, Union, and Warren Counties, see New York City)

(For all other NJ Counties, see Philadelphia's FJIC Listing)

NEW MEXICO
Albuquerque: Fed. Bldg., 505 Marquette Ave., Ste. 910, 87102, (505) 766-2906, Staff on Duty: M-Th/8-4

NEW YORK
New York City: Jacob B. Javits Fed. Bldg., 26 Federal Plaza 10278, (212) 264-0422/0423, Staff on Duty: M-F/10-2

Syracuse: P.O. Box 7267, James M. Hanley Fed. Bldg., 100 S. Clinton St. 13260, (315) 423-5660, Self Service: M-F/9-3

NORTH CAROLINA
Raleigh: 4407 Bland Rd., Ste. 202, 27609-6296, (919) 790-2822, Self Service: M-F/8-4:30

NORTH DAKOTA
See Minnesota FJIC Listing

OHIO
Dayton: Fed. Bldg., 200 W. 2nd St., Rm. 506, 45402, (513) 225-2720, Self Service: M-F/7-6 (For Van Wert, Auglaize, Harden, Marion, Crawford, Richland, Ashland, Wayne, Stark, Carrol, Columbiana counties and farther north, see Michigan FJIC)

OKLAHOMA
(See San Antonio, TX 406-231-4848)

OREGON
Portland: Federal Bldg., 1220 SW 3rd Ave., Rm. 376, 97204, (503) 326-4141 Staff on Duty: M-F/12-3, Self Service: M-F/8-12

PENNSYLVANIA
Harrisburg: Federal Bldg., Rm. 168, P.O. Box 761, 17108, (717) 782-4494, Staff on Duty: MTThF/8-12

Philadelphia: Wm J. Green, Jr., Fed Bldg., 600 Arch St., Rm. 1416, 19106 (215) 597-7440, Staff on Duty: M-F/10:30-2:30, Self service: M-F/8:30-3:30

Pittsburgh: Fed. Bldg., 1000 Liberty Ave., Rm. 119, 15222, Self-Service: M-F/9-4. (Walk-in only. For mail or telephone, see Philadelphia listing)

PUERTO RICO
San Juan: U.S. Federal Bldg., Rm. 340, 150 Carlos Chardon Ave., Hato Rey 00918-1710, (809) 766-5242, Staff on Duty: M-F/7:30-Noon

RHODE ISLAND
See Massachusetts Listing

SOUTH CAROLINA
See Raleigh, North Carolina FJIC

SOUTH DAKOTA
See Minnesota FJIC Listing

TENNESSEE
Memphis: 200 Jefferson Ave., Suite 1312, 38103, Self Service: M-F/8-4 (Walk-in only. For mail or telephone, see Alabama listing.)

TEXAS
Corpus Christi (See San Antonio)

Dallas: 6B10, 1100 Commerce St. 75242, (214) 767-8035, Self-Service: M-F/8-4:30

Houston: (See San Antonio listing)

San Antonio: 8610 Broadway, Rm. 305, 78217, (210) 229-6611 or 6600. For forms call (210) 229-6618. Staff on Duty: M-F/7:30-4:30

UTAH
See Colorado FJIC Listing

VERMONT
See Massachusetts FJIC Listing

VIRGIN ISLANDS
See Puerto Rico. (809) 774-8790

VIRGINIA
Norfolk: Fed. Bldg., Rm. 220, Granby Mall 23510-1886, (804) 441-3355, Self Service: M-F/9-4

Norfolk VEC Job Service Office, 5145 E. Virginia Beach Blvd., OPM Staff on Duty: M-F/8:15-4:30

WASHINGTON
Seattle: Fed. Bldg., 915 Second Ave., Rm. 110, 98174, (206) 220-6400, Staff on Duty: M-F/12-3:30, Self Service: M-F/8-Noon

WEST VIRGINIA
See Ohio FJIC Listing

WISCONSIN
For Counties in close proximity to Milwaukee, (312) 353-6189. All others refer to Minnesota Listing.

WYOMING
See Colorado FJIC Listing

APPENDIX C

FEDERAL AGENCY CONTACT LIST

This Appendix provides a functional summary and general employment information for the three branches of the government and for eighteen federal departments under the Executive Branch. Larger independent agencies are also listed.

The information and statistics in this appendix were extracted from The United States Government Manual 1992/93, Federal Civilian Workforce Statistics Employment & Trends as of March 1993, The Federal Career Directory - S/N 006-000-01339-2, and the Central Personnel Data File, Office of Workforce Information.

NOTICE

Many government agencies are converting their telephone lines to a less expensive service. In the process many agency telephone numbers will change. The telephone numbers listed throughout this guide were accurate up through July of 1993. If you call a number that is not in service you may receive a recorded message. Some recorded messages give the new number, others do not.

If you're unable to reach an agency at the listed number, call directory assistance in that city. Directory assistance can be reached by dialing the area code plus 555-1212. For directory assistance in the metropolitan DC area call (202) 555-1212, Virginia (703) 555-1212, and (301) 555-1212 for agencies located in Maryland in close proximity to the District of Columbia.

The Clinton/Gore National Performance Review Report suggests numerous proposals to consolidate services and reduce inefficiency throughout government. The President has executive powers to implement specific actions and agencies are being directed to reorganize. Many agencies will consolidate offices and functions over the next two to five years. If the office you are trying to contact closes, call the agency's Washington DC headquarters for employment information.

LEGISLATIVE BRANCH

The Congress of the United States was created by Article 1, section 1, of the Constitution. All legislative powers are vested in the Congress of the United States, which consists of a Senate and House of Representatives. The Legislative Branch has 37,430 full-time, 538 part-time, and 413 intermittent employees.

The Senate is comprised of 100 members, 2 from each state. Senators are elected for a six year term. The House of Representatives is made up of 435 Representatives. Each state elects Representatives based on population distribution. The larger the state the more Representatives they have.

The Vice President of the United States is the Presiding Officer of the Senate. The following offices are under the Legislative Branch (The number employed by each office is noted in parentheses):

Congress	**(20,298)**
Architect of the Capital	**(2,360)**
United States Botanical Garden	**(51)**
General Accounting Office	**(5,123)**
Government Printing Office	**(4,809)**
Library of Congress	**(4,941)**
Office of Technology Assessment	**(214)**
Congressional Budget Office	**(230)**
Copyright Royalty Tribunal	**(9)**

ARCHITECT OF THE CAPITOL
U.S. Capitol Building, Washington D.C. 20515
(202)-225-1200

The Architect of the Capitol is responsible for the care and maintenance of the Capitol Building and nearby buildings and grounds.

GENERAL ACCOUNTING OFFICE
Office of Public Information General Accounting Office, 441 G St. NW., Washington DC 20548
(202) 275-5067

The General Accounting Office is the investigative arm of Congress and is charged with examining all matters related to the receipt and disbursement of public funds.

LIBRARY OF CONGRESS
Recruitment & Placement Office
101 Independence Ave. SE.
Washington, DC 20540
(202) 707-6080

The Library of Congress is the national library of the United States, offering diverse materials for research including comprehensive historical collections. Direct applications and inquiries to this office. An employment message is recorded on (202) 707-5295.

CONGRESSIONAL BUDGET OFFICE
Second & D Streets SW
Washington, DC 20515
(202) 226-2621

Provides Congress with assessments of the economic impact of the federal budget.

UNITED STATES BOTANIC GARDENS
Office of Director, 245 First St. SW., Washington
D.C. 20024
(202) 225-8333

The United States Botanic Garden collects and grows various vegetable productions of this and other countries for exhibition and public display, student study, scientists, and garden clubs.

GOVERNMENT PRINTING OFFICE
Chief, Employment Branch
North Capitol & H Streets NW
Washington, DC 20401
(202) 512-1198

This office prints, binds, and distributes the publications of the Congress as well as the executive departments. Employment primarily in administrative, clerical and technical fields. Hires through OPM registers.

OFFICE OF TECHNOLOGY ASSESSMENT
600 Pennsylvania Ave SE
Washington, DC 20510-8025
(203) 224-9241

This office reports to the Congress on the scientific and technical impact of government policies and proposed legislative initiatives.

COPYRIGHT ROYALTY TRIBUNAL
1111 Twentieth Street NW
Washington, DC 20036
(202) 606-4400

Establishes and monitors copyright royalty rates for various published and recorded material.

JUDICIAL BRANCH

Article III, section 1, of the Constitution of the United States provides that "the judicial power of the United States, shall be vested in one supreme Court, and in such inferior Courts as the Congress may from time to time ordain and establish." The Supreme Court was established on September 24, 1789. This Branch employs 28,018 legal professionals, clerks, administrative personnel, secretaries, and other related specialties.

The following offices are under this Branch:

The Supreme Court of the United States
Lower Courts
Special Courts
Administrative Office of the United States Courts
Federal Judicial Center

THE SUPREME COURT
U.S. SUPREME COURT BUILDING
1 First Street NE
Washington, DC 20543
(202) 479-3000

Comprised of the Chief Justice & eight Associate Justices that are nominated by the President of the United States.

SPECIAL COURTS
Clerk Special Courts
717 Madison Place NW., Washington, DC
20005. (202) 633-7257

Consists of the United States Claims Court, Court of International Trade, Court of Military Appeals, United States Tax Court, Temporary Emergency Court of Appeals, Court of Veterans Appeals, and Other Courts.

LOWER COURTS
Administrative Office of the U.S. Courts, 1 First Street NE, Washington, DC 20543
(202) 633-6236

The twelve districts include all states. There are 121 district offices located throughout the country. Consult your local telephone book for offices located near you. Includes Court of Appeals, U.S. District Courts, Territorial Courts, and the Judicial Panel on Multidistrict Litigation.

ADMINISTRATIVE OFFICE OF U.S. COURTS
Personnel Division
Washington, DC 20544
(202) 633-6236

Charged with the nonjudicial, administrative business of U.S. Courts. Includes the following divisions; Bankruptcy, Court Admin., Defender Services, Financial Management, General Counsel, Magistrates, Personnel, Probation and Statistical Analysis.

EXECUTIVE BRANCH

The president is the administrative head of the executive branch and is responsible for numerous agencies as well as 14 executive departments. The administration of this vast bureaucracy is handled by the president's cabinet that includes the heads of the 14 executive departments. The Executive Branch consists of 2,975,315 employees distributed among the 14 departments and numerous independent agencies.

The following offices, departments, and over 63 independent agencies are under the executive branch: (The number employed by each office is noted in parentheses)

Executive Office of the President	**(2,056)**
The White House Office	**(595)**
Office of Management and Budget	**(567)**
Council of Economic Advisors	**(36)**
National Security Council	**(69)**
Office of Policy Development	**(45)**
U. S. Trade Representative	**(193)**
Council on Environmental Quality	**(28)**
Office of Science & Technology Policy	**(38)**
Office of Critical Materials Council	**(2)**
Office of Administration	**(267)**
Office of the Vice President	**(21)**

THE WHITE HOUSE OFFICE
1600 Pennsylvania Avenue NW.
Washington, DC 20500
(202) 456-1414

This office assists the president in the performance
of the many duties and responsibilities of the office.
The staff facilitates and maintains communication
with the Congress, other agencies and the public.

OFFICE OF MANAGEMENT & BUDGET
Executive Office Building
Washington, DC 20503
(202) 395-3080

Evaluates, formulates, and coordinates management
procedures and program objectives within and
among federal departments and agencies.
Employment inquiries - Personnel Division, Office
of Administration, Washington, DC (202) 395-
3765.

NATIONAL SECURITY COUNCIL
Old Executive Bldg.
Washington, DC 20506
(202) 395-4974

Advises the president with respect to the integration
of domestic, foreign, and military policies relating
to national security.

OFFICE OF POLICY DEVELOPMENT
1600 Pennsylvania Ave. NW.
Washington, DC 20500
(202) 456-1414

Advises the president in the formulation,
evaluation, and coordination of long-range domestic
and economic policy.

UNITED STATES TRADE REPRESENTATIVE
600 Seventeenth Street NW.
Washington, DC 20506
(202) 395-3230

Responsible for the direction of all trade
negotiations of the United States and for the
formulation of trade policy for the United States.

ENVIRONMENTAL QUALITY COUNCIL
722 Jackson Place NW.
Washington, DC 20503
(202) 395-5750

Develops and recommends to the president national
policies that further environmental quality.

**OFFICE OF SCIENCE & TECHNOLOGY
POLICY**
New Executive Office Bldg.
Washington, DC 20506
(202) 395-7347

Provides scientific, engineering, and technological
analysis and judgement for the president with
respect to major policy, plans, and programs.

**OFFICE OF CRITICAL MATERIALS
COUNCIL**
Eighteenth & C Streets NW
Washington, DC 20240
(202) 343-1847

Ensures that sufficient supplies of strategic minerals
and materials are maintained for national security,
economic well-being, and industrial productivity.

OFFICE OF ADMINISTRATION
Old Executive Building
Washington, DC 20500
(202) 456-7050

Provides administrative support to all units within
the Executive Office of the President.

OFFICE OF THE VICE PRESIDENT
Old Executive Office Building
Washington, DC 20501
(202) 456-2326

The executive functions of the vice president
include participation in Cabinet meetings and, by
statute, membership on the National Security
Council and the Board of Regents of the
Smithsonian Institution.

THE 14 EXECUTIVE DEPARTMENTS

Agriculture	**(114,251)**
Commerce	**(38,261)**
Defense - nonmilitary	**(958,976)**
Education	**(4,949)**
Energy	**(20,695)**
Health & Human Services	**(131,625)**
Housing & Urban Development	**(13,309)**
Interior	**(78,383)**
Justice	**(97,830)**
Labor	**(17,642)**
State	**(25,992)**
Transportation	**(69,974)**
Treasury	**(172,606)**
Veterans Affairs	**(263,427)**

DEPARTMENT OF AGRICULTURE
Fourteenth Street and Independence Avenue SW
Washington, DC 20250
(202) 720-5626

This department works to maintain and improve farm income and develop and expand markets abroad for agricultural products. Helps curb and cure poverty, hunger, and malnutrition. Enhances the environment and maintains production capacity through efforts to protect the soil, water, forests, and other natural resources.

General employment inquiries may be sent to the Staffing & Personnel Information Systems Staff, Office of Personnel, Department of Agriculture, Washington, DC 20250. Phone (202) 720-5626.

EMPLOYMENT INFORMATION - Employment opportunities within the Food & Nutrition Service can be researched by contacting their national headquarters in Washington, DC. Phone (703) 305-2351. Regional offices are located in Atlanta, Chicago, Dallas, San Francisco, Denver, Boston, and NJ. For these locations look up the Department of Agriculture, Food & Nutrition Services in the above cities' phone directory or obtain addresses from their headquarters in Washington, DC.

Field meat and poultry inspector units are located throughout the country in hundreds of metropolitan areas. Employment opportunities exist at hundreds of locations that are administered from the central offices listed in this appendix.

Persons interested in employment in the Office of the Inspector General should contact the USDA Office of Personnel, Room 31-W, Administration Bldg., Washington, DC 20250. Phone (202) 720-5781.

FIELD OFFICES - FOREST SERVICE

There are ten (10) National Forest Service Regions. The Regional Forester can be contacted for job opportunities at these locations:

Northern Region	Federal Bldg., (P.O. Box 7669), Missoula, MT 59807
Rocky Mountain Region	11177 W. 8th Ave., (P.O. Box 25127), Lakewood, CO 80225
Southwestern Region	517 Gold Ave. SW., Albuquerque, NM 87102.
Intermountain Region	324 25th St., Ogden, UT 84401
Pacific Region	630 Sansome St., San Francisco, CA 94111
Pacific Northwest Region	319 SW. Pine St., (P.O. Box 3623), Portland, OR 97208
Southern Region	1720 Peachtree Rd., NW., Atlanta GA 30367
Eastern Region	310 W. Wisconsin Ave., Milwaukee, WI 53203
Alaska Region	Federal Office Bldg., (P.O. Box 21628), Juneau, AK 99802

* Note: There is no region 7.

AREA OFFICES - AGRICULTURAL RESEARCH SERVICE

Office	Address
BELTVILLE AREA - Beltville Agricultural Research Center, National Arboretum, Washington, DC	Bldg. 003, Beltville Agricultural Research Center, W. Beltsville, MD 20705
MIDSOUTH AREA - AL, KY, LA, MS, WI	P.O. Box 225, Stoneville, MS 38776
NORTHERN PLAINS AREA - CO, NM, UT, WY, KS. MT, ND, NE, SD	2625 Redwing Rd., Ft. Collins, CO 80526
NORTH ATLANTIC AREA - CT, DE, ME, MD, MA, NH, NJ, NY, PA, RI, VT, WV	600 E. Mermaid Lane, Philadelphia, PA 19118
PACIFIC WEST AREA - CA, HI, AK, AZ, ID, NV, OR, WA	800 Buchanan St., Albany, CA 94710
SOUTH ATLANTIC AREA - FL, GA, NC, PR, SC, VA, Virgin Islands	P.O. Box 5677, Athens, GA 30613
SOUTHERN PLAINS AREA - AR, NM, OK, TX	7607 Eastmark Dr., College Sta., TX 77840

The Agricultural Research Service administers fundamental and applied research to solve animal and plant protection and production problems. Research activities are carried out at 138 domestic locations. Contact the above offices for hiring information.

DEPARTMENT OF COMMERCE
**Fourteenth Street between Constitution Ave. and E Street NW.,
Washington, DC 20230
(202) 377-3827**

This department promotes the nation's international trade, economic growth, and technological advancement. The Department of Commerce provides assistance and information to increase America's competitiveness in the world economy, administers programs to prevent unfair foreign trade competition, provides research and support for the increased use of scientific engineering and technological development. Other responsibilities include the granting of patents and registration of trademarks, development of policies and conducting various research projects.

DEPARTMENT OF COMMERCE OFFICES, AGENCIES AND BUREAUS

■   **BUREAU OF THE CENSUS**
This bureau is a general purpose, statistical agency that collects, tabulates, and publishes a wide variety of statistical data about people and the economy of the nation.

FIELD ORGANIZATIONS - BUREAU OF CENSUS

ATLANTA - Ste. 3200, 101 Marietta, St. NW, GA 30303
CHARLOTTE - 222 S. Church St., NC 28202
DENVER - 6900 W. Jefferson Ave., CO 80227
DETROIT - 231 W. Lafayette, MI 48226
NEW YORK - 26 Federal Plaza, NY 10278
SEATTLE - Suite 500, 101 Stewart St., WA 98101

BOSTON - 10 Causeway St., Boston, MA 02222
CHICAGO - 175 W. Jackson Blvd., Chicago, IL 60604
DALLAS - Ste. 210, 6303 Harry Hines Blvd., TX 75235
KANSAS CITY - 4th & State, Kansas City, KS 66101
LOS ANGELES - 15350 Sherman Way, Van Nuys, CA 91406
PHILADELPHIA - 105 S. 7th St., PA 19106

■   **BUREAU OF ECONOMIC ANALYSIS**
This bureau provides a clear picture of the U. S. economy. For additional information contact the Public Information Office, Bureau of Economic Analysis, Dept. of Commerce, Washington, DC 20230. Phone (202) 523-0777.

■ **BUREAU OF EXPORT ADMINISTRATION**

The major functions of this agency are to process export license applications, conduct foreign availability studies, and enforce the U.S. export laws.

FIELD OFFICES - BUREAU OF EXPORT ADMINISTRATION

BOSTON, MA	Rm. 350, 10 Causeway St., 02222
DALLAS, TX	Rm. 622, 525 Griffin St., 75202
DES PLAINES, IL	Suite 300, 2400 E. Devon St., 60018
FORT LAUDERDALE, FL	Suite 500, 200 S. Andrews Ave., 33301
IRVINE, CA	Ste. 310, 2601 Main St., 92714
NASHUA, NH	547 Amherst St., 03063
NEW YORK, NY	Rm. 3704, 26 Federal Plaza, 10278
NEWPORT BEACH, CA	Suite 345, 3300 Irvine Blvd., 92660
PORTLAND, OR	Rm 241, 121 SW Salman St., 97204
SAN JOSE, CA	Ste. 250, 96 N. 3rd St., 95112
SANTA CLARA, CA	Ste. 226, 5201 Great America Pkwy., 95054
SPRINGFIELD, VA	Rm. 201, 8001 Forbes Pl., 22161

■ **ECONOMIC DEVELOPMENT ADMINISTRATION**

This agency was created to generate new jobs, to help protect existing jobs, and to stimulate commercial and industrial growth in economically distressed areas.

REGIONAL OFFICES - ECONOMIC DEVELOPMENT ADMINISTRATION

ATLANTA, GA	Suite 750, 1365 Peachtree St. NE., 30308
AUSTIN, TX	611 E. 6th St., 78701
CHICAGO, IL	Ste. 855, 111 N. Canal, 60606
DENVER, CO	Ste. 670, 1244 Speer Blvd., 80204
PHILADELPHIA, PA	105 S. 7th St., 19106
SEATTLE, WA	Rm. 1856, 915 2d Ave., 98174

* For further information contact the Economic Development Administration, Department of Commerce, Washington, DC 20230. Phone, (202) 377-5113.

■ **INTERNATIONAL TRADE ADMINISTRATION**

The International Trade Administration was established in 1980 to strengthen the international trade and investment position of the United States. There are 47 district offices located throughout the country. A complete listing of district offices and specific employment information can be obtained through The International Trade Administration, Department of Commerce, Washington, DC 20230. Phone, (202) 482-5138.

■ **MINORITY BUSINESS DEVELOPMENT AGENCY**
This agency was created to assist minority enterprise in achieving effective and equitable participation in the American free enterprise system. Provides management and technical assistance to minority firms on request, primarily through a network of minority business development centers.

REGIONAL OFFICES - MINORITY BUSINESS DEVELOPMENT AGENCY

ATLANTA, GA	Ste. 1930, 401 W. Peachtree St., NW., 30308
CHICAGO, IL	Ste. 1440, 33 E. Monroe St., 60603
DALLAS, TX	Ste. 7823, 1100 Commerce St. 75242
NEW YORK, NY	Ste. 37-20, 26 Federal Plaza 10278
SAN FRANCISCO, CA	Rm. 1280, 221 Main St. 91405
WASHINGTON, DC.	Rm. 6723, 14th & Constitution Ave. NW. 20230

■ **NATIONAL OCEANIC AND ATMOSPHERIC ADMINISTRATION (NOAA)**
NOAA's mission is to explore, map, and chart the global ocean and its living resources and to manage, use, and conserve those resources. Predicts atmospheric conditions, ocean, sun, and space environment. Maintains weather stations including an electronic maintenance staff to service weather radar systems and other related weather equipment. NOAA, U.S, Career Resource Center, 1335 East-West Hwy, Rm 2262, Silver Spring MD 20910. Phone, (301)-713-0677.

■ **PATENT AND TRADEMARK OFFICE**
Examines applications for patents and trademarks. Issued 78,000 patents in 1988 and registered 52,500 trademarks in that same year. Sells printed copies of issued patents and trademark registrations, records and indexes documents transferring ownership, maintains a scientific library and search files containing over 27 million documents.
Office of Personnel, 2011 Crystal Drive, Arlington, VA 22202. Phone (703)-305-8231.

■ **NATIONAL INSTITUTE OF STANDARDS AND TECHNOLOGY**
Conducts research for the nation's physical and technical measurement systems as well as scientific and technological measurement systems. Admin. Bldg., Rm A123, Gaithersburg, MD 20899. Phone, (301) 975-3007.

The Department of Commerce has four additional offices: National Telecommunications and Information Administration, Patent and Trademark Office, National Institute of Standards and Technology, and the National Technical Information Service. For employment information with these agencies contact the number listed for the Department of Commerce.

The Department of Commerce has field employment offices at the Western Administrative Support Center, 7600 Sand Point Way NE., Bin C15700, Seattle, WA 98115 (phone, 206-526-6053); the Mountain Administrative Support Center, 325 Broadway, Boulder, CO 80303 (phone, 303-497-6305); the Central Administrative Support Center, 601 East Twelfth Street, Kansas City, MO 64106 (phone, 816-426-2056); and the Eastern Administrative Support Center, 253 Monticello Avenue, Norfolk, VA 23510 (phone, 804-441-6516).

DEPARTMENT OF DEFENSE (DOD)
The Pentagon
Washington, DC 20301-1155
(703) 545-6700

Responsible for providing the military forces needed to deter war and protect the security of the United States. Major elements are the Army, Navy, Marine Corps, and Air Force, consisting of close to 2 million men and women on active duty. In case of emergency, they are backed up by 1.7 million members of the reserve forces. In addition, there are about 958,976 civilian employees in the Defense Department.

The DOD is composed of the Office of the Secretary of Defense; the military departments and the military services within those departments; the Organization of the Joint Chiefs of Staff; the unified and specified combatant commands; the Armed Forces Policy Council; the Defense agencies and various DOD field facilities.

This Executive Branch Department is the largest civilian employer. The jobs are interspersed through the United States and at several hundred installations overseas.

For overseas locations and employment contacts see Chapter Seven. The jobs in the United States are distributed throughout every state including the District of Columbia. The majority of military installations hire civilian personnel. Many are hired off of OPM's federal registers and others are special appointments for hiring veterans, spouses and family members of military personnel, the handicapped, minorities and others.

Locate military installations in your area in the yellow pages of your phone directory under GOVERNMENT. Also the blue pages in the back of the white page telephone directory provide comprehensive listings of government offices including military installations in your area.

The following list includes the larger military installations in the United States. Write the Civilian Personnel Office (CPO) at the address provided for employment information and to request open job announcements. The majority of the jobs stateside are filled through OPM registers.

ABBREVIATIONS LIST

AFB Air Force Base   **NF**   Naval Facility
AS   Air Station   **NS**   Naval Station
NAF Naval Air Facility   **NSA** Naval Support Activity
NAS Naval Air Station   **NSF** Naval Support Facility

MILITARY INSTALLATIONS IN THE U.S.A.
FACILITY, CITY, AND ZIP CODE

ALABAMA (AL)
Anniston Army Depot, Anniston 36201
Birmingham Municipal Airport, Birmingham 35217
Dannelly Field, Montgomery 36105
Fort McClellan, 36205
Fort Rucker, 36362
Hall ANG Station, Gadsden, 35954
Maxwell AFB, 36112
Redstone Arsenal, 35809
ALASKA (AK)
Eilson AFB, 99702
Elmendorf AFB, 99506
Fort Greely, Delta Junction, 98733
Fort Richardson, 99505
Fort Wainwright, Fairbanks, 99703
Kulis ANG Base, Anchorage, 99502
Adak NAS, 98791
Shemya AFB, Aleutians, 98736
ARIZONA (AZ)
Davis-Monthan AFB, 85707
Fort Huachucha, 85613
Gila Bend Air Force Auxiliary, Gila Bend, 85337
Luke AFB, 85309
Phoenix ANG, Phoenix, 85034
Sky Harbor Municipal Airport, Phoenix, 85034
Tucson Int'l Airport, Tucson, 85706
Yuma Marine Corps AS, Yuma, 85364
Yuma Proving Grounds, Yuma, 85364
CALIFORNIA (CA)
Alameda NAS, Alameda 94501
Almaden AFS, New Almaden 95042
Barslow Marine Corps Logistics Base, Barstow 92311
Bay Area Military Ocean Terminal, Oakland 94626
Beale AFB 95903
Camp Pendleton Marine Corps Base, Camp Pendleton 92055
China Lake Naval Weapons Center, China Lake 93555
Concord NWS, Concord 94520
Edwards AFB 93523
El Toro MCAS, El Toro 92709
Fleet Post Office, San Francisco 94105
Fort Hunter Liggett, Jolon 93928
Fort Irwin 92310
Fort Winfield Scott, Presidio of San Francisco 94129

Fresno ANG Base, Fresno 93727
Lenmore NAS, Lenmore 93245
Los Angeles AFS, Worldway Postal Center, Los Angeles 90009
March AFB 92508
Mare Island Naval Shipyard, Vallejo 94592
Marine Combat Center, 29 Palms 92278
McClellan AFB 95652]
Miramar NAS, San Diego 92145
Monterey, Presidio of 93940
Mount Leguna AFS, Mount Laguna 92408
Naval Construction Battalion, Port Hueneme 93043
Navy Postgraduate School, Monterey 93940
North Highland ANG Station, San Diego 92135
Oakland Army Base, Oakland 94626
Oakland Naval Hospital, Oakland 94627
Oakland Naval Supply Center, Oakland 94625
Ontario Int'l Airport, Ontario 91761
Point Mugu NAS, Point Mugu 93042
Recruit Training Command, San Diego 92133
San Diego NAS, San Diego 92136
Seal Beach Naval Weapons Station, Seal Beach 90740
Sharpe Army Depot, Lathrop 95331
Sierra Army Depot, Herlong 96113
Tracy Defense Depot, Tracy 95376
Travis AFB 94535
Treasure Island Naval Support Activity, San Francisco 94130
Vanderburg AFB 93437
COLORADO (CO)
Air Force Accounting & Finance Center, Denver 80279
Air Reserve Personnel Center, Denver 80280
Buckley ANG Base, Aurora 80045
Fitzsimmons Army Medical Center, Aurora 80045
Fort Carson 80913
Peterson AFB, Colorado Springs 80914
Pueblo Army Depot, Pueblo 81001
Rocky Mountain Arsenal, Denver 80240
United States Air Force Academy 80840
CONNECTICUT (CT)
Bradley ANG Base, Windsor Locks 06096
Naval Submarine Base, Groton 06340
Orange ANG Communications Station, Orange 06477
United States Coast Guard Academy, New London 06320

DELAWARE (DE)
Dover AFB 19902
DISTRICT OF COLUMBIA (DC)
Andrews AFB, Washington 20331
Bolling AFB, Washington 20332
Department of Defense, The Pentagon, Washington 20301
Fort Lesley J. McNair, Washington 20319
Naval Air Facility, Washington 20390
Walter Reed Army Medical Center, Washington 20012
FLORIDA (FL)
Cape Canaveral AFS 32925
Cecil Field NAS, Cecil Field 32215
Eglin AFB, 32542
Jacksonville NAS, Jacksonville 32212
Key West NAS, Key West 33040
MacDill AFB 33608
Mayport Naval Station, Mayport 32228
Patrick AFB 32925
Pensacola NAS, Pensacola 32508
Tyndall AFB 32403
Whiting Field NAS, Milkton 32570
GEORGIA (GA)
Atlanta NAS, Marietta 30060
Dobbins AFB 30069
Fort Benning 31905
Fort Gillem, Forest Park 30050
Fort Gordon 30905
Fort McPherson 30330
Fort Stewart, Hinesville 31314
Hunter Army Air Field, Savannah 31409
King's Bay Submarine Base, Albany 31704
Moody AFB 31699
Robins AFB, 31098
HAWAII (HI)
Barbers Point NAS, Barbers Point 96862
Camp H.M. Smith USMC, Honolulu 96861
Fort Shafter 96858
Hickam AFB 96853
Kaneohe Marine Corps Air Station, Kailua 96863
Pearl Harbor Naval Base, Pearl Harbor 96860
Schofield Barracks, Wahiawa 96857
IDAHO (ID)
Boise Air Terminal, Boise 83701
Mountain Home AFB 83648
ILLINOIS (IL)
Joilet Army Ammunition Plant, joilet 60436
Glenview NAS, Glenview 60026
Recruit Training Command, Great Lakes 60088
Rock Island Arsenal, Rock Island 61299
Savanna Army Depot, Savanna 61074
Scott AFB 62225
INDIANA (IN)
Crane Naval Weapons Support Center, Craine 47552
Fort Wayne Municipal Airport, Fort Wayne 46809
Hulman Field, Terra Haut 47803
Indiana Army Ammunition Plant, Charleston 47111
Naval Avionics Center, Indianapolis 46218
Newport Army Ammunition Plant, Newport 47966
IOWA (IA)
Iowa Army Ammunition Plant, Burlington 53601
Sioux City Municipal Airport, Sergeant Bluff 51504

KANSAS (KS)
Forbes Field AGS, Topeka 66620
Fort Leavenworth 66027
Fort Riley 66442
Kansas Army Ammunition Plant, Parsons 67357
McConnell AFB 67221
KENTUCKY (KY)
Blue Grass Depot Activity, Lexington 40507
Fort Campbell 42223
Fort Knox 40121
Naval Ordnance Station, Louisville 40214
Standford Field, Louisville 40213
LOUISIANA (LA)
Barksdale AFB 71110
Fort Polk 71549
Lake Charles AFS, Lake Charles 70601
Louisiana Army Ammunition Plant, Shreveport 71102
New Orleans NAS, New Orleans 70146
8th Marine Corps District, New Orleans 70146
MAINE (ME)
Brunswick NAS, Brunswick 04011
Bucks Harbor AFS, Bucks Harbor 04618
Caswell AFS, Limestone 04750
Charleston AFS 04422
South Portland ANG Station, South Portland 04106
MARYLAND (MD)
Aberdeen Proving Ground 21005
Andrews AFB, Camp Springs 20331
Bethesda Naval Hospital, Bethesda 20014
Fort Detrick, Frederick 21701
Fort George G. Meade 20755
Fort Holabird 21219
Fort Richie 21719
Indian Head Naval Ordnance Station, Indian Head 20640
National Naval Medical Center, Bethesda 20014
Patuxent River NAS, Patuxent River 20670
United States Naval Academy, Annapolis 21402
MASSACHUSETTS (MA)
Army Materials Research Center, Watertown 02172
Fort Devens 01433
Hanscom AFB, Bedford 01731
Natick Research & Development Center, Natick 01760
Otis AGB 02542
South Weymouth NAS, South Weymouth 02190
Wellesley ANG Station, Wellesley 02181
Westover AGB 01022
Worshester ANG Base, Worchester 01605
MICHIGAN (MI)
Detroit Arsenal, Warren 48090
Detroit Naval Air Facility, Mt. Clemens 48043
K.I. Sawyer AFB 49843
Muskegon Army Engine Plant, Muskegon 49443
Selfridge ANG Base 48045
MINNESOTA (MN)
Duluth ANG Station, Duluth 55811
MISSISSIPPI (MS)
Columbus AFB 39701
Gulfport Naval Construction Center, Gulfport 39501
Keesler AFB, Biloxi 39534
Meridian NAS, Meridian 39301
Naval Oceanography Command, Bay St. Louis 39529

MISSOURI (MO)
Fort Leonard Wood 65473
Gateway Army Communication Plant, St. Louis 63143
Marine Corps Finance Center, Kansas City 64197
National Personnel Record Center, St. Louis 63132
Saint Louis Army Ammunition Plant, Saint Louis 63120
U.S. Army Administration Center, Saint Louis 63132
U.S. Army Reserve Personnel Admin Center, Saint Louis 63132
Whiteman AFB 65305

MONTANA (MT)
Lewiston AFS, Lewiston 59457
Malmstrom AFB 59042

NEBRASKA (NE)
Cornhusker Army Ammunition Plant, Grand Island 68801
Offutt AFB 68113

NEVADA (NE)
Indian Springs Air Force Auxiliary Field Indian Springs 89018
Fallen NAS, Fallon 89406
Nellis AFB 89191
Tonopah AFS, Tonopah 89049

NEW HAMPSHIRE (NH)
Pease AGS 03803
Portsmouth Naval Shipyard, Portsmouth 03804

NEW JERSEY (NJ)
Bayonne Military Ocean Terminal, Bayonne 07002
Earle Naval Weapons Station, Colts Neck 07722
Fort Dix 08640
Fort Monmouth 07703
Lakehurst Naval Air Engineering Center, Lakehurst 08733
McGuire AFB 08641
Naval Air Propulsion Center, Trenton 08628
Picatinny Arsenal, Dover 07801

NEW MEXICO (NM)
Cannon AFB 88101
Holloman AFB, 88330
Kirtland AFB, Albuquerque 87116
White Sands Missle Range 88002

NEW YORK (NY)
Fort Drum, Watertown 13601
Fort Hamilton 11252
Griffis AFB 13441
Hancock Field, Syracuse 13225
Hawthorne Army Ammunition Plant, Hawthorn 10532
Naval Support Activity, Brooklyn 11251
Plattsburgh AFB 12903
Roslyn ANG Station, Roslyn 11576
Seneca Army Depot, Romulus 14541
United States Military Academy, West Point 10996
Watertown AFS, Watertown 13601

NORTH CAROLINA (NC)
Badin ANG Station, Badin 28009
Camp Lejeune Marine Corps Air Base, Camp Lajeune 28542
Cherry Point Marine Corps Air Station, Cherry Point 28533
Fort Bragg 28307
Jacksonville Marine Corps Air Station, Jacksonville 28545
Pope AFB 28308
Seymour Johnson AFB 27531
Sunny Point Military Ocean Terminal, Southport 28461

NORTH DAKOTA (ND)
Cavalier AFS, Moountain 58221
Grand Forks AFB 58205
Minot AFB 58705

OHIO (OH)
Blue Ash ANG Station, Cincinnati 45242
Camp Perry ANG Station, Port Clinton 43452
Cleveland Army Tank - Automotive Plant, Cleveland 44135
Gentile Defense Electronics Supply Center, Dayton 45444
Mansfield Lahm Airport, Mansfield 44901
Navy Finance Center, Cleveland 44199
Newark AFS, Newark 43055
Wright Patterson AFB 45433

OKLAHOMA (OK)
Altus AFB 73523
Fort Sill 73503
Mcalester Army Ammunition 74501
Tinker AFB 73145
Vance AFB 73701

PENNSYLVANIA (PA)
Carlisle Barracks 17013
Defense Personnel Support Center, Philadelphia 19105
Fort Indiantown Gap, Anneville 17003
Letterkenny Army Depot, Chambersburg 17201
Mechanicsburg Defense Depot, Mechanicsburg 17055
Navy Fleet Material Support Office, Mechanicsburg 17055
New Cumberland Army Depot, New Cumberland 17070
Tobyhanna Army Depot, Tobyhanna 18466
Valley Forge General Hospital, Phoenixville 19460
Warminster Naval Air Development Center, Warminster 18974
Willow Grove NAS, Willow Grove 19090
4th Marine Corps District, Philadelphia 19112

RHODE ISLAND (RI)
Naval Education & Training Center, Newport 02840

SOUTH CAROLINA (SC)
Beaufort Marine Corps Air Station, Beaufort 29902
Beaufort Naval Hospital, Beaufort 29902
Charleston AFB, 29404
Charleston Naval Base, Charleston 29408
Fort Jackson 29207
McEntire ANG Base, Eastover 29044

SOUTH DAKOTA (SD)
Elmsworth AFB 5770
Joe Foss Field, Sioux Falls 57104

TENNESSEE (TN)
Alcoa ANG Station, Alcoa 37701
Arnold AFS 37389
Memphis Defense Depot, Memphis 38115
Memphis NAS, Millington 38054

TEXAS (TX)
Army & Air Force Exchange Service, Dallas 75266
Beeville NAS, Beeville 78103
Brooke Army Medical Center, Fort Sam Houston 78234
Brooks AFB 78235
Corpus Christi Army Depot, Corpus Christi 78419
Corpus Christi NAS, Corpus Christi 78419
Dallas NAS, Dallas 75211
Dyess AFB 79607
Ellington AFB 77209
Fort Bliss 79916
Fort Hood 76544
Fort Sam Houston 78234
Garland ANG Station, Garland 75040
Goodfellow AFB 76908
Kelly AFB 78241
Kingsville NAS, Kingsville 78363

Laporte ANG Station, La Porte 77571
Lackland AFB 78236
Laredo AFB 78040
Laughlin AFB 78843
Longhorn Army Ammunition Plant, Marshall 75670
Randolph AFB 78150
Red River Army Depot, Texarkana 75501
Reese AFB 79489
San Antonio AFS, San Antonio 78208
Sheppard AFB 76311
U.S. Army Depot, Corpus Christi 78419
UTAH (ut)
Dugway Proving Grounds, Dugway 84002
Hill AFB 84056
Ogden Defense Depot, Ogden 84407
Tooele Army Depot, Toole 84074
VIRGINIA (VA)
Armed Forces Staff College, Norfolk 23511
Camp Elmore USMC, Norfolk 23511
Defense General Supply Center, Richmon 23219
Fleet Tng Command Center, Virginia Beach 23461
Fort A. P. Hill, Bowling Green 22427
Fort Belvior 22060
Fort Eustis 23604

Fort Lee AFS, Fort Lee 23801
Fort Monroe 23651
Fort Myer 22211
Fort Picket, Blackstone 23824
Fort Story 23459
Langley AFB 23665
Little Creek Naval Amphibious Base, Norfolk 23521
Norfolk NAS, Norfolk 23511
Norfolk Naval Shipyard, Portsmouth 23709
Norfolk Naval Supply Center, Norfolk 23512
Oceana NAS, Virginia Beach 23460
Quantico Marine Corps Air Facility, Quantico 22134
U.S. Marine Corps HDQ, Arlington 22214
WASHINGTON (WA)
Fairchild AFB 99011
Fort Lewis 98433
McChord AFB 98438
Navy Undersea Warfare Station, Keyport 98345
Whidbey Island NAS, Oak Harbor 98278
WISCONSIN (WI)
Badger Army Ammunition Plant, Baraboo 53913
Volk Field ANG Base, Camp Douglas 54618
WYOMING (WY)
F.E. Warren AFB 82005

EMPLOYMENT INFORMATION - Additional employment information can be obtained by writing to the Chief, Staffing and Support Programs, Directorate for Personnel and Security, Rm 3B347, The Pentagon, Washington, DC 20301-1155. Phone (703) 697-4211.

DEPARTMENT OF EDUCATION
400 Maryland Avenue S.W.
Washington, DC 20202
(202) 401-0559

The Department of Education is the Cabinet-level department that establishes policy for, administers, and coordinates most federal assistance to education. Total employment within this department is less than 5,000. There are ten regional offices located in: Atlanta, Boston, Chicago, Dallas, Denver, Kansas City, New York, Philadelphia, San Francisco, and Seattle.

EMPLOYMENT INFORMATION - Employment inquiries and applications should be directed to the Personnel Management Service at the above address.

DEPARTMENT OF ENERGY
1000 Independence Avenue SW
Washington, DC 20585
(202) 586-8580

The Department of Energy provides a balanced national energy plan through the coordination and administration of the energy functions of the federal Government. The department is responsible for long-term, high-risk research and development of energy technology; the marketing of federal power, energy conservation; the nuclear weapons program, energy regulatory programs, and a central energy data collection and analysis program.

The majority of the department's energy research and development activities are carried out by contractors who operate government-owned facilities. Management and administration of these government-owned, contractor operated facilities are the major responsibility of the department's eight Operations Offices:

Albuquerque, NM 87115, P.O. Box 5400	(505) 646-7231
Argonne, IL 60439, 9800 S. Cass Avenue	(708) 972-2110
Fernald, OH 45030, 7400 Willey Rd	(513) 738-6655
Idaho Falls, ID 83402, 785 Doe Place	(208) 526-1322
Las Vegas, NV 89193-8518, P.O. Box 98518	(702) 295-3211
Oak Ridge, TN 37831, P.O. Box 2001	(615) 576-4444
Richland, WA 99352, 825 Jadwin Avenue	(509)-376-7395
Oakland, CA 94612, 1333 Broadway	(415) 273-7111
Aiken, SC 29802, P.O. Box A	(803) 725-2277

DEPARTMENT OF HEALTH AND HUMAN SERVICES (HHS)
200 Independence Avenue SW
Washington, DC 20201
(202) 619-2560

The Department of Health and Human Services touches the lives of more Americans than any other Federal agency. This department advises the President on health, welfare, and income security plans, policies, and programs of the Federal government. These programs are administered through five operating divisions, which include: the Social Security Administration, the Health Care Financing Administration, the Office of Human Development Services, the Public Health Service, and the Family Support Administration.

REGIONAL OFFICES - HHS

1. John F. Kennedy Federal Bldg., Boston, MA 02203	(617) 565-1500
2. 26 Federal Plaza, New York, NY 10278	(212) 264-4600
3. 3535 Market St., Philadelphia, PA. 19101	(215) 596-6492
4. 101 Marietta Tower, Atlanta, GA 30323	(404) 331-2442
5. 105 W. Adams St., Chicago, IL 60603	(312) 353-5160
6. 1200 Main Tower, Dallas, TX 75202	(214) 767-3301
7. 601 E. 12th St., Kansas City, MO 64106	(816) 374-2821
8. 1961 Stout St., Denver, CO 80294	(303) 844-3372
9. Federal Office Bldg., San Francisco, CA 94501	(415) 556-6746
10. 2901 3rd Avenue, Seattle, WA 98101	(206) 553-0420

DEPARTMENT OF HOUSING AND URBAN DEVELOPMENT (HUD)
451 Seventh Street SW
Washington, DC 20410
(202) 619-2560

This department is the federal agency responsible for programs concerned with the nation's housing needs, the development and preservation of the nation's communities, and the provisions of equal housing opportunity.

The department administers a wide variety of programs, including: Federal Housing Administration mortgage insurance programs, rental assistance programs for lower income families; the Government National Mortgage Association mortgage-backed securities programs and other assistance programs. Regional offices are located in Boston, New York City, Philadelphia, Atlanta, Fort Worth, Kansas City, Denver, San Francisco, and Seattle.

> **EMPLOYMENT INFORMATION** - Inquiries and applications should be directed to the Headquarters Office of Personnel or the nearest Regional Office Personnel Division.

DEPARTMENT OF THE INTERIOR
1800 C Street NW
Washington, DC 20240
(202) 343-3171

The nation's principal conservation agency, the Department of the Interior has responsibility for most of our nationally owned public lands and natural resources. This includes fostering the wisest use of our land and water resources, protecting our fish and wildlife, preserving the environmental and cultural values of our national parks and historical places, and providing for the enjoyment of life through outdoor recreation.

BUREAUS, SERVICES AND OTHER OFFICES

■ UNITED STATES FISH & WILDLIFE SERVICE

This service is composed of a headquarters office in Washington, DC, 7 regional offices in the lower 48 states and Alaska, a regional research structure, and a variety of field units and installations. These include 450 National Wildlife Refuges and 150 Waterfowl Protection Areas, 25 major fish and wildlife laboratories and centers, 36 cooperative research units at universities, 70 National Fish Hatcheries, and a nationwide network of wildlife law enforcement agents. Division of Personnel mgmt., 1849 C St. NW, Mail Stop ARLSQ-100, Washington, DC 20240. Phone, (703) 358-1743.

REGIONAL OFFICES - U.S. FISH & WILDLIFE SERVICE

ALBUQUERQUE, NM (P.O. Box 1306, 87103)	(505) 766-2321
ANCHORAGE, AK (1011 E. Tudor Rd., 99503)	(907) 786-3542
ATLANTA, GA (75 Spring St. SW., 30303)	(404) 331-3588
BOSTON, MA (Suite 700, 1 Gateway Center, Newton Corner, 02158	(617) 965-5100
DENVER, CO (P.O. Box 25486, 80225	(303) 236-7920
PORTLAND, OR (Suite 1692, 500 NE. Multnomah St., 97232)	(503) 231-6118
TWIN CITIES, MN (Federal Bldg., Fort Snelling, 55111)	(612) 725-3500
WASHINGTON, DC (1800 C St. NW., 20240)	(703) 358-1801

■ NATIONAL PARK SERVICE

The National Park Service has a service center in Denver; and a center for production of exhibits in Harpers Ferry, WV. There are more than 350 units in the National Parks and monuments, scenic parkways, riverways, seashores, lakeshores, recreation areas, and reservoirs; and historic sites. This Service develops and implements park management plans and staffs the areas under its administration. Phone, (202) 619-7256.

REGIONAL OFFICES - NATIONAL PARK SERVICE

ALASKA	(2525 Gambell St., Anchorage, AK, 99503)
MID-ATLANTIC	(143 S. 3d St., Philadelphia, PA 19106)
MIDWEST	(1709 Jackson St., Omaha, NE 68102)
NATIONAL CAPITAL	(1100 Ohio Dr. SW., Washington, DC 20242)
NORTH ATLANTIC	(15 State St., Boston, MA 02109)
PACIFIC NORTHWEST	(83 S. King St., Suite 212, Seattle, WA 98104)
ROCKY MOUNTAIN	(P.O. Box 25287, Denver, CO 80225)
SOUTHEAST	(75 Spring St. SW., Atlanta, GA 30303)
WESTERN	(450 Golden Gate Ave., San Francisco, CA 94102)

EMPLOYMENT INFORMATION - Direct inquiries and applications to the Personnel Office, National Parks Service, Department of the Interior, Washington, DC, 20240. **Applications for seasonal employment** must be received between September 1 and January 15 and should be sent to the Division of Personnel Management, National Parks Service, P.O. Box 37127, Washington, DC 20013-7127.

■ BUREAU OF MINES

This Bureau is primarily a research and fact finding agency. Research is conducted to provide technology for the extraction, processing, use, and recycling of the nation's nonfuel resources at a reasonable cost and without harm to the environment. Contact the Bureau of Mines at 810 Seventh St. NW., Washington, DC 20241 for additional employment information.

■ GEOLOGICAL SURVEY

The primary responsibilities of this service are to identify the nation's land, water, energy, and mineral resources.

EMPLOYMENT INFORMATION - Direct inquiries to the following:

215 National Center, 12201 Sunrise Valley Dr., Reston, VA 22092, (703) 648-6131.
Ate. 160, Holcomb Bridge Rd., Norcross, GA 30092, (404) 409-7750.
1400 Independence Rd., Rolla, MO 65401, (314) 341-0810.
Federal Center, Bldg. 25, Denver, CO 80225, (303) 236-5900.
345 Middlefield Rd., Menlo Park, CA 94025. Phone (415) 329-4104.

■ BUREAU OF INDIAN AFFAIRS - The principal objectives of the Bureau are to actively encourage and train Indian and Alaska Native people to manage their own affairs under the trust relationship to the federal government.

AREA OFFICES - BUREAU OF INDIAN AFFAIRS

Aberdeen, SD	115 4th Ave. SE., 57401
Albuquerque, NM	P.O. Box 26567, 615 N. 1st St., 87125-6567
Anadarko, OK	P.O. Box 368, 73005
Billings, MT	316 N. 26th St., 59101
Juneau, AK	Box 3-8000, 99802
Minneapolis, MN	331 2d Ave., S., 55401
Muskogee, OK	Old Federal Bldg., 74401
Navajo Area	P.O. Box M, Window Rock, AZ 86515
Phoenix, AZ	P.O. Box 10, 1 N. 1st St., 85001
Portland, OR	1002 NE. Hollady St., 97232
Sacramento, CA	2800 Cottage Way, 95825
EASTERN AREA	Ste. 260, 3701 N. Fairfax Dr., Arlington, VA 22203

EMPLOYMENT INFORMATION - Direct inquiries to the Branch of Personnel Services. Phone, 202-208-2547.

■ BUREAU OF LAND MANAGEMENT - The bureau is responsible for the total management of 272 million acres of public lands. These lands are located primarily in the West and Alaska. Resources managed by the bureau include timber, solid minerals, oil and gas, geothermal energy, wildlife habitat, endangered plant & animal species, vegetation, etc.

FIELD OFFICES - BUREAU OF LAND MANAGEMENT

ALASKA	Box 13, 701 C St., Anchorage, 99513	(907) 271-5076
ARIZONA	P.O. Box 16563, Phoenix, 85011	(602) 241-5501
CALIFORNIA	Rm. E-2841, 2800 Cottage Way, Sacramento, 95825	(916) 987-4743
COLORADO	2850 Youngfield St., Lakewood, 80215	(303) 239-3700

EASTERN STATES	350 S. Pickett St., Alexandria, VA 22304	(703) 461-1400
IDAHO	3380 Americana Terrace, Boise, 83706	(208) 384-3001
MONTANA	P.O. Box 36800, 222 N 32nd St., Billings, 59107	(406) 255-2904
NEVADA	P.O. Box 12000, 850 Harvard Way, Reno, 89520	(702) 785-6590
NEW MEXICO	P.O. Box 1449, S. Federal Pl., Sante Fe, 87504	(505) 438-7501
OREGON	1300 NE. 44th Ave., Portland, 97208	(503) 280-7024
UTAH	324 S. State St., Salt Lake City, 84111-2303	(801) 539-4010
WYOMING	P.O. Box 1828, 2515 Warren Ave., Cheyenne, 82003	(307) 775-6001

EMPLOYMENT INFORMATION - The following OPM announcements are applicable to most professional positions within the bureau. Announcement # 421, Biological and Agricultural Sciences; Announcement # 424, Engineering, Physical Sciences and Related Professions. The Mid-Level and Senior-Level registers are also used. Inquiries should be directed to any Bureau of Land Management Office, or to the Personnel Officer, Bureau of Land Management, Department of the Interior, Washington, DC 20240.

DEPARTMENT OF JUSTICE
Constitution Avenue & Tenth St. NW
Washington, DC 20530
(202) 514-6813

The Department of Justice is the largest law firm in the nation and serves as counsel for its citizens. It represents them in enforcing the law in the public interest. This department conducts all suits in the Supreme Court in which the United States is concerned. The Attorney General supervises and directs these activities, as well as those of the U.S. attorney and U.S. Marshalls in the various districts around the country.

DIVISIONS - DEPARTMENT OF JUSTICE

ANTITRUST - Responsible for promoting and maintaining competitive markets by enforcing the federal antitrust laws. This division has field offices at the federal buildings in Atlanta, GA; Chicago, IL; Cleveland, OH; Dallas, TX; New York, NY; Philadelphia, PA; and San Francisco, CA.

CIVIL - Litigation involves cases in Federal district courts, the U.S. Courts of Appeals, the U.S. Claims Court, etc.. This division represents the United States, its departments and agencies, Members of Congress, Cabinet officers, and other Federal employees. There are three field office facilities. The Commercial Litigation Branch has two field offices. One is at 26 Federal Plaza, New York, NY 10007 and the other at 450 Golden Gate Ave., San Francisco, CA 94102. The TORTS Branch (Admiralty & Shipping Litigation) is located at 26 Federal Plaza, New York, NY 10007.

CRIMINAL - Formulates criminal law enforcement policies, enforces and exercises general supervision over all federal criminal laws except those assigned to the other divisions.

BUREAUS & SERVICES

■ FEDERAL BUREAU OF INVESTIGATION (FBI)
Ninth St. & Pennsylvania Ave.
Washington, DC 20535
(202) 324-4981

The FBI is the principal investigative arm of the United States Department of Justice. It is charged with gathering and reporting facts, locating witnesses, and compiling evidence in cases involving federal jurisdiction. The Bureau's investigations are conducted through 58 field offices.

EMPLOYMENT INFORMATION - Direct inquiries to the Federal Bureau of Investigation, Director, Washington, DC 20535. You can also contact any of the 58 field offices. Consult your local telephone directory for the office nearest you.

■ BUREAU OF PRISONS
HOLC Building, Rm 161
Washington, DC 20534
(202) 307-1304

Responsible to maintain secure, safe, and humane correctional institutions for individuals placed in the care and custody of the Attorney General. Maintains and staffs all Federal Penal & Correctional Institutions.

REGIONAL OFFICES

MID-ATLANTIC - Ste. 100N, 10010 Junction Dr., Annapolis, MD 20701	(301) 317-7000
NORTH CENTRAL - 10920 Ambassador Dr., Kansas City, MO 64153	(816) 891-7007
NORTHEAST - 7th Fl., 2d and Chestnut Sts., Philadelphia, PA 19106	(215) 597-6317
SOUTH CENTRAL - 211 Cedar Springs Rd., Dallas, TX 75219	(214) 767-9700
SOUTHEAST - 5213 McDonough Blvd. SE., Atlanta, GA 30315	(404) 624-5202
WESTERN - 7950 Dublin Blvd., Dublin, CA 94568	(510) 803-4700

EMPLOYMENT INFORMATION - Direct inquiries to the Bureau of Prisons, Central Office, 320 First St. NW., Washington, DC 20534. You can also contact the regional offices listed above.

■ UNITED STATES MARSHALL SERVICE
600 Army Navy Drive
Arlington, VA 22202-4210
(202) 307-9629

The presidentially appointed marshals and their support staff of just over 3,400 deputy marshalls and administrative personnel operate from 427 office locations in all 94 federal judicial districts nationwide, from Guam to Puerto Rico, and from Alaska to Florida.

■ IMMIGRATION AND NATURALIZATION SERVICE
425 I Street NW
Washington, DC 20536
(202) 514-2530

This service provides information and service to the public, while concurrently exercising its enforcement responsibilities. The Immigration and Naturalization Service assists persons to the United States as visitors or as immigrants, provides assistance to those seeking permanent residence, prevents unlawful entry, and removes illegal aliens from the country. Major occupations include: Border Patrol Agent, Special Agent, Immigration Examiner, Immigration Inspector, Deportation Officer, Attorney, Computer Specialist and administrative positions. **Many jobs require employees to speak Spanish.**

REGIONAL OFFICES

EASTERN	70 Kimbell Ave., Burlington, VT 05403
NORTHERN	Fed. Bldg., Fort Snelling, Twin Cities, MN 55111
SOUTHERN	7701 N. Stemmons Frwy., Dallas, TX 75247
WESTERN	24000 Avila Rd., Laguna Niguel, CA 92677

EMPLOYMENT INFORMATION - Contact the regional offices listed above or direct inquiries to the Immigration & Naturalization Service, Central Office, 425 I St. NW, Washington, DC 20536.

■ DRUG ENFORCEMENT ADMINISTRATION
700 Army Navy Drive
Arlington, VA 22202
(202) 307-4055

The Drug Enforcement Administration is the lead federal agency in enforcing narcotics and controlled substances laws and regulations. The administration has offices throughout the United States and in 43 foreign countries. Special agents conduct criminal investigations and prepare for the prosecution of violators of the drug laws. Entry level is at the GS-7 or GS-9 grade with progression to GS-12 in three years.

This administration uses accountants, engineers, computer scientists, language majors, chemists, history majors, mathematicians, and other specialties for special agents, investigators, intelligence research and administrative positions are also filled.

EMPLOYMENT INFORMATION - Contact the Office of Personnel, Drug Enforcement Administration at the address listed above.

DEPARTMENT OF LABOR
200 Constitution Avenue
Washington, DC 20210
(202) 523-6666

The Department of Labor was created " to foster, promote and develop the welfare of the wage earners of the United States, to improve their working conditions, and to advance their opportunities for profitable employment." The department administers a variety of federal labor laws guaranteeing workers rights to safe and healthful working conditions.

This department has 17,642 employees and ranks eleventh out of the fourteen departments in total numbers of employees. Yet, the Department of Labor effects every worker in the United States through one of their many internal components; the Pension and Welfare Benefits Administration, Office of Labor - Management Standards, Office of Administrative Law Judges, Benefits Review Board, Bureau of International Labor Affairs, The Bureau of Labor Statistics, Women's Bureau, Employment Standards Administration, Employment and Training Administration, Mine Safety and Health Administration, Veterans' Employment and Training Service, and Occupational Safety and Health Administration (OSHA).

EMPLOYMENT INFORMATION - Personnel offices use lists of eligibles from the clerical, scientific, technical, and general examinations of the Office of Personnel Management. Inquiries and applications may be directed to address listed above or consult your telephone directory (under U.S. Government - Department of Labor) for field offices nearest you.

DEPARTMENT OF STATE
2201 C Street NW
Washington, DC 20520
(202) 647-7284 (24 hour job vacancy hot line)

"The Department of State advises the president in the formulation and execution of foreign policy." The department's primary objective is to promote long-range security and well-being of the United States.

There were 144 U.S Embassies, 9 missions, 71 consulates general, 26 consulates, 1 branch office, 23 consular agencies throughout the world in April of 1990 manned by several thousand

Foreign Service Officers of the Department of State. The State Departments' total employment exceeds 25,900 full time employees assigned stateside and overseas in administrative, personnel, management, engineering, communications electronics, security, and career Foreign Service Officer positions. Five Regional Bureaus consist of the Bureaus of African Affairs, European & Canadian Affairs, East Asian and Pacific Affairs, and the Near Eastern and South Asian.

EMPLOYMENT INFORMATION - For Foreign Service Opportunities contact: Foreign Service, Recruitment Division, PER/REE/REC, PO Box 9317, Rosslyn Station, Arlington, VA 22210. Phone (703) 875-7490.
For Civil Service Opportunities: Staffing Services Division, Office of Civil Service Personnel (PER/CSP), Department of State, P.O. Box 18657, Washington, DC 20036.

DEPARTMENT OF TRANSPORTATION
400 Seventh Street, SW
Washington, DC 20590
(202) 366-9394

"The U.S. Department of Transportation establishes the nation's overall transportation policy. There are nine administrations whose jurisdiction includes highway planning; urban mass transit; railroads; aviation; and the safety of waterways, ports, highways, and oil and gas pipelines."

ADMINISTRATIONS & OFFICES OF THE DOT

U.S. COAST GUARD
FEDERAL AVIATION ADMINISTRATION
FEDERAL HIGHWAY ADMINISTRATION
FEDERAL RAILROAD ADMINISTRATION
NATIONAL HIGHWAY TRAFFIC SAFETY ADMINISTRATION
FEDERAL TRANSIT ADMINISTRATION
ST. LAWRENCE SEAWAY DEVELOPMENT CORPORATION
MARITIME ADMINISTRATION
RESEARCH AND SPECIAL PROGRAMS ADMINISTRATION

■ **UNITED STATES COAST GUARD**
Civilian Personnel Division, Rm 4100
Transpoint Building
2100 Second Street, SW
Washington, DC 20593 (202) 267-1726

The U.S. Coast Guard is responsible for maritime service to the nation through search and rescue operations, preservation of navigational aids, merchant marine safety, environmental protection, maritime law enforcement, and boating safety.

EMPLOYMENT INFORMATION - Inquiries for information on the U.S. Coast Guard Academy should be directed to the Director of Admissions, U.S. Coast Guard Academy, New London, CT 06320.

■ FEDERAL AVIATION ADMINISTRATION (FAA)
Headquarters
800 Independence Avenue, SW
Washington, DC 20591
(202) 267-3870

"The Administration is charged with regulating air commerce, controlling the use of navigable airspace, promoting civil aeronautics, research and development, installing and operating air navigation facilities, air traffic control, and environmental impact of air navigation."

REGIONAL OFFICES - FAA

ALASKA	701 C St., BOX 14, Anchorage, AK 90513
CENTRAL	601 East 12th St., Kansas City, MO 64106
EASTERN	JFK Int'l Airport, Jamaica, NY 11430
GREAT LAKES	2300 East Devon, Des Plaines, IL 60018
NEW ENGLAND	12 New England Exec., Burlington, MA 01803
NORTHWEST MOUNTAIN	1601 Lind Ave. SW., Renton, WA 98055
SOUTHERN REGION	PO Box 20636, Atlanta, GA 30320
SOUTHWEST	PO Box 1689, Fort Worth, TX 76101
WESTERN-PACIFIC	Box 92007, Los Angeles, CA 90009

EMPLOYMENT INFORMATION: Entry level engineers start at the GS-5/7/9 grade depending on college grades and work experience. Engineers progress to the GS-11 or 12 pay grade. Air Traffic Control Specialists start at the GS-7 pay grade and can progress through the GS-14 grade and higher. Electronics technicians start at the GS-5/7/9 pay grade and can progress through the GS-13 grade. A large number of administrative, clerical, and personnel specialists are also needed.

■ FEDERAL HIGHWAY ADMINISTRATION
400 Seventh Street, SW
Washington, DC 20590
(202) 366-0630

"This agency is concerned with the total operation and environment of highway systems." Civil/Highway Engineers, Motor Carrier Safety Specialists, Accountants, Contract Specialists, Computer Programmers, and administrative and clerical skills are needed by the administration. Regional offices are located in Albany, NY, Baltimore, MD, Atlanta, GA, Homewood, IL, Fort Worth, Kansas City, MO, Lakewood, San Francisco, and Portland, OR.

> **EMPLOYMENT INFORMATION** - Major occupations include Civil/Highway Engineer, Motor Carrier Safety Specialists, Accountants, Contract Specialists, Computer Programmers, Administrative and Clerical.

■ FEDERAL RAILROAD ADMINISTRATION
Office of Personnel
400 Seventh Street, SW, Rm 8232
Washington, DC 20509
(202) 366-4000

The Federal Railroad Administration enforces railroad safety, conducts research and development, provides passenger and freight services, and staffs and maintains the Transportation Test Center.

> **EMPLOYMENT INFORMATION** - Major occupations include Economist, Contract Specialist, Accountant, Attorney, Law Clerk, Administrative and Clerical.

■ NATIONAL HIGHWAY TRAFFIC SAFETY ADMINISTRATION
Office of Personnel, Rm 5306
400 Seventh Street, SW
Washington, DC 20590
(202) 366-9550

"The National Highway Traffic Safety Administration was established to reduce the number of deaths, injuries, and economic losses resulting from traffic accidents on national highways."

> **EMPLOYMENT INFORMATION** - Major occupations include Attorney Advisor, Law Clerk, Highway Safety Specialist, Mathematical Statistician, Mechanical Engineer, Safety Standard Engineer, Administrative and Clerical.

■ URBAN MASS TRANSPORTATION ADMINISTRATION
Office of Personnel, Rm 7101
400 Seventh Street, SW
Washington, DC 20590
(202) 366-2513

"Their mission is to assist in the development of improved mass transportation, to encourage the planning and establishment of areawide urban mass transit systems, and to provide assistance to state and local governments in financing such systems."

EMPLOYMENT INFORMATION - Transportation Specialist, Civil Engineer, General Engineer, Contract Specialist, Administrative and Clerical.

■ RESEARCH & SPECIAL PROGRAMS ADMINISTRATION
Personnel Office, Rm 8401
400 Seventh Street, SW
Washington, DC 20509
(202) 366-4433

"This Administration consists of the Office of Hazardous Materials Transportation; the office of Pipeline Safety; the Office of Civil Rights; the Office of the Chief Council; the Transportation Systems Center in Cambridge, Massachusetts; the Office of Emergency Transportation; the Office of Aviation Information Management; and the Office of Administration."

EMPLOYMENT INFORMATION - Major occupations include Transportation Specialist, General Engineer (Pipeline), Mechanical Engineer, Chemical Engineer, Writer/Editor, Administrative and Clerical.

DEPARTMENT OF THE TREASURY
1500 Pennsylvania Avenue NW
Washington, DC 20220
(202) 377-9205

"The Department of the Treasury performs four basic functions: formulating and recommending economic, financial, tax, and fiscal policies; serving as financial agent for the U.S Government; enforcing the law; and manufacturing coins and currency."

BUREAUS, SERVICES, & OFFICES OF THE TREASURY

INTERNAL REVENUE SERVICE
U.S. CUSTOMS SERVICE
BUREAU OF ALCOHOL, TOBACCO, & FIREARMS
BUREAU OF ENGRAVING AND PRINTING
FINANCIAL MANAGEMENT SERVICE
FEDERAL LAW ENFORCEMENT TRAINING CENTER
U.S. MINT
OFFICE OF THE COMPTROLLER OF THE CURRENCY
BUREAU OF THE PUBLIC DEBT
SAVINGS BOND DIVISION
U.S. SECRET SERVICE

■ **INTERNAL REVENUE SERVICE (IRS)**
1111 Constitution Avenue NW
Washington, DC 20224
(202) 566-6151

"The Internal Revenue Service has more than 100,000 employees and is the largest organization in the Department of the Treasury. Approximately 7,000 of these employees work in Washington, DC. Others are employed in hundreds of offices throughout the U. S. There is an IRS Office in or near every town."

EMPLOYMENT INFORMATION - "Almost every major field of study has some application to the work of the IRS. A substantial number of positions are in accounting, business administration, finance, economics, criminology, and law. There are also a great number of persons whose college major was political science, public administration, education, liberal arts, or other fields not directly related to business or law."

■ **THE U.S. CUSTOMS SERVICE**
Office of Human Resources
1301 Constitution Avenue, NW
Washington, DC 20229
(202) 634-5270

The Customs Service collects the revenue from imports and enforces customs and related laws. Customs also administers the Tariff Act of 1930. They also enforce trademark, copyright, and patent privileges. "The 50 states, plus the Virgin Islands and Puerto Rico, are divided into seven regions. Contained within these regions are 44 subordinate district offices or area offices under which there are approximately 240 ports of entry."

EMPLOYMENT INFORMATION - The Customs Service recruits through the Treasury Enforcement Agent examination. Address employment inquiries to 2120 L. St., NW., 6th fl., Washington, DC 20037. There are approximately 14,000 Customs employees.

■ **BUREAU OF ALCOHOL, TOBACCO, & FIREARMS**
Personnel Staffing Specialist, Rm 1215
1200 Pennsylvania Avenue, NW
Washington, DC 20336
(202) 927-8500

"The Bureau is responsible for enforcing and administering firearms and explosives laws, as well as those covering the production, use, and distribution of alcohol and tobacco products." There are approximately 3,500 employees most of which are Special Agents and Inspectors.

■ BUREAU OF ENGRAVING & PRINTING
Office of Industrial Relations
14TH and C Streets, SW
Washington, DC 20228
(202) 847-3019

"The Bureau of Engraving & Printing designs, prints, and finishes a large variety of security products including Federal Reserve notes, U.S. postage stamps, Treasury securities, identification cards, and certificates. The bureau is the largest printer of security documents in the world; over 40 billion documents are printed annually. The bureau's headquarters and most of its production operations are located in Washington, DC. A second currency plant is in Fort Worth, TX."

> **EMPLOYMENT INFORMATION** - Selections are highly competitive. Major occupations include Police Officer, Computer Specialist, Engineer, Contract Specialist, Engraver, Production Manager, Security Specialist, Accountant, Auditor, and Administrative and Clerical positions.

■ U.S. MINT
Chief of Staffing
633 Third Street, NW, Suite 655
Washington, DC 20220
(202) 874-6450

The U.S. Mint employs some 2,300 employees at six locations including Washington, DC. Field facilities are located in Philadelphia, PA, Denver, CO, San Francisco, CA, West Point, NY, and Fort Knox, KY. The U.S. Mint produces bullion and domestic and foreign coins, distributes gold and silver, and safeguards and controls bullion.

■ BUREAU OF PUBLIC DEBT
300 13th Street, SW, Rm 446
Washington, DC 20239-1400
(202) 219-3302

"The bureau administers the public debt by borrowing money through the sale of United States Treasury securities. The sale, service, and processing of Treasury securities involves the Federal Reserve Banks and their branches, which serve as fiscal agents of the Treasury." This bureau also manages the U.S. Savings Bond program through it's U.S. Savings Bonds Division.

> **EMPLOYMENT INFORMATION** - The major occupations include Accountant, Operating Accountant, Computer Systems Analyst, Computer Programmer, Computer Analyst.

■ **SAVINGS BOND DIVISION**
1111 20th Street, NW (Personnel)
Washington, DC 20226
(202) 634-5389

This Division has field offices located throughout the United States. Field offices are managed through 18 district offices.

EMPLOYMENT INFORMATION - The Division occasionally has vacancies for people with college training and degrees. No specific degrees or majors are required.

■ **SECRET SERVICE**
Chief of Staffing
1800 G Street, NW, Rm 912
Washington, DC 20223
(202) 435-5708

The Secret Service has over 4,000 employees operating from 65 field offices. Agents protect the President, Vice President, and numerous government officials including the heads of foreign governments. They also enforce counterfeiting laws, and fraud and forgery of government checks.

EMPLOYMENT INFORMATION - Major occupations include Corrections, Criminology, Law Enforcement, and Special Agent.

DEPARTMENT OF VETERANS AFFAIRS
810 Vermont & Avenue NW
Washington, DC 20420
(202) 233-3771

"The Department of Veterans Affairs operates programs to benefit veterans and members of their families. Benefits include compensation payments for disabilities or death related to military service; pensions; education and rehabilitation; home loan guaranty; burial; and a medical care program incorporating nursing homes, clinics, and medical centers."

Approximately 90 percent of VA's 263,427 employees are involved with providing medical care. Nearly 36,000 registered nurses work for the VA.

EMPLOYMENT INFORMATION - All medical occupations are needed by the VA. Other major occupations include Accounting, all BS, BA Majors, Architecture, Business, Computer Science, Engineering, Law, Statistics, and numerous Administrative and Clerical positions. There are hundreds of national Veterans Affairs facilities within the United States. Consult your local telephone directory for the facility nearest you.

INDEPENDENT AGENCIES (Partial List)

ENVIRONMENTAL PROTECTION AGENCY
Recruitment Center (PM-224)
401 M Street, SW
Washington, DC 20460
(202) 260-2090

CENTRAL INTELLIGENCE AGENCY
Office of Personnel
Washington, DC 20505
(703) 874-4400

COMMISSION OF CIVIL RIGHTS
Personnel Office
1121 Vermont Avenue, NW
Washington, DC 20425
(202) 376-8364

CONSUMER PRODUCT SAFETY COMMISSION
Division of Personnel Management
5401 Westbard Avenue, Rm 329
Bethesda, MD 20207
(301) 492-6580

FARM CREDIT ADMINISTRATION
Human Resources Division
1501 Farm Credit Drive
McLean, VA 22102-5090
(703) 883-4139

FEDERAL COMMUNICATIONS COMMISSION
Human Resource Management
1919 M Street, NW
Washington, DC 20554
(202) 632-7104

FEDERAL DEPOSIT INSURANCE CORPORATION
Director of Personnel
Washington, DC 20929
(202) 898-8890

FEDERAL EMERGENCY MANAGEMENT
Office of Personnel, Rm 816
500 C. Street, SW
Washington, DC 20472
(202) 646-3970

FEDERAL MARITIME COMMISSION
1100 L Street, NW, Rm 10103
Washington, Dc 20573-0001
(202) 523-5773

FEDERAL TRADE COMMISSION
Division of Personnel, Rm 151
Sixth & Pennsylvania Ave., NW
Washington, DC 20580
(202) 326-2020

GENERAL SERVICES ADMINISTRATION
Office of Personnel, Central Office
18th and F Streets, NW
Washington, DC 20405
(202) 501-0370

GOVERNMENT PRINTING OFFICE
Chief, Employment Branch, Stop: PSE
North Capital & H Streets, NW
Washington, DC 20401
(202) 512-0000

MERIT SYSTEMS PROTECTION BOARD
Personnel Division, Rm 850
1120 Vermont Ave., NW
Washington, DC 20419
(202) 254-8013

NATIONAL AERONAUTICS & SPACE ADMINISTRATION (NASA)
NASA Headquarters, DP
Washington, DC 20546
(202) 453-8478

NATIONAL CREDIT UNION ADMINISTRATION
Personnel Management Specialist
1776 G Street, NW
Washington, DC 20456
(202) 682-9720

NATIONAL ENDOWMENT FOR THE HUMANITIES
Personnel Management Specialist, Rm 417
1100 Pennsylvania Ave., NW
Washington, DC 20506
(202) 786-0415

NATIONAL LABOR RELATIONS BOARD
Personnel Operations
1717 Pennsylvania Ave., NW
Washington, DC 20570
(202) 254-9044

NATIONAL SCIENCE FOUNDATION
Division of Personnel Management
1800 G. St., NW, Rm 208
Washington, DC 20550
(202) 357-7602

OFFICE OF PERSONNEL MANAGEMENT (OPM)
Recruitment/Employment, Rm 1469
1900 E. Street, NW
Washington, DC 20415
(202) 606-2424

SECURITIES AND EXCHANGE COMMISSION (SEC)
Office of Personnel
450 Fifth St., NW
Washington, DC 20549
(202) 272-2550

SMALL BUSINESS ADMINISTRATION
Central Personnel Office, Rm 300
1441 L Street, NW
Washington, DC 20416
(202) 653-6504

APPENDIX D

FEDERAL OCCUPATION LISTS

The government's classification system includes an occupational structure which groups similar jobs together. There are 22 occupational groups comprising 441 different white-collar occupations under the General Schedule; GS-000 through GS-2100. Each occupational group is further subdivided into specific numerical codes (for example: GS-856, Electronics Technician, GS-318, Secretary Series, etc.). The Wage Grade Trades and Labor Schedule offers an additional 36 occupational families; WG-2500 through WG-9000.

This Appendix presents a comprehensive listing of both GS and WG occupational groups, families and related series. First, locate the occupational group or groups in which you have specific knowledge, skill, and or training. Then, review each job series under the primary occupation group or Family.[1]

More than a quarter (457,761 or 28.1 percent) of all white-collar workers had an occupation in the General Administrative, Clerical and Office Services group. The three other large white-collar groups are: Engineering and Architecture (169,769 or 10.4 percent); Medical, Hospital, Dental and Public Health (142,292 or 8.7 percent); and Accounting and Budget (142,286 or 8.7 percent).

Certain white-collar occupations are concentrated in particular federal agencies. The Department of Agriculture employed 66.5 percent of Biological Science employees and 94.8 percent of Veterinary Medical Science workers. The Department of Health and Human Services was the major employer of the Social Science, Psychology and Welfare group (39.5 percent) and the Legal and Kindred group (39 percent). The Veterans Administration employed 73.9 percent of the Medical, Hospital, Dental and Public Health group. The Department of Commerce employed 79.9 percent of the Copyright, Patent and Trademark group. The Department of Transportation had 60.5 percent of the Transportation group employees. The Library of Congress and Department of Defense together employed 55.8 percent of the Library and Archives group. The Department of Treasury and Justice together employed 66.7 percent of the Investigative group. The Department of Defense was the major employer in all the other white collar occupational groups.

---

[1] References for the General Schedule Occupational Groups and Series are the Handbook of Occupational Groups & Series, September 1992 published by the U.S. Office of Personnel Management and Pamphlet TS-56.

GENERAL SCHEDULE (GS) OCCUPATIONAL GROUPS

GS-000: MISCELLANEOUS - This group includes all classes of positions, the duties of which are to administer, supervise, or perform work which cannot be included in other occupational groups either because the duties are unique, or because they are complex and come in part under various groups.

GS-100: SOCIAL SCIENCE, PSYCHOLOGY, AND WELFARE GROUP - This group includes all classes of positions, the duties of which are to advise on, administer, supervise, or perform research or other professional and scientific work, subordinate technical work, or related clerical work in one or more of the social sciences; in psychology; in social work; in recreational activities; or in the administration of public welfare and insurance programs.

GS-200: PERSONNEL MANAGEMENT AND INDUSTRIAL RELATIONS GROUP - This group includes all classes of positions, the duties of which are to advise on, administer, supervise, or perform work involved in the various phases of personnel management and industrial relations.

GS-300: GENERAL ADMINISTRATIVE, CLERICAL, & OFFICE SERVICES GROUP-This group includes all classes of positions the duties of which are to administer, supervise, or perform work involved in management analysis; stenography, typing, correspondence, and secretarial work; mail and file work; the operation of office appliances; the operation of communications equipment, use of codes and ciphers, and procurement of the most efficient communications services; the operation of microform equipment, peripheral equipment, duplicating equipment, mail processing equipment, duplicating equipment, and copier/duplicating equipment; and other work of a general clerical and administrative nature.

GS-400: BIOLOGICAL SCIENCE GROUP - This group includes all classes of positions, the duties of which are to advise on, administer, supervise, or perform research or other professional and scientific work or subordinate technical work in any of the fields of science concerned with living organisms, their distribution, characteristics, life processes, and adaptations and relations to the environment; the soil, its properties and distribution, and the living organisms growing in or on the soil; and the management, conservation, or utilization thereof for particular purposes or uses.

GS-500: ACCOUNTING AND BUDGET GROUP - This group includes all classes of positions, the duties of which are to advise on, administer, supervise, or perform professional, technical, or related clerical work of an accounting, budget administration, related financial management, or similar nature.

GS-600: MEDICAL, HOSPITAL, DENTAL, AND PUBLIC HEALTH GROUP - This group includes all classes of positions, the duties of which are to advise on, administer, supervise, or perform research or other professional and scientific work, subordinate technical work, or related clerical work in the several branches of medicine, surgery, and dentistry or in related patient care services such as dietetics, nursing, occupational therapy, physical therapy, pharmacy, and others.

GS-700: VETERINARY MEDICAL SCIENCE GROUP - This group includes all classes of positions, the duties of which are to advise and consult on, administer, manage, supervise, or perform research or other professional and scientific work in the various branches of veterinary medical science.

GS-800: ENGINEERING AND ARCHITECTURE - This group includes all classes of positions, the duties of which are to advise on, administer, supervise, or perform professional, scientific, or technical work concerned with engineering or architectural projects, facilities, structures, systems, processes, equipment, devices, material or methods. Positions in this group require knowledge of the science or art, or both, by which materials, natural resources, and power are made useful.

GS-900: LEGAL AND KINDRED GROUP - This group includes all classes of positions, the duties of which are to advise on, administer, supervise, or perform professional legal work in the preparation for trial and the trial and argument of cases, the presiding at formal hearings afforded by a commission, board, or other body having quasi-judicial powers, as part of its administrative procedure, the administration of law entrusted to an agency, the preparation or rendering of authoritative or advisory legal opinions or decisions to other federal agencies or to administrative officials of own agency, the preparation of various legal documents; and the performance of other work requiring training equivalent to that represented by graduation from a recognized law school and in some instances requiring admission to the bar; or quasi-legal work which requires knowledge of particular laws, or of regulations, precedents, or departmental practice based thereon, but which does not require such legal training or admission to the bar.

GS-1000: INFORMATION AND ARTS GROUP - This group includes positions which involve professional, artistic, technical, or clerical work in (1) the communication of information and ideas through verbal, visual, or pictorial means, (2) the collection, custody, presentation, display, and interpretation of art works, cultural objects, and other artifacts, or (3) a branch of fine or applied arts such as industrial design, interior design, or musical composition. Positions in this group require writing, editing, and language ability; artistic skill and ability; knowledge of foreign languages; the ability to evaluate and interpret informational and cultural materials; the practical application of technical or aesthetic principles combined with manual skill and dexterity; or related clerical skills.

GS-1100: BUSINESS AND INDUSTRY GROUP - This group includes all classes of positions, the duties of which are to advise on, administer, supervise, or perform work pertaining to and requiring a knowledge of business and trade practices, characteristics and use of equipment, products, or property, or industrial production methods and processes, including the conduct of investigations and studies; the collection, analysis, and dissemination of information; the establishment and maintenance of contacts with industry and commerce; the provision of advisory services; the examination and appraisement of merchandise or property; and the administration of regulatory provisions and controls.

GS-1200: COPYRIGHT, PATENT, AND TRADE-MARK GROUP - This group includes all classes of positions, the duties of which are to advise on, administer, supervise, or perform professional scientific, technical, and legal work involved in the cataloging and registration of copyright, in the classification and issuance of patents, in the registration of trade-marks, in the prosecution of applications for patents before the Patent Office, and in the giving of advice to government officials on patent matters.

GS-1300: PHYSICAL SCIENCE GROUP - This group includes all classes of positions, the duties of which are to advise on, administer, supervise, or perform research or other professional and scientific work or subordinate technical work in any of the fields of science concerned with matter, energy, physical space, time, nature of physical measurement, and fundamental structural particles; and the nature of the physical environment.

GS-1400: LIBRARY AND ARCHIVES GROUP - This group includes all classes of positions, the duties of which are to advise on, administer, supervise, or perform professional and scientific work or subordinate technical work in the various phases of library archival science.

GS-1500: MATHEMATICS AND STATISTICS GROUP - This group includes all classes of positions, the duties of which are to advise on, administer, supervise, or perform research or other professional and scientific work or related clerical work in basic mathematical principals, methods, procedures, or relationships, including the development and application of mathematical methods for the investigation and solution of problems; the development and application of statistical theory in the selection, collection, classification, adjustment, analysis, and interpretation of data; the development and application of mathematical, statistical, and financial principles to programs or problems involving life and property risks; and any other professional and scientific or related clerical work requiring primarily and mainly the understanding and use of mathematical theories, methods, and operations.

GS-1600: EQUIPMENT, FACILITIES, AND SERVICES GROUP - This group includes positions the duties of which are to advise on, manage, or provide instructions and information concerning the operation, maintenance, and use of equipment, shops, buildings, laundries, printing plants, power plants, cemeteries, or other government facilities, or other work involving services provided predominantly by persons in trades, crafts, or manual labor operations. Positions in this group require technical or managerial knowledge and ability, plus a practical knowledge of trades, crafts, or manual labor operations.

GS-1700: EDUCATION GROUP - This group includes positions which involve administering, managing, supervising, performing, or supporting education or training work when the paramount requirement of the position is knowledge of, or skill in, education, training, or instruction processes.

GS-1800: INVESTIGATION GROUP - This group includes all classes of positions the duties of which are to advise on, administer, supervise, or perform investigation, inspection, or enforcement work primarily concerned with alleged or suspected offenses against the laws of the United States, or such work primarily concerned with determining compliance with laws and regulations.

GS-1900: QUALITY ASSURANCE, INSPECTION, AND GRADING GROUP - This group includes all classes of positions, the duties of which are to advise on, supervise, or perform administrative or technical work primarily concerned with the quality assurance or inspection of material, facilities, and processes; or with the grading of commodities under official standards.

GS-2000: SUPPLY GROUP - This group includes positions which involve work concerned with finishing all types of supplies, equipment, material, property (except real estate), and certain services to components of the federal government, industrial, or other concerns under contract to the government, or receiving supplies from the federal government. Included are positions concerned with one or more aspects of supply activities from initial planning, including requirements analysis and determination, through acquisition, cataloging, storage, distribution, utilization to ultimate issue for consumption or disposal. The work requires a knowledge of one or more elements or parts of a supply system, and/or supply methods, policies, or procedures.

GS-2100: TRANSPORTATION GROUP - This group includes all classes of positions, the duties of which are to advise on, administer, supervise, or perform work which involves two or more specialized transportation functions or other transportation work not specifically included in other series of this group.

GENERAL SCHEDULE GROUPS & RELATED SERIES
GS-000-Miscellaneous Occupations Group (Not Elsewhere Classified)

Correctional Institution Administration Series	GS-006	Chaplain Series	GS-060
Correctional Officer	GS-007	Clothing Design Series	GS-062
Bond Sales Promotion Series	GS-011	Fingerprint Identification Series	GS-072
Safety and Occupational Health Management Series	GS-018	Security Administration Series	GS-080
Safety Technician Series	GS-019	Fire Protection and Prevention Series	GS-081
Community Planning Series	GS-020	United States Marshall Series	GS-082
Community Planning Technician Series	GS-021	Police Series	GS-083
Outdoor Recreation Planning Series	GS-023	Nuclear Materials Courier Series	GS-084
Park Ranger Series	GS-025	Security Guard Series	GS-085
Environmental Protection Specialist Series	GS-028	Security Clerical Assistance Series	GS-086
Environmental Protection Assistant Series	GS-029	Guide Series	GS-090
Sports Specialist Series	GS-030	Foreign Law Specialist Series	GS-095
Funeral Directing Series	GS-050	General Student Trainee Series	GS-099

GS-100-SOCIAL SCIENCE, PSYCHOLOGY, AND WELFARE GROUP

Social Science Series	GS-101	Geography Series	GS-150
Social Science Aid and Technician Series	GS-102	Civil Rights Analysis Series	GS-160
Social Insurance Administration Series	GS-105	History Series	GS-170
Unemployment Insurance Series	GS-106	Psychology Series	GS-180
Economist Series	GS-110	Psychology Aid and Technician Series	GS-181
Economics Assistant Series	GS-119	Sociology Series	GS-184
Food Assistance Program Specialist Series	GS-120	Social Work Series	GS-185
Foreign Affairs Series	GS-130	Social Services Aid and Assistant Series	GS-186
International Relations Series	GS-131	Social Services Series	GS-187
Intelligence Series	GS-132	Recreation Specialist Series	GS-188
Intelligence Aid and Clerk Series	GS-134	Recreation Aid and Assistant Series	GS-189
Foreign Agricultural Affairs Series	GS-135	General Anthropology Series	GS-190
International Cooperation Series	GS-136	Archeology Series	GS-193
Manpower Research and Analysis Series	GS-140	Social Science Student Trainee Series	GS-199
Manpower Development Series	GS-142		

GS-200-PERSONNEL MANAGEMENT AND INDUSTRIAL RELATIONS GROUP

Personnel Management Series	GS-201	Employee Development Series	GS-235
Personnel Clerical and Assistance Series	GS-203	Mediation Series	GS-241
Military Personnel Clerical and Technician Series	GS-204	Apprenticeship and Training Series	GS-243
Military Personnel Management Series	GS-205	Labor Management Relations Examining Series	GS-244
Personnel Staffing Series	GS-212	Contractor Industrial Relations Series	GS-246
Position Classification Series	GS-221	Wage and Hour Compliance Series	GS-249
Occupational Analysis Series	GS-222	Equal Employment Opportunity Series	GS-260
Salary and Wage Administration Series	GS-223	Federal Retirement Benefits Series	GS-270
Employee Relations Series	GS-230	Personnel Management Student Trainee Series	GS-299
Labor Relations Series	GS-233		

GS-300-GENERAL ADMINISTRATION, CLERICAL, AND OFFICE SERVICES GROUP

Miscellaneous Administration and Program Series	GS-301	Clerk-Typist Series	GS-322
Messenger Series	GS-302	Office Automation Clerical and Assistance Series	GS-326
Miscellaneous Clerk and Assistant Series	GS-303	Computer Operation Series	GS-332
Information Receptionist Series	GS-304	Computer Specialist Series	GS-334
Mail and File Series	GS-305	Computer Clerk and Assistant Series	GS-335
Correspondence Clerk Series	GS-309	Program Management Series	GS-340
Clerk-Stenographer and Reporter Series	GS-312	Administrative Officer Series	GS-341
Work Unit Supervising Series	GS-313	Support Services Administration Series	GS-342
Secretary Series	GS-318	Management and Program Analysis Series	GS-343
Closed Microphone Reporting Series	GS-319	Management Clerical and Assistance Series	GS-344
Logistics Management Series	GS-346	Electric Accounting Machine Project Planning Series	GS-362
Equipment Operator Series	GS-350	Telephone Operating Series	GS-382
Printing Clerical Series	GS-351	Telecommunications Processing Series	GS-390
Data Transcriber Series	GS-356	Telecommunications Series	GS-391
Coding Series	GS-357	General Communications Series	GS-392
Electric Accounting Machine Operation Series	GS-359	Communications Clerical Series	GS-394
Equal Opportunity Compliance Series	GS-360	Administration & Office Support Student Trainee Series	
Equal Opportunity Assistance Series	GS-361	Series	GS-399

GS-400-BIOLOGICAL SCIENCES GROUP

General Biological Science Series	GS-401	Range Conservation Series	GS-454
Microbiology Series	GS-403	Range Technician Series	GS-455
Biological Science Technician Series	GS-404	Soil Conservation Series	GS-457
Pharmacology Series	GS-405	Soil Conservation Technician Series	GS-458
Agricultural Extension Series	GS-406	Irrigation System Operation Series	GS-459
Ecology Series	GS-408	Forestry Series	GS-460
Zoology Series	GS-410	Forestry Technician Series	GS-462
Physiology Series	GS-413	Soil Science Series	GS-470

Entomology Series	GS-414	Agronomy Series	GS-471
Toxicology Series	GS-415	Agricultural Management Series	GS-475
Plant Protection Technician Series	GS-421	General Fish and Wildlife Administration Series	GS-480
Botany Series	GS-430	Fishery Biology Series	GS-482
Plant Pathology Series	GS-434	Wildlife Refuge Management Series	GS-485
Plant Physiology Series	GS-435	Wildlife Biology Series	GS-486
Plant Protection and Quarantine Series	GS-436	Animal Science Series	GS-487
Horticulture Series	GS-437	Home Economics Series	GS-493
Genetics Series	GS-440	Biological Science Student Trainee Series	GS-499

GS-500 ACCOUNTING AND BUDGET GROUP

Financial Administration and Program Series	GS-501	Voucher Examining Series	GS-540
Financial Clerical and Assistance Series	GS-503	Civilian Pay Series	GS-544
Financial Management Series	GS-505	Military Pay Series	GS-545
Accounting Series	GS-510	Budget Analysis Series	GS-560
Auditing Series	GS-511	Budget Clerical and Assistance Series	GS-561
Internal Revenue Agent Series	GS-512	Financial Institution Examining Series	GS-570
Accounting Technician Series	GS-525	Tax Examining Series	GS-592
Tax Technician Series	GS-526	Insurance Accounts Series	GS-593
Cash Processing Series	GS-530	Financial Management Student Trainee Series	GS-599

GS-600-MEDICAL, HOSPITAL, DENTAL, AND PUBLIC HEALTH GROUP

General Health Science Series	GS-601	Diagnostic Radiologic Technologist Series	GS-647
Medical Officer Series	GS-602	Therapeutic Radiologic Technologist Series	GS-648
Physician's Assistant Series	GS-603	Medical Instrument Technician Series	GS-649
Nurse Series	GS-610	Medical Technical Assistant Series	GS-650
Practical Nurse Series	GS-620	Respiratory Therapist Series	GS-651
Nursing Assistant Series	GS-621	Pharmacist Series	GS-660
Medical Supply Aide and Technician Series	GS-622	Pharmacy Technician Series	GS-661
Autopsy Assistant Series	GS-625	Optometrist Series	GS-662
Dietitian and Nutritionist Series	GS-630	Restoration Technician Series	GS-664
Occupational Therapist Series	GS-631	Speech Pathology and Audiology Series	GS-665
Physical Therapist Series	GS-633	Orthotist and Prosthetist Series	GS-667
Corrective Therapist Series	GS-635	Podiatrist Series	GS-668
Rehabilitation Therapy Assistant Series	GS-636	Medical Records Administration Series	GS-669
Manual Arts Therapist Series	GS-637	Health System Administration Series	GS-670
Recreation/Creative Arts Therapist Series	GS-638	Health System Specialist Series	GS-671
Educational Therapist Series	GS-639	Prosthetic Representative Series	GS-672
Health Aid and Technician Series	GS-640	Hospital Housekeeping Management Series	GS-673
Nuclear Medicine Technician Series	GS-642	Medical Records Technician Series	GS-675
Medical Technologist Series	GS-644	Medical Clerk Series	GS-679
Medical Technician Series	GS-645	Dental Officer Series	GS-680
Pathology Technician Series	GS-646	Dental Assistant Series	GS-681
Dental Hygiene Series	GS-682	Industrial Hygiene Series	GS-690
Dental Laboratory Aid and Technician Series	GS-683	Consumer Safety Series	GS-696
Public Health Program Specialist Series	GS-685	Environmental Health Technician Series	GS-698
Sanitarian Series	GS-688	Medical and Health Student Trainee Series	GS-699

GS-700-VETERINARY MEDICAL SCIENCE GROUP

Veterinary Medical Science Series	GS-701	Veterinary Student Trainee Series	GS-799
Animal Health Technician Series	GS-704		

GS-800-ENGINEERING AND ARCHITECTURE GROUP

General Engineering Series	GS-801	Computer Engineering Series	GS-854
Engineering Technician Series	GS-802	Electronics Engineering Series	GS-855
Safety Engineering Series	GS-803	Electronics Technician Series	GS-856
Fire Protection Engineering Series	GS-804	Biomedical Engineering Series	GS-858
Materials Engineering Series	GS-806	Aerospace Engineering Series	GS-861

Landscape Architecture Series	GS-807	Naval Architecture Series	GS-871
Architecture Series	GS-808	Ship Surveying Series	GS-873
Construction Control Series	GS-809	Mining Engineering Series	GS-880
Civil Engineering Series	GS-810	Petroleum Engineering Series	GS-881
Surveying Technician Series	GS-817	Agricultural Engineering Series	GS-890
Engineering Drafting Series	GS-818	Ceramic Engineering Series	GS-892
Environmental Engineering Series	GS-819	Chemical Engineering Series	GS-893
Construction Analyst Series	GS-828	Welding Engineering Series	GS-894
Mechanical Engineering Series	GS-830	Industrial Engineering Technician Series	GS-895
Nuclear Engineering Series	GS-840	Industrial Engineering Series	GS-896
Electrical Engineering Series	GS-850	Engineering and Architecture Student Trainee Series	GS-899

GS-900-LEGAL AND KINDRED GROUP

Law Clerk Series	GS-904	Legal Clerical and Assistance Series	GS-986
General Attorney Series	GS-905	Tax Law Specialist Series	GS-987
Estate Tax Examining Series	GS-920	General Claims Examining Series	GS-990
Hearings and Appeals Series	GS-930	Workers' Compensation Claims Examining Series	GS-991
Clerk of Court Series	GS-945	Loss and Damage Claims Examining Series	GS-992
Paralegal Specialist Series	GS-950	Social Insurance Claims Examining Series	GS-993
Pension Law Specialist Series	GS-958	Unemployment Compensation Examining Series	GS-994
Contact Representative Series	GS-962	Dependents and Estates Claims Examining Series	GS-995
Legal Instruments Examining Series	GS-963	Veterans Claims Examining Series	GS-996
Land Law Examining Series	GS-965	Claims Clerical Series	GS-998
Passport and Visa Examining Series	GS-967	Legal Occupations Student Trainee Series	GS-999

GS-1000-INFORMATION AND ARTS GROUP

General Arts and Information Series	GS-1001	Music Specialist Series	GS-1051
Interior Design Series	GS-1008	Theater Specialist Series	GS-1054
Exhibits Specialist Series	GS-1010	Art Specialist Series	GS-1056
Museum Curator Series	GS-1015	Photography Series	GS-1060
Museum Specialist and Technician Series	GS-1016	Audiovisual Production Series	GS-1071
Illustrating Series	GS-1020	Writing and Editing Series	GS-1082
Office Drafting Series	GS-1021	Technical Writing and Editing Series	GS-1083
Public Affairs Series	GS-1035	Visual Information Series	GS-1084
Language Specialist Series	GS-1040	Editorial Assistance Series	GS-1087
Language Clerical Series	GS-1046	Information and Arts Student Trainee Series	GS-1099

GS-1100-BUSINESS AND INDUSTRY GROUP

General Business and Industry Series	GS-1101	Property Disposal Series	GS-1104
Contracting Series	GS-1102	Purchasing Series	GS-1105
Industrial Property Management Series	GS-1103	Procurement Clerical and Technician Series	GS-1106
Property Disposal Clerical and Technician Series	GS-1107	Crop Insurance Administration Series	GS-1161
Public Utilities Specialist Series	GS-1130	Crop Insurance Underwriting Series	GS-1162
Trade Specialist Series	GS-1140	Insurance Examining Series	GS-1163
Commissary Store Management Series	GS-1144	Loan Specialist Series	GS-1165
Agricultural Program Specialist Series	GS-1145	Internal Revenue Officer Series	GS-1169
Agricultural Marketing Series	GS-1146	Realty Series	GS-1170
Agricultural Market Reporting Series	GS-1147	Appraising and Assessing Series	GS-1171
Industrial Specialist Series	GS-1150	Housing Management Series	GS-1173
Production Control Series	GS-1152	Building Management Series	GS-1176
Financial Analysis Series	GS-1160	Business and Industry Student Trainee Series	GS-1199

GS-1200-COPYRIGHT, PATENT, AND TRADE-MARK GROUP

Patent Technician Series	GS-1202	Patent Attorney Series	GS-1222
Copyright Series	GS-1210	Patent Classifying Series	GS-1223
Copyright Technician Series	GS-1211	Patent Examining Series	GS-1224
Patent Administration Series	GS-1220	Design Patent Examining Series	GS-1226

Patent Advisor Series	GS-1221	Copyright and Patent Student Trainee Series	GS-1299

GS-1300-PHYSICAL SCIENCES GROUP

General Physical Science Series	GS-1301	Oceanography Series	GS-1360
Health Physics Series	GS-1306	Navigational Information Series	GS-1361
Physics Series	GS-1310	Cartography Series	GS-1370
Physical Science Technician Series	GS-1311	Cartographic Technician Series	GS-1371
Geophysics Series	GS-1313	Geodesy Series	GS-1372
Hydrology Series	GS-1315	Land Surveying Series	GS-1373
Hydrologic Technician Series	GS-1316	Geodetic Technician Series	GS-1374
Chemistry Series	GS-1320	Forest Products Technology Series	GS-1380
Metallurgy Series	GS-1321	Food Technology Series	GS-1382
Astronomy and Space Science Series	GS-1330	Textile Technology Series	GS-1384
Meteorology Series	GS-1340	Photographic Technology Series	GS-1386
Meteorological Technician Series	GS-1341	Document Analysis Series	GS-1397
Geology Series	GS-1350	Physical Science Student Trainee Series	GS-1399

GS-1400-LIBRARY AND ARCHIVES GROUP

Librarian Series	GS-1410	Archivist Series	GS-1420
Library Technician Series	GS-1411	Archives Technician Series	GS-1421
Technical Information Services Series	GS-1412	Library and Archives Student Trainee	GS-1499

GS-1500-MATHEMATICS AND STATISTICS GROUP

Actuary Series	GS-1510	Statistical Assistant Series	GS-1531
Operations Research Series	GS-1515	Cryptography Series	GS-1540
Mathematics Series	GS-1520	Cryptanalysis Series	GS-1541
Mathematics Technician Series	GS-1521	Computer Science Series	GS-1550
Mathematical Statistician Series	GS-1529	Mathematics and Statistics Student Trainee Series	GS-1599
Statistician Series	GS-1530		

GS-1600-EQUIPMENT, FACILITIES, AND SERVICES GROUP

General Facilities and Equipment Series	GS-1601	Steward Series	GS-1667
Cemetery Administration Series	GS-1630	Equipment Specialist Series	GS-1670
Facility Management Series	GS-1640	Equipment & Facilities Mgmt Student Trainee Series	GS-1699
Printing Management Series	GS-1654		
Laundry and Dry Cleaning Plant Management Series	GS-1658		

GS-1700-EDUCATION GROUP

General Education and Training Series	GS-1701	Training Instruction Series	GS-1712
Education and Training Technician Series	GS-1702	Vocational Rehabilitation Series	GS-1715
Educational and Vocational Training Series	GS-1710	Education Program Series	GS-1720
Public Health Educator Series	GS-1725	Instructional Systems Series	GS-1750
Education Research Series	GS-1730	Education Student Trainee Series	GS-1799
Education Services Series	GS-1740		

GS-1800-INVESTIGATION GROUP

General Inspection Investigation & Compliance Series	GS-1801	Consumer Safety Inspection Series	GS-1862
Compliance Inspection and Support Series	GS-1802	Food Inspection Series	GS-1863
General Investigating Series	GS-1810	Public Health Quarantine Inspection Series	GS-1864
Criminal Investigating Series	GS-1811	Customs Patrol Officer Series	GS-1884
Game Law Enforcement Series	GS-1812	Import Specialist Series	GS-1889
Air Safety Investigating Series	GS-1815	Customs Inspection Series	GS-1890
Immigration Inspection Series	GS-1816	Customs Entry and Liquidating Series	GS-1894
Mine Safety and Health Series	GS-1822	Customs Warehouse Officer Series	GS-1895
Aviation Safety Series	GS-1825	Border Patrol Agent Series	GS-1896
Securities Compliance Examining Series	GS-1831	Customs Aid Series	GS-1897

Agricultural Commodity Warehouse Examining Series	GS-1850	Admeasurement Series	GS-1898
Alcohol, Tobacco and Firearms Inspection Series	GS-1854	Investigation Student Trainee Series	GS-1899

GS-QUALITY ASSURANCE, INSPECTION, AND GRADING GROUP

Quality Assurance Series	GS-1910	Agricultural Commodity Aid Series	GS-1981
Agricultural Commodity Grading Series	GS-1980	Quality Inspection Student Trainee Series	GS-1999

GS-2000-SUPPLY GROUP

General Supply Series	GS-2001	Packaging Series	GS-2032
Supply Program Management Series	GS-2003	Supply Cataloging Series	GS-2050
Supply Clerical and Technician Series	GS-2005	Sales Store Clerical Series	GS-2091
Inventory Management Series	GS-2010	Supply Student Trainee Series	GS-2099
Distribution Facilities and Storage Management Series	GS-2030		

GS-2100-TRANSPORTATION GROUP

Transportation Specialist Series	GS-2101	Transportation Loss and Damage Claims	
Transportation Clerk and Assistant Series	GS-2102	Examining Series	GS-2135
Transportation Industry Analysis Series	GS-2110	Cargo Scheduling Series	GS-2144
Transportation Rate and Tariff Examining Series	GS-2111	Transportation Operations Series	GS-2150
Railroad Safety Series	GS-2121	Dispatching Series	GS-2151
Motor Carrier Safety Series	GS-2123	Air Traffic Control Series	GS-2152
Highway Safety Series	GS-2125	Air Traffic Assistance Series	GS-2154
Traffic Management Series	GS-2130	Marine Cargo Series	GS-2161
Freight Rate Series	GS-2131	Aircraft Operation Series	GS-2181
Travel Series	GS-2132	Air Navigation Series	GS-2183
Passenger Rate Series	GS-2133	Aircrew Technician Series	GS-2185
Shipment Clerical and Assistance Series	GS-2134	Transportation Student Trainee Series	GS-2199

(WAGE GRADE) TRADES & LABOR JOB FAMILIES & OCCUPATIONS

The Government's Personnel Classification System includes Wage Grade occupations grouped into families of like jobs. The 36 occupational families range from WG-2500 to WG-9000. Each occupational family has its own group number and title which makes it distinctive from every other family grouping. The following is a list of the Wage Grade families.

Each occupational family has a three part identifier: the Pay System, Occupational Group Number and Title. In the example, WG-2500, Wire Communications Equipment Installation and Maintenance Family, WG means the job is in the Wage Grade Schedule (or blue collar) pay system; 2500 is the Occupational Family Number; and Wire Communications Equipment Installation and Maintenance is the Occupational Family Title. Each occupational family lists the individual jobs that comprise the family with their corresponding Job Series Numbers and Titles.

[2]A brief description is provided for each of the occupational Wage Grade families. Following each family description, the jobs within that family are listed.

---

[2]The Wage Grade listing is taken from the Government Printing Office publication TS-56 dated March 1990, titled PART 3, DEFINITIONS OF TRADES AND LABOR JOB FAMILIES AND OCCUPATIONS.

WG-2500 - Wire Communications Equipment Installation and Maintenance Family

This job family includes occupations involved in the construction, installation, maintenance, repair and testing of all types of wire communications systems and associated equipment which are predominantly electrical-mechanical. Work involved in the installation and repair of communications equipment which requires in-depth knowledge of operating electronic principles should be coded to electronic equipment installation and maintenance family, 2600.

WG-2502   Telephone Mechanic
WG-2504   Wire Communications Cable Splicing

WG-2508   Communications Line Installing/Repairing
WG-2511   Wire Communications Equip. Install/Repair

WG-2600 - Electronic Equipment Installation and Maintenance Family

This job family includes occupations involved in the installation, repair, overhaul, fabrication, tuning, alignment, modification, calibration, and testing of electronic equipment and related devices, such as radio, radar, loran, sonar, television, and other communications equipment; industrial controls; fire control, flight/landing control, bombing-navigation, and other integrated systems; and electronic computer systems and equipment.

WG-2602   Electronic Measurement Equip. Mech.
WG-2604   Electronics Mechanic
WG-2606   Electronic Industrial Controls Mechanic

WG-2698   Electronic Digital Computer Mechanic
WG-2610   Electronic Integrated Systems Mechanic

WG-2800 Electrical Installation & Maintenance Family

This job family includes occupations involved in the fabrication, installation, alteration, maintenance, repair, and testing of electrical systems, instruments, apparatus, and equipment.

WG-2800   Electrician
WG-2810   Electrician (High Voltage)

WG-2854   Electrical Equipment Repairing
WG-2892   Aircraft Electrician

WG-3100 Fabric & Leather Work Family

This job family includes occupations involving the fabrication, modification, and repair of clothing and equipment made of (a) woven textile fabrics of animal, vegetable, or synthetic origin; (b) plastic film and filaments; (c) natural and simulated leather; (d) natural and synthetic fabrics; and (e) paper. Work involves use of handtools and mechanical devices and machines to lay out, cut, sew, rivet, mold, fit, assemble, and attach bindings to articles such as uniforms, rain gear, hats, belts, shoes, brief cases, holsters, equipage articles, tents, gun covers, bags, parachutes, upholstery, mattresses, brushes, etc.

WG-3103   Shoe Repairing
WG-3105   Fabric Working
WG-3106   Upholstering

WG-3111   Sewing Machine Operating
WG-3119   Broom & Brush Making

WG-3300 Instrument Work Family

This job family includes occupations that involve fabricating, assembling, calibrating, testing, installing, repairing, modifying, and maintaining instruments and instrumentation systems for measuring, regulating, and computing physical quantities such as moment, force, acceleration, displacement, stress, strain, vibration or oscillation frequency, phase and amplitude, linear or angular velocity, voltage, current, power, impedance, etc.

Examples of such instruments and equipment are: gyro, optical, photographic, timekeeping, electrical, metered, pressure, and geared instruments, test equipment, and navigation, flight control, and fuel totalizing systems. The work requires knowledge of electrical, electronic, mechanical, optical, pneumatic, and/or hydraulic principals. Work that primarily involves fabricating and repairing electronic instruments should be coded to the electronic equipment installation and maintenance family, 2600.

WG-3306 Optical Instrument Repairing
WG-3314 Instrument Making
WG-3341 Scale Building, Install/Repair

WG-3359 Instrument Mechanic
WG-3364 Projection Equipment Repairing

WG-3400 Machine Tool Work Family

This job family includes occupations that involve setting up and operating machine tools and using handtools to make or repair (shape, fit, finish, assemble) metal parts, tools, gages, models, patterns, mechanisms, and machines; and machining explosives and synthetic materials.

WG-3414 Machining
WG-3416 Toolmaking
WG-3417 Tool Grinding

WG-3422 Power Saw Operator
WG-3428 Die Sinker
WG-3431 Machine Tool Operating

WG-3500 General Services & Support Work Family

This job family includes occupations not specifically covered by another family that require little or no specialized training or work experience to enter. These occupations usually involve work such as moving and handling material (e.g., loading, unloading, digging, hauling, hoisting, carrying, wrapping, mixing, pouring, spreading); washing and cleaning laboratory apparatus, cars, and trucks, etc.; cleaning and maintaining living quarters, hospital rooms and ward, office buildings, grounds, and other areas; and doing other general maintenance work, by hand or using common handtools and power equipment. They may involve heavy or light physical work and various skill levels. Skills are generally learned through job experience and instruction from supervisors or, in some instances, formal training programs lasting a few days or weeks or longer.

WG-3502 Laboring
WG-3506 Summer Aid/Student Aid
WG-3508 Pipeline Working
WG-3511 Laboratory Working
WG-3513 Coin/Currency Checking

WG-3515 Laboratory Support Working
WG-3543 Stevedoring
WG-3546 Railroad Repairing
WG-3566 Custodial Working

WG-3600 Structural & Finishing Work Family

This job family includes occupations not specifically covered by another family that involve doing structural and finishing work in construction, maintenance, and repair of surfaces and structures, e.g., laying brick, block, and stone; setting tile; finishing cement and concrete; plastering; installing, maintaining, and repairing asphalt, tar, and gravel; roofing; insulating and glazing.

WG-3602 Cement Finishing
WG-3603 Masonry
WG-3604 Tile Setting
WG-3605 Plastering
WG-3604 Roofing
WG-3609 Floor Covering Installing

WG-3610 Insulating
WG-3611 Glazing
WG-3653 Asphalt Working

WG-3700 Metal Processing Family

This job family includes occupations which involve processing or treating metals to alter their properties or produce desirable qualities such as hardness or workability, using processes such as welding, plating, melting, alloying, annealing, heat treating, and refining.

WG-3702 Flame/Arc Cutting	WG-3720 Brazing & Soldering
WG-3703 Welding	WG-3722 Cold Working
WG-3705 Nondestructive Testing	WG-3725 Battery Repairing
WG-3707 Metalizing	WG-3727 Buffing & Polishing
WG-3708 Metal Process Working	WG-3735 Metal Phototransferring
WG-3711 Electroplating	WG-3736 Circuit Board Making
WG-3712 Heat Treating	WG-3741 Furnace Operating
WG-3716 Leadburning	WG-3769 Shot Preening Machine Operating

WG-3800 Metal Working Family

This job family includes occupations involved in shaping and forming metal and making and repairing metal parts or equipment. Includes such work as the fabrication and assembly of sheet metal parts and equipment; forging and press operations; structural iron working, stamping, etc. Doesn't include machine tool work.

WG-3802 Metal Forging	WG-3819 Airframe Jig Fitting
WG-3804 Coppersmithing	WG-3820 Shipfitting
WG-3806 Sheet Metal Mechanic	WG-3830 Blacksmithing
WG-3807 Structural/Ornamental Iron Working	WG-3832 Metal Making
WG-3808 Boilermaking	WG-3833 Transfer Engraving
WG-3809 Mobile Equipment Metal Mechanic	WG-3858 Metal Tank & Radiator Repairing
WG-3815 Pneumatic Tool Operating	WG-3869 Metal Forming Machine Operating
WG-3816 Engraving	WG-3872 Metal Tube Making & Installing
WG-3818 Springmaking	

WG-3900 Motion Picture, Radio, Television, and Sound Equipment Operation Family

This job family includes occupations involved in setting up, testing, operating, and making minor repairs to equipment such as microphones, sound and radio controls, sound recording equipment, lighting and sound effect devices, television cameras, magnetic video tape recorders, motion picture projectors, and broadcast transmitters used in the production of motion pictures and radio and television programs. Also includes occupations that involve related work such as operating public address system equipment.

WG-3910 Motion Picture Projection	WG-3940 Broadcasting Equipment Operating
WG-3911 Sound Recording Equipment Operating	WG-3941 Public Address Equipment Operating
WG-3919 Television Equipment Operating	

WG-4000 Lens and Crystal Work Family

This job family includes occupations involved in making precision optical elements, crystal blanks or wafers, or other items of glass, polished metals, or similar materials, using such methods as cutting, polishing, etc.

WG-4005 Optical Element Working	WG-4015 Quartz Crystal Working
WG-4010 Prescription Eyeglass Making	

WG-4100 Painting & Paperhanging Family

This job family includes occupations which involve hand or spray painting and decorating interiors and exteriors of buildings, structures, aircraft, vessels, mobile equipment, fixtures, furnishings, machinery, and other surfaces; finishing hardwoods, furniture, and cabinetry; painting signs; covering interiors of rooms with strips of wallpaper or fabric, etc.

WG-4102 Painting

WG-4103 Paperhanging

WG-4104 Sign Painting

WG-4157 Instrument Dial Painting

WG-4200 Plumbing & Pipefitting Family

This job family includes occupations that involve the installation, maintenance, and repair of water, air, steam, gas, sewer, and other pipelines and systems, and related fixtures, apparatus, and accessories.

WG-4204 Pipefitting

WG-4206 Plumbing

WG-4255 Fuel Distribution Systems Mechanic

WG-4300 Pliable Materials Work Family

This job family includes occupations involved in shaping, forming, and repairing items and parts from non-metallic moldable materials such as plastic, rubber, clay, wax, plaster, glass, sand, or other similar material.

WG-4351 Plastic Molding Equipment Operating

WG-4352 Plastic Fabricating

WG-4360 Rubber Products Molding

WG-4361 Rubber Equipment Repairing

WG-4370 Glassblowing

WG-4371 Plaster Pattern Casting

WG-4373 Molding

WG-4374 Core Making

WG-4400 Printing Family

This job family includes occupations involved in letterpress (relief), offset- lithographic, gravure (intaglio), or screen printing; including layout, hand composition, typesetting from hot metal type, platemaking, printing, and finishing operations.

WG-4402 Bindery Work

WG-4403 Hand Composing

WG-4405 Film Assembly-Stripping

WG-4406 Letterpress Operating

WG-4407 Linotype Machine Operating

WG-4413 Negative Engraving

WG-4414 Offset Photography

WG-4416 Platemaking

WG-4417 Offset Press Operating

WG-4419 Silk Screen Making & Printing

WG-4422 Dot Etching

WG-4425 Photoengraving

WG-4441 Bookbinding

WG-4445 Bank Note Designing

WG-4446 Bank Note Engraving

WG-4447 Sculptural Engraving

WG-4448 Sidergraphic Transferring

WG-4449 Electrolytic Intaglio Platemaking

WG-4450 Intaglio Die & Plate Finishing

WG-4454 Intaglio Press Operating

WG-4600 Wood Work Family

This occupation includes jobs involved in blocking, bracing, staying, and securing cargo for shipment by land, sea, or air. It requires skill in construction, placing, and installing wooden blocks, wedges, bracing, structures, and other staying devices, as well as skill in securing items using wires, ropes, chains, cables, plates, and other hardware.

WG-4602   Blocking & Bracing
WG-4604   Wood Working
WG-4605   Wood Crafting
WG-4607   Carpentry
WG-4616   Patternmaking

WG-4618   Woodworking Machine Operating
WG-4620   Shoe Lasting Repairing
WG-4639   Timber Working
WG-4654   Form Block Making

WG-4700 General Maintenance & Operations Work Family

This job family includes occupations which (1) consist of various combinations of work such as are involved in constructing, maintaining and repairing buildings, roads, grounds, and related facilities; manufacturing, modifying, and repairing items or apparatus made from a variety of materials or types of components; or repairing and operating equipment or utilities; and (2) require the application of a variety of trade practices associated with occupations in more than one job family (unless otherwise indicated), and the performance of the highest level of work in at least two of the trades involved.

WG-4714   Model Making
WG-4715   Exhibits Making/Modeling
WG-4716   Railroad Car Repairing
WG-4717   Boat Building and Repairing
WG-4737   General Equipment Mechanic

WG-4741   General Equipment Operating
WG-4742   Utility Systems Repairing-Operating
WG-4745   Research Laboratory Mechanic
WG-4749   Maintenance Mechanic
WG-4754   Cemetery Caretaking

WG-4800 General Equipment Maintenance Family

This job family includes occupations involved in the maintenance or repair of equipment, machines, or instruments which are not coded to other job families because the equipment is not characteristically related to one of the established subject-matter areas such as electronics, electrical, industrial, transportation, instruments, engines, aircraft, ordnance, etc., or because the nature of the work calls for limited knowledge/skill in a variety of crafts or trades as they relate to the repair of such equipment, but not a predominate knowledge of any one trade or craft.

WG-4802   Musical Instrument Repairing
WG-4804   Locksmithing
WG-4805   Medical Equipment Repairing
WG-4806   Office Appliance Repairing
WG-4807   Chemical Equipment Repairing
WG-4808   Custodial Equipment Servicing
WG-4812   Saw Reconditioning
WG-4816   Protective/Safety Equipment Fabrication
WG-4818   Aircraft Survival/Flight Equipment
WG-4819   Bowling Equipment Repairing
WG-4820   Vending Machine Repairing

WG-4839   Film Processing Equipment Repairing
WG-4840   Tool & Equipment Repairing
WG-4841   Window Shade Assembling, Repairing
WG-4843   Navigation Aids Repairing
WG-4844   Bicycle Repairing
WG-4845   Orthopedic Appliance Repairing
WG-4848   Mechanical Parts Repairing
WG-4850   Bearing Reconditioning
WG-4851   Reclamation Working
WG-4855   Domestic Appliance Repairing

WG-5000 Plant and Animal Work Family

This job family includes occupations involved in general or specialized farming operations; gardening, including the general care of grounds, roadways, nurseries, greenhouses, etc.; trimming and felling trees; and propagating, caring for, handling, and controlling animals and insects, including pest species.

WG-5002   Farming
WG-5003   Gardening
WG-5026   Pest Controlling

WG-5031   Insects Production Working
WG-5034   Dairy Farming
WG-5035   Livestock Ranching/Wrangling

WG-5042 Tree Trimming and Removing
WG-5048 Animal Caretaking

WG-5200 Miscellaneous Occupations Family

This job family includes occupations which are not covered by the definition of any other job family or which are of such a general or miscellaneous character as to preclude placing them within another job family.

WG-5205 Gas and Radiation Detecting
WG-5210 Rigging
WG-5220 Shipwright

WG-5221 Lofting
WG-5222 Diving
WG-5235 Test Range Tracking

WG-5300 Industrial Equipment Maintenance Family

This job family includes occupations involved in the general maintenance, installation, and repair of portable and stationary industrial machinery, tools, and equipment such as sewing machines, machine tools, woodworking and metal working machines, printing equipment, processing equipment, driving machinery, power generating equipment, air conditioning equipment, heating and boiler plant equipment, and other types of machines and equipment used in the production of goods and services.

WG-5306 Air Conditioning Equipment Mechanic
WG-5309 Heating and Boiler Plant Mechanic
WG-5310 Kitchen/Bakery Equipment Repairing
WG-5312 Sewing Machine Repairing
WG-5313 Elevator Mechanic
WG-5317 Laundry/Dry Cleaning Equip. Repairing
WG-5318 Lock & Dam Repairing
WG-5323 Oiling & Greasing
WG-5324 Powerhouse Equipment Repairing
WG-5326 Drawbridge Repairing

WG-5330 Printing Equipment Repairing
WG-5334 Marine Machinery Mechanic
WG-5335 Wind Tunnel Mechanic
WG-5341 Industrial Furnace Building & Repairing
WG-5350 Production Machinery Mechanic
WG-5352 Industrial Equipment Mechanic
WG-5364 Door Systems Mechanic
WG-5365 Physiological Trainer Mechanic
WG-5378 Powered Support Systems Mechanic
WG-5384 Gasdynamic Facility Installing/ Repairing

WG-5400 Industrial Equipment Operation Family

This job family includes occupations involved in the operation of portable and stationary industrial equipment, tools, and machines to generate and distribute utilities such as electricity, steam, and gas for heat or power; treat and distribute water; collect, treat, and dispose of waste; open and close bridges, locks and dams; lift and move workers, materials, and equipment; manufacture and process materials and products; etc.

WG-5402 Boiler Plant Operating
WG-5403 Incinerator Operating
WG-5406 Utility Systems Operating
WG-5407 Electric Power Controlling
WG-5408 Sewage Disposal Plant Operating
WG-5409 Water Treatment Plant Operating
WG-5413 Fuel Distribution System Operating
WG-5414 Baling Machine Operating
WG-5415 Air Conditioning Equipment Operating
WG-5419 Stationary-Engine Operating
WG-5423 Sandblasting
WG-5424 Weighing Machine Operating
WG-5426 Lock and Dam Operating

WG-5427 Chemical Plant Operating
WG-5430 Drawbridge Operating
WG-5433 Gas Generating Plant Operating
WG-5435 Carton/Bag Making Machine Operating
WG-5438 Elevator Operating
WG-5439 Testing Equipment Operating
WG-5440 Packaging Machine Operating
WG-5444 Food/Feed Processing Equip. Operating
WG-5446 Textile Equipment Operating
WG-5450 Conveyor Operating
WG-5454 Solvent Still Operating
WG-5455 Paper Pulping Machine Operating
WG-5473 Oil Reclamation Equipment Operating

WG-5478 Portable Equipment Operating
WG-5479 Dredging Equipment Operating
WG-5484 Counting Machine Operating

WG-5485 Aircraft Weight & Balance Operating
WG-5486 Swimming Pool Operating

WG-5700 Transportation/Mobile Equipment Operation Family

This job family includes occupations involved in the operation and operational maintenance of self-propelled transportation and other mobile equipment (except aircraft) used to move materials or passengers, including motor vehicles, engineering and construction equipment, tractors, etc. some of which may be equipped with power takeoff and controls to operate special purpose equipment; ocean-going and inland waterway vessels, harbor craft, and floating plants; and trains, locomotives, and train cars.

WG-5703 Motor Vehicle Operating
WG-5704 Fork Lift Operating
WG-5705 Tractor Operating
WG-5706 Road Sweeper Operating
WG-5707 Tank Driver
WG-5716 Engineering Equipment Operating
WG-5725 Crane Operating
WG-5729 Drill Rig Operating

WG-5731 Mining/Tunneling Machine Operating
WG-5736 Braking-Switching & Conducting
WG-5737 Locomotive Engineering
WG-5738 Railroad Maintenance Vehicle Operating
WG-5767 Airfield Clearing Equipment Operating
WG-5782 Ship Operating
WG-5784 Riverboat Operating
WG-5786 Small Craft Operating
WG-5788 Deckhand

WG-5800 Heavy Mobile Equipment Mechanic

This job family includes occupations involved in repairing, adjusting, and maintaining self-propelled transportation and other mobile equipment (except aircraft), including any special-purpose features with which they may be equipped.

WG-5803 Heavy Mobile Equipment Mechanic
WG-5806 Mobile Equipment Servicing

WG-5823 Automotive Mechanic
WG-5876 Electromotive Equipment Mechanic

WG-6500 Ammunition, Explosives, & Toxic Materials Work Family

This job family includes occupations involved in the manufacturing, assembling, disassembling, renovating, loading, deactivating, modifying, destroying, testing, handling, placing, and discharging of ammunition, propellants, chemicals and toxic materials, and other conventional and special munitions and explosives.

WG-6502 Explosives Operating
WG-6505 Munitions Destroying

WG-6511 Missile/Toxic Materials Handling
WG-6517 Explosives Test Operating

WG-6600 Armament Work Family

This job family includes occupations involved in the installation, repair, rebuilding, adjusting, modification, and testing of small arms and artillery weapons and allied accessories. Artillery includes, but is not limited to, field artillery, antitank artillery, antiaircraft weapons, aircraft and shipboard weapons, recoilless rifles, rocket launchers, mortars, cannon, and allied accessories. Small arms includes, but is not limited to, rifles, carbines, pistols, revolvers, helmets, body armor, shoulder-type rocket launchers, machine guns, and automatic rifles.

WG-6605 Artillery Repairing
WG-6606 Artillery Testing
WG-6610 Small Arms Repairing

WG-6641 Ordnance Equipment Mechanic
WG-6652 Aircraft Ordnance Systems Mechanic
WG-6656 Special Weapons Systems Mechanic

WG-6900 Warehousing & Stock Handling Family

This family includes occupations involved in physically receiving, storing, handling, and issuing supplies, materials, and equipment; handling, marking, and displaying goods for customer selection; identifying and condition classifying materials and equipment; and routing and expediting movement of parts, supplies, and materials in production and repair facilities.

WG-6902 Lumber Handling
WG-6903 Coal Handling
WG-6904 Tools and Parts Attending
WG-6907 Materials Handling
WG-6910 Materials Expediting

WG-6912 Materials Examining & Identifying
WG-6915 Store Working
WG-6941 Bulk Money Handling
WG-6968 Aircraft Freight Loading

WG-7000 Packing and Processing Family

This job family includes occupations involved in determining the measures required to protect items against damage during movement or storage; selecting proper method of packing, including type and size of container; cleaning, drying, and applying preservatives to materials, parts, or mechanical equipment; and packing, equipment, parts, and materials.

WG-7002 Packing
WG-7004 Preservation Packaging
WG-7006 Preservation Servicing

WG-7009 Equipment Cleaning
WG-7010 Parachute Packing

WG-7300 Laundry, Dry Cleaning, & Pressing Family

This job family includes occupations involved in receiving, sorting, washing, drying, dry cleaning, dyeing, pressing, and preparing for delivery clothes, linens, and other articles requiring laundering, dry cleaning, or pressing.

WG-7304 Laundry Working
WG-7305 Laundry Machine Operating

WG-7306 Pressing
WG-7307 Dry Cleaning

WG-7400 Food Preparation & Servicing Family

This job family includes occupations involved in the preparation and serving of food.

WG-7402 Baking
WG-7404 Cooking
WG-7405 Bartending

WG-7407 Meatcutting
WG-7408 Food Service Working
WG-7420 Waiter

WG-7600 Personal Services Family

This job family includes occupations concerned with providing grooming, beauty, or other personal services to individuals, patrons, guests, passengers, entertainers, etc., or attending to their personal effects.

WG-7603 Barbering
WG-7640 Bus Attending

WG-7641 Beautician

WG-8200 Fluid Systems Maintenance Family

Includes occupations involving repair, assembly, and testing of fluid systems and components of aircraft, aircraft engines, missiles, and mobile and support equipment. These fluid systems store, supply, distribute, and move gases or liquids to produce power, transmit force, and pressurize, cool, and condition cabins.

WG-8255 Pneudraulic Systems Mechanic
WG-8268 Aircraft Pneudraulic Systems Mechanic

WG-8600 Engine Overhaul Family

This job family includes occupations concerned primarily with the manufacture, repair, modification, and major overhaul of engines (except where covered by another job family) including the disassembly, reassembly, and test phases of engine overhaul programs.

WG-8602   Aircraft Engine Mechanic

WG-8610   Small Engine Mechanic
WG-8675   Liquid Fuel Rocket Engine Mechanic

WG-8800 Aircraft Overhaul Family

This job family includes occupations concerned primarily with the overhaul of aircraft, including the disassembly, reassembly, and test phases of aircraft overhaul programs.

WG-8810 Aircraft Propeller Mechanic
WG-8840 Aircraft Mechanical Parts Repairing
WG-8852 Aircraft Mechanic

WG-8862 Aircraft Attending
WG-8863 Aircraft Tire Mounting
WG-8882 Airframe Test Operating

WG-9000 Film Processing Family

This job family includes occupations that involve processing film, for example, operating motion picture developers and printers; cleaning, repairing, matching, cutting, splicing, and assembling films; and mixing developing solutions. Does not include processing work that requires specialized subject-matter knowledge or artistic ability.

WG-9003 Film Assembling and Repairing
WG-9004 Motion Picture Machine Operating

WG-9055 Photographic Solution Mixing

"The Lord gave us two ends — one to sit on and the other to think with. Success depends on which one we use the most."

Ann Landers

INDEX

CAREER RESOURCES

THE BOOK OF U.S. GOVERNMENT JOBS, 5th Ed., by Dennis Damp

$15.95, 1994, 224 pages

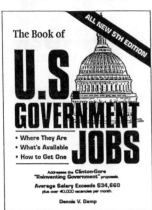

Where They Are, What's Available, & How to Get One. The all new 5th edition is an easy to follow, step-by-step guide to high-paying jobs with the U.S. government. Filled with everything you need to know about obtaining a federal government job, this book guides you through Uncle Sam's unique hiring world..

"A comprehensive how-to-guide. Recommended ... A worthy, affordable addition to career collections." — **LIBRARY JOURNAL**

" Anyone interested in obtaining government employment will find the Book of U.S. Government Jobs a TREASURE TROVE OF INFORMATION,"
— **BOOKWATCH**

HEALTH CARE JOB EXPLOSION! Career In The 90's by Dennis V. Damp.

$14.95, 1993, 384 pages

Audiologist
Chiropractor
Clinical Laboratory Technologist
Dental Hygienist
Dental Laboratory Technician
Dentist
Dietitian
Dispensing Optician
EEG & EKG Technologist
Emergency Medical Technician
Homemaker-Home Health Aides
Human Service Worker
Licensed Practical Nurse
Medical Assistants
Medical Record Technician
Nuclear Medicine Technologist
Nursing Aide
Nutritionist
Occupational Therapist
Ophthalmic Lab Technician
Optometrist
Pharmacist
Psychiatric Aide
Physical Therapist
Physician
Physician Assistant
Radiologic Technologist
Recreational Therapist
Registered Nurse
Respiratory Therapists
Social Worker
Speech-Language Pathologist
Surgical Technologist
Veterinarian

The health care job market is **EXPLODING**. Currently, seven out of every one hundred Americans work in health services. By the year 2005 that figure will increase to nine out of every one hundred, that's **3,900,000 NEW JOBS!**

Health Care Job Explosion! by Dennis V. Damp is a comprehensive **career guide** and **job finder** that steers readers to where they can actually find job openings; periodicals with job ads, placement services, directories, associations, job fairs, and job hotlines. All major health care groups are explored including the nature of work for each occupation, describing:

- Typical working conditions
- Training/advancement potential
- Job outlook and earnings

- Employment opportunities
- Necessary qualifications
- Related occupations

PLUS more than 1,000 verified job resources

"...With the growth of the health-care industry, this book will be a boon to those seeking jobs. Well rounded... Recommended for general collections; this book will be in demand. — LIBRARY JOURNAL

GOVERNMENT JOB FINDER by Daniel Lauber

$16.95, 336 pages

The perfect companion to The Book Of U.S. Government Jobs. A one-stop shopping center for federal, state, and local government positions in the U.S. and abroad. It shows you how to use over 1,400 specialty periodicals, job-matching services, job hotlines, and directories to find the government vacancies in your specialty.

"Dynamite job hunting tool... the most complete compendium of resources for government jobs I've ever seen."   **Joyce Lain Kennedy, careers columnist**

NON-PROFIT'S JOB FINDER by Daniel Lauber

$16.95, 320 pages

Takes you to over 1,000 sources of job vacancies, internships, and grant opportunities in the non-profit sector: education, social services, the arts, advocacy, environment, research, foundations, religion, public interest groups, and dozens more specialties. Armed with this book, you'll no longer have to rely solely on word-of-mouth to find these jobs. **Recommended by Career World Magazine.**

PROFESSIONAL'S PRIVATE SECTOR JOB FINDER by Daniel lauber

$18.95, 520 pages (6 x 9)

You'll learn how to use over 2,000 of the best job sources to find job vacancies in all aspects of the private sector: health care, science, and engineering, media, computers, manufacturing, law, management, business, banking, and dozens of other fields.

"... One of the most complete sources of information that I have seen." - **Search Bulletin: Career Opportunities for Executives and Professionals**

THE ULTIMATE JOB FINDER (Computer Program) by Daniel Lauber

$59.95, 4,500+ job sources on disk

This software package brings over 4,500 of the best job sources that comprise the hidden job market into one easy-to-use search-and-retrieval software program for your IBM-compatible, MS-DOS personal computer with a hard disk drive. Just type your occupation into a box and hit the enter key. Then a detailed description of every job source for your specialty will instantly appear on the screen. You can browse through the descriptions and print out the ones you want. Also provides advice on resumes, cover letters and interviewing.

Comes with both 3.5" and 5.25" disks. It will run on any IBM-compatible, MS-DOS personal computer with at lease 2 megabytes of free space on the hard drive.

HOW TO FIND AN OVERSEAS JOB WITH THE U.S. GOVERNMENT
by Will Cantrell & Francine Modderno

$28.95, 421 pages

There are over 72,000 Americans assigned overseas in a civilian capacity by various agencies of the U.S. Government. Additional thousands work for the United Nations. Whatever you do, from accounting to writing, chances are there's someone with your skills enjoying comfortable government employment in a stimulating foreign setting.

Aside from its comprehensive coverage of internship, entry and mid-level employment opportunities, the book offers invaluable insight on how to prepare for, and pass, the annual Foreign Service written and oral examinations.

INTERNATIONAL INTERNSHIPS AND VOLUNTEER PROGRAMS
by Will Cantrell & Francine Modderno

$18.95, 233 pages

"Internationalists" at all carer stages will find dozens of international opportunities throughout this reference. This book contains applications procedures and program descriptions for organizations that sponsor internship and volunteer opportunities of international scope, including: business; private voluntary organizations; religious organizations; international development firms; educational institutions; government agencies and institutions.

GUIDE TO CAREERS IN WORLD AFFAIRS by the Editors of the Foreign Policy Association

$14.95, 331 Pages (6 x 9)

Completely revised for the 1990s, this outstanding careers book reveals hundreds of opportunities in the international job market. Thoroughly researched, the book identifies major international employers in the fields of business, consulting, finance, banking, journalism, law, translation/interpretation, nonprofit organizations, federal and state government, and the United Nations. Special chapters outline internship opportunities, international graduate programs, and job hunting strategies appropriate for the international job market.

GREAT CONNECTIONS - Networking for Business people by Anne Baber and Lynne Waymon

$11.95, 194 pages

"Highly Recommended." Midwest Book Review. Here's the unique book that reveals how to use small talk to make great connections that are vital for business success in the 1990s. The authors explain practical small talk techniques anyone can learn and apply quickly; join a group of people who are already talking, strike up conversations, remember people's names, come up with topics, revive dying conversations, recover when saying something they wish they hadn't, close conversations easily, and much more.

DYNAMITE ANSWERS TO INTERVIEW QUESTIONS by Drs. Caryl and Ron Krannich

$9.95, 168 pages

Shows how to turn possible negative responses into positive answers that can mean the difference between being accepted or rejected for the job. Includes numerous questions interviewees need to answer and ask about themselves, the employer, organization, position, & salary expectations.

INTERVIEW FOR SUCCESS (3rd Edition) by Drs. Caryl & Ron Krannich

$11.95, 218 pages (6 x 9)

"ONE OF THE BEST CAREER BOOKS."- **Career Opportunity News.** This is the first book to place the job interview in the context of job skills, objectives, resumes, and networking. Shows how to prepare for interviews, handle stress, observe etiquette, gather information, formulate questions, rehearse tough questions, dress appropriately, communicate and listen, discuss salary, and handle the post-interview period.

DISCOVER THE RIGHT JOB FOR YOU! by Drs. Ron & Caryl Krannich

$11.95, 1992, 185 pages
  Shows job seekers how to identify their interests, skills, and abilities and formulate them into a powerful objective related to specific jobs and careers. Complete with tests and self-assessment exercises, the book addresses the **fundamentals** central to developing an effective job search. 181 pages. ISBN: 0-942710-33-9

THE BOOK OF U.S. POSTAL EXAMS
How to Score 95-100% and Get a Job!
by Veltisezar Bautista

$13.95, 272 pages (8 1/2 x 11)
  Here's the only Postal exam book you'll ever need. The guide includes the most commonly-given exams for 44 job classifications. This book has won the nationally acclaimed **Benjamin Franklin Award** and it has received excellent reviews from national magazines to individuals that have benefitted from this valuable reference.

THE BOOK OF $16,000 - $60,000 Post Office Jobs
Where They Are, What They Pay, & How to Get Them
by Veltisezar Bautista

$14.95, 186 pages (8 1/2 x 11)
  Amazingly, the U.S. Postal Service had never issued a complete book of approximately 300 job classifications. Because you have the right to know about these opportunities we put together a comprehensive directory detailing these occupations.
  Find out how you can get a high-paying Postal job, whether you are a high school graduate, a student, a mechanic, an engineer, truck driver, computer program, or any one of the 300 occupations available today. This is the only guide to nearly 300 specific Postal job classifications.

QUICK & EASY 171's by Datatech

$49.95 (Personal Version) **DOS and WINDOWS** Versions available.
  Computer software that fills out and manages your SF-171 federal employment application. Customize your SF-171 to fit the requirements of the position that you are applying for. You can easily edit your experience and qualifications to reflect the demands of the position that you want, and keep as many versions of your SF-171 on disk as you want. Quick & easy for the SF-171 is not just another fill in the blanks forms program. It is a complete system with word processing and spell check specifically designed to fill in and manage the SF-171.
  If you have any one of 53 dot matrix printers, an HP Deskjet, or a LaserJet compatible laser printer, Quick & Easy can automatically print both the SF-171 forms and your data on blank paper. The pages are exact including all fonts,point sizes, bold and italic on the original form.

HARDWARE REQUIREMENTS

  IBM-PC/XT/AT - 640K - DOS 3.0 or greater. One Floppy Drive and a Hard Drive and Monitor - Any printer except Canon including: ALPS, Brother, Citizen, C. Itoh, Epson, Facit, Fujitsu, HP Deskjet, LaserJet II & III, Proprinter, M. Talley, NEC, Panasonic, Seikosha, and Toshiba.

ORDERING INFORMATION

Use this order form to purchase the following titles. Include shipping charges and sales tax, if appropriate, in accordance with the instructions on the following pages and enclose your check or money order. Individuals must prepay before we can ship your order. Purchase orders are accepted only from bookstores, libraries, universities, and government offices. Please call or write for resale prices.

ORDER FORM

QTY TITLE   __TOTAL__

___ $15.95 Book of U.S. Government Jobs _____

___ $14.95 Health Care Job Explosion _____

___ $16.95 Government Job Finder _____

___ $18.95 Professional's Job Finder _____

___ $16.95 Non-Profits' Job Finder _____

___ $59.95 The Ultimate Job Finder _____

___ $28.95 How to Find an Overseas Job With the U.S. Government _____

___ $18.95 International Internships & Volunteer Programs _____

___ $14.95 Guide to Careers in World Affairs _____

___ $11.95 Great Connections _____

___ $11.95 Network Your Way to Careers & Success _____

___ $11.95 Interview For Success _____

___ $13.95 The Book of U.S. Postal Exams _____

___ $14.95 The Book of $16,000 to $60,000 Post Office Jobs _____

___ $ 9.95 Dynamite Answers to Interview Questions _____

___ $11.95 Discover the Right Job For You _____

___ $49.95 Quick & Easy SF-171 Software Package _____
   (Check Preferences)
   ☐ 3.5" Disk ☐ 5.25" Disk - ☐ WIN ☐ DOS

                __SUBTOTAL $___.___

☞ Shipping/handling: ($3.75 for first book.
 $1.00 for each additional book.)   __$ 3.75__

☞ Additional Books, ___ x $1.00 $___.___

☞ Pennsylvania residents add 6% sales tax $___.___

☞   **TOTAL** $___.___

☞ Please continue on the other side.

SHIP TO:

(PLEASE PRINT)

Name _____

Address _____

City-State-Zip _____

Orders from individuals or private businesses must be prepaid. Purchase orders are accepted only from libraries, colleges and universities, bookstores, and government offices.

☐ I enclose check or money order for $ _____
Made payable to: D-Amp Publications

**Send orders to: D-Amp Publications
P.O. Box 1243, Dept. US5, Coraopolis, PA 15108**

D-AMP PUBLICATIONS

P.O. Box 1243
Coraopolis, PA 15108

(412) 262-5578